THE VNR
INVESTOR'S
DICTIONARY

THE VNR
INVESTOR'S
DICTIONARY

DAVID M. BROWNSTONE
IRENE M. FRANCK

A HUDSON GROUP BOOK,

 VAN NOSTRAND REINHOLD COMPANY
NEW YORK   CINCINNATI   ATLANTA   DALLAS   SAN FRANCISCO
LONDON   TORONTO   MELBOURNE

Van Nostrand Reinhold Company Regional Offices:
New York Cincinnati Atlanta Dallas San Francisco

Van Nostrand Reinhold Company International Offices:
London Toronto Melbourne

Library of Congress Catalog Card Number: 80–23841
ISBN: 0–442–21578–9

Manufactured in the United States of America

Published by Van Nostrand Reinhold Company
135 West 50th Street, New York, N.Y. 10020

Published simultaneously in Canada by Van Nostrand Reinhold Ltd.

15 14 13 12 11 10 9 8 7 6 5 4 3 2 1

Library of Congress Cataloging in Publication Data

Brownstone, David M.
    The VNR investor's dictionary.

    "A Hudson Group book."
    1. Investments—Dictionaries. I. Franck, Irene M.,
joint author. II. Title.
HG4513.B76   332.6'03'21   80–23841
ISBN 0–442–21578–9

Preface

In recent years, the special language of the investment world has grown by leaps and bounds, as investors and investment professionals search out and work with a rapidly increasing body of investment tools and techniques. Investment language today is full of words and phrases that either did not exist 10 years ago, were used exclusively by a few specialists, or have taken on new meanings. For instance, there are new kinds of bonds and new ways of investing in them; new combined insurance and investment vehicles; and several new kinds of mutual funds. There are also many terms drawn from the worlds of art, antiques, and collectibles. In addition, many terms previously in wide use have become obsolete, as the slang of the investment world has changed.

As a result, the need has grown for a clear, complete, concise, up-to-date investor's dictionary, containing all the key words and phrases encountered in the course of investment, work, and study—yet no such dictionary has been in print.

The VNR Investor's Dictionary is our attempt to fill that need. It contains all those key words and phrases, drawn from the many sources providing language to the world of investment and finance. Areas included are securities, finance, banking, business, accounting, law, real estate, statistics, and government. These areas are sources for the language encountered when dealing with such investment tools and techniques as stocks, bonds, mutual funds, savings, real estate, gold and other commodities, currency, futures, options, tax shelters, tax havens, insurance, pension and profit-sharing plans, estate plans, art, antiques, and collectibles. Throughout the dictionary, we have included practical examples of current usage.

We have made every attempt to be clear and concise. Whenever appropriate, we have tried to consolidate several related words into one usable definition, rather than define several forms of the same word.

This dictionary is for investors, investment and banking professionals, students, teachers, librarians, and library users. In short, it is designed for people at all levels who need a concise investor's dictionary, written in easy-to-understand business English.

To minimize page-flipping by busy readers, we have most often briefly defined terms that might otherwise have been cross-referenced. However, where appropriate, key words in the definitions will lead interested readers to wider definitions. Where two or more terms are synonymous, in general the most commonly used term is defined, and the less commonly used terms are cross-referenced.

The alphabetizing style we have chosen is "letter by letter" rather than "word by word." This method should enable users to find desired words and phrases quickly and easily.

Many commonly encountered terms have quite different meanings in different contexts. Sometimes, these differ from each other as well as from general noninvestment usages. For such terms, we have numbered the various meanings in order of importance, giving the most general meanings first, except where a narrow meaning is the one most often encountered.

Some of the terms and definitions found in this book are also found in the authors' VNR Dictionary of Business and Finance, which is intended for a more general business use.

This dictionary is by its very nature selective, reflecting the authors' decisions regarding which terms will prove most useful to its users. While including as many new terms as possible, we have tried to select mainly those terms of lasting value and to exclude the jargon of the moment. We hope that there are no significant omissions.

DAVID M. BROWNSTONE
IRENE M. FRANCK

THE VNR INVESTOR'S DICTIONARY

A

abandonment: The total, irrevocable and voluntary giving up of any property and of all possible rights to that property. Once abandoned, the property becomes the possession of the first to claim it.

abatement: 1. A decrease; for example, a reduction in taxes on real property due to special circumstances or on imported goods due to spoilage in transit; also a legally acceptable decrease in payments due or received for any reason. **2.** The total destruction of a plaintiff's cause of action at law, but leaving the plaintiff the ability to commence another cause of action based on the same set of facts.

ab initio: Latin for "from the beginning," describing the legal status of a condition or transaction, whether by its very nature or constructed from subsequent matters, as applied to a contract that is void from the start, or to a legal entry later construed to have been a trespass from the start due to the subsequent actions of the trespasser.

above par: Above listed, or par, value. Any stock selling for more than its listed value is selling above par.

above the line: Describing any normal, customary item on an accounting statement; unusual items are described as *below the line*.

abrogation: The destruction or repeal of an existing law, whether by legislative, judicial, or executive act, or by practice.

absentee bid: At an auction, a bid left with the autioneer by a bidder who is unable to attend the auction; often but not always required by the auction to be accompanied by a deposit.

absentee ownership: The ownership of wealth-producing assets by those who neither work nor manage those assets, a common form of industrial ownership. Often used as term of opprobrium by local people who feel that absentee owners care little about local people and their interests but only about profits.

absolute sale: A sale which is consummated in full at the moment of formal agreement, with no conditions of any kind accompanying the sale, as distinct from a "conditional" sale, which becomes fully consummated only upon the occurrence of specified later events.

absorb: In describing an investment vehicle or a market, to be able to ingest selling and buying transactions without appreciable price moves; for example, a widely held stock, such as American Telephone and Telegraph, will move up or down in response to buying or selling pressure far less quickly, thus absorbing more, than a narrowly held stock.

absorbed cost: Any additional, determinable cost which might either be passed on whole to the buyer or paid by the seller, but which is paid by the seller, such as postage or handling charges

absorption costing: A method of allocating all or part of fixed and variable production costs to goods in production, goods sold, and inventory.

accelerated depreciation: Any method of calculating depreciation of land, buildings, or other fixed assets so that the stated value of the asset diminishes faster than if it lost its value in equal proportions, period after period, as is the case when *straight line* depreciation is used. It is used widely as a tax avoidance device, especially in real estate and generally throughout American industry.

acceleration clause: A clause in a debt instrument, such as a mortgage, which make the entire amount of the debt due and payable on demand if the conditions stated in the clause are not met. For example, the entire amount of a mortgage may become immediately due if a single payment of interest or principal is missed.

acceleration principle: The theory that when demand for consumer goods rises, investment in capital equipment rises even faster; conversely, that when consumer demand drops, capital equipment investment drops faster.

acceptance: Agreement to a transaction with intent to carry through that transaction. It is usually expressed and indicated by acts such as signing a contract, writing ''accepted'' on the face of a time draft or bill of exchange, receiving and holding delivered goods, or registering a deed. Acceptance may be implied, conditional, or partial, as when property is received and held, but the question of the receivers' intent to keep it can be disputed. Some common examples are banker's acceptances, bills of exchange, and trade acceptances.

acceptance bank: A banking firm that specializes in handling bills of exchange.

accommodation endorsement: See accommodation party.

accommodation paper: A debt instrument which is co-signed by one who does not receive the borrowings, but who is signing as guarantor that the borrower will repay or, if not, that the co-signer will repay the debt.

accommodation party: One who signs a debt instrument and undertakes co-liability for borrowings while not receiving any of the proceeds of those borrowings.

account: 1. A written record of transactions, kept in one or more ledgers and usually, though not always, expressed in money or money equivalents. 2. A customer, one who has a bank or brokerage account, or one who regularly buys and is extended some kind of business credit.

account balance: See balance.

account executive: An employee responsible for handling the relationship between a firm and one or more of its clients; widely used in advertising, but also in other service industries, such as consulting, securities, and insurance.

accounting: 1. Reporting, classifying, summarizing, and interpreting transactions, partly or wholly of a financial nature. **2.** Any formal report of an entity's transactions during a specific period, usually including a summary of the entity's current status as of the beginning of the period.

accounting period: Any period for which an accounting is prepared, usually monthly, quarterly, and yearly.

accounting practice: The normal and generally accepted practices of accountants regarding commonly encountered professional matters.

accounts payable: Money a firm owes others for goods purchased and not yet paid for; does not include such obligations as notes, bonds, and other debts.

accounts receivable: Money owed a firm by its customers for goods purchased and not yet paid for; does not include income from such sources as investments and bank deposits.

accounts receivable financing: Use of money owed a firm in receivables to secure funds, either by the sale of those receivables to others, a process known as factoring, or by their use as loan collateral.

accretion: In general, any gradual increase in size; in business the meaning has expanded to mean any increase in value of any asset for any reason and at any rate of speed.

accrual: 1. The process of adding to and accumulating. Also refers to anything that is added to and accumulates. **2.** In accounting, continuous or periodic change in the amount of any account, including increases and decreases, income and expenses. Also refers to the specific account item that is changed by the process of accrual.

accrual basis: An accounting method which records income and expenses for accounting purposes when they are earned and incurred rather than on a cash basis, when they are actually received and spent. For example, on the accrual basis, goods bought are charged against the day they are actually bought rather than the day they are paid for, which may be considerably later; goods sold are recorded as income, minus any necessary reserves for uncollectibles, when sold rather than when the money due for them is collected.

accrue: 1. To increase, accumulate and accrete over some extended period of time. **2.** To reach the point where an increase is gained, as when pension rights accrue to their holders at the moment of vesting, or inheritance rights accrue to their holders on the death of the testator. **3.** In accounting, to record accruals in the appropriate accounts.

accrued: Describing any item which, for accounting purposes, has been earned or incurred but which has not yet been received or spent.

accrued dividend: Dividends thought to be due, undeclared, and unpaid. In fact, dividends are not due until declared by a firm's board of directors, so this phase describes a situation that can exist only in certain private securities sales situations.

accrued expense: An expense incurred and recorded in one accounting period which is due and payable in a future accounting period, under an accrual basis accounting method.

accrued income: Income earned and recorded in one accounting period which is to be actually received in a future accounting period, under an accrual basis accounting method.

accrued interest: Interest earned that is not yet due and payable, as with fixed interest bonds earning interest every day which is payable quarterly or semi-annually.

accumulated dividend: See dividend in arrears.

accumulated income: Net and undistributed corporate income which is not offset by losses. How much corporate income can be held undistributed without being subject to tax is the focus of a considerable body of tax law.

accumulated profits: See accumulated income.

accumulated surplus: See accumulated income.

accumulation: The acquisition of marketable securities or goods over a period of time, in such fashion as to avoid public notice, which might drive up the market price of that which is being accumulated. For example, securities might be so acquired during a period of depressed prices; a kind of collectible might be accumulated before it becomes popular; or the shares of a company might be accumulated by a potential acquirer in anticipation of a takeover attempt.

ACH: See automated clearing house.

acid test: The ratio of liquid assets, including cash, trade receivables, and marketable securities, to current liabilities. Used to assess the credit-worthiness and liquidity of a business, with a ratio of 1:1 generally thought acceptable. Also called quick ratio.

acquired surplus: Accumulated income of a company which is taken over when that company is acquired by another.

acquisition: 1. The process of gaining ownership of anything. Also that which is acquired.   **2.** In business, the process of gaining full or partial but controlling ownership of a business entity. Also, the business entity which is acquired.

acquisition candidate: A company that others are seriously thinking of acquiring or trying to acquire, whether or not that company desires to be acquired.

acquittance: A document that completely discharges a financial debt or other performance obligation; usually issued upon settlement of a financial obligation.

across the board: Referring to a group of numbers that have all risen or fallen together; for example, the prices of securities listed on an exchange or uniform wage increases for all employees in a plant or industry.

action: The pursuit of a claimed legal right by any kind of legal process in a court of law. Also refers to the legal proceeding itself.

active account: An account that is used relatively often, with transactions occurring fairly regularly, such as an often used stock brokerage account.

active market: Any market in which trading is heavy. Examples are, a day of large share turnover on the New York and other stock exchanges; a period of heavy trading on the commodities exchanges; or a week of active trading in currencies.

active partner: A partner who participates in the normal functioning of a business; for example, a securities firm partner who is active in the conduct of the firm's affairs.

activity charge: A monthly bank service charge on a depositor's checking account, where the average monthly balance in the account is below the minimum which the bank sets to cover the costs of handling the depositor's checks. Special checking accounts have no minimum but charge a flat sum per check drawn.

adaptation: An object constructed to be used in some different way than originally designed; for example, a table constructed from a ship's hatch cover.

additional capital: See paid in surplus.

address of record: An address stated for legal purposes, such as a legal residence statement for tax and voting purposes, or an address stated for purposes of legal notification under the terms of a contract.

adjusted gross income: For income tax purposes, gross income minus all deductions from gross income provided by statute, such as business and some other expenses connected with property and wealth.

administered price: A price mainly controlled by one or more organizations rather than by marketplace supply and demand factors. While direct price-fixing collusion among companies is prohibited by law, groups of companies in substantial control of industries can and do informally set narrow price ranges for many of their products, amounting to effectively administered prices.

administration: 1. The management of matters, businesses, and other organizations. **2.** The organizational entity created to accomplish the work of managing matters, companies and other organizations. **3.** In law, the process of managing an estate

administrative budget: Management's operating budget, controlling normal ongoing business operations, usually on a yearly basis.

administrative expenses: Expenses incurred to accomplish the management of matters and organizations. In business, the expenses of management as management, rather than by specific productive functions.

administrator: One who manages matters and organizations. In business, an executive in charge of some aspect of management. In law, one who manages an estate.

ADR: See American Depositary Receipt.

ad valorem tax: A tax computed on the basis of the value of the taxed item; usually expressed as a percentage of that value. Examples are many excise, most property, and all value-added taxes.

advance: To move forward, as in a general rise of stock prices.

advance-decline index: An attempt to represent graphically the relationship between the number of securities advancing and the number declining in a given period.

advance refunding: An offer by a bond issuer to bondholders to exchange new bonds for old bonds at favorable rates, to forestall early redemption of the old bonds. Treasury bondholders often take advantage of advance refunding offers.

affiliate: A company that is closely associated with another company, through partial stock ownership, largely shared boards of directors, shared marketing facilities, or other such relationships, but that stops short of subsidiary status, which requires majority stock control.

affluent society: John Kenneth Galbraith's ironic term for an American society rich in material goods but poor in social services and human values. Now often merely used as a synonym for wealthy society.

after: See manner of.

after date: Describing when a debt is due to be repaid, a specific time after it is incurred; for example, a note payable 90 days after the date on which it was executed and the money loaned is payable 90 days "after date."

after market: The market for a new securities issue during the period just after issue; after a brief and indeterminate time, the security is no longer a new issue and the "after market" designation drops away. Then the security is thought of as being normally traded in its markets as other securities are.

after sight: Describing when a debt is due to be repaid, a specific time after legal presentation and acceptance of the debt instrument; for example, in "This note is payable 30 days after sight," the debt is due 30 days after acceptance of the note.

agency: A relationship in which one party acts for or represents another, under authority granted by the other. The agency may be express or implied, exclusive or shared, general or limited.

agency agreement: A formal and written contract between principal and agent, setting forth all terms and conditions of the agency arrangement; for example, the agreement between an insurance company and one of its general agents.

agency contract: See agency agreement.

agent: 1. One who acts for or represents another, under authority granted by the other. Where the agency is a formal business relationship, it is usually governed in every major way by the provisions of an agency contract.   **2.** One who buys or sells good and services for another, as do purchasing, insurance, real estate, and other agents.

agio: The premium paid for exchanging one nation's currency for another's, or for handling a foreign bill of exchange.

agribusiness: Those industries, companies, and individuals engaged in agriculture and agriculture-related activities, as big business, including farming and other agricultural production, processing, distribution, equipment, and supporting financial and service functions; in contrast to small family farming.

AIB: See American Institute of Banking.

air rights: Proprietary rights to air space above owned land. Often leased or sold to others for building purposes, as in the instance of apartment buildings over bridge approaches in some major cities.

allocate: 1. To distribute according to a plan or set of rules, as in distribution of scarce commodities by government in time of emergency.   **2.** To distribute expenditures and revenues according to function among various accounts in an accounting system. For example, the direct costs attributable to order processing may be distributed among the various products for which orders were processed.

allocation: See allotment.

all or any part: In underwriting new securities issues, a term indicating that a firm bidding for the issue will buy the entire issue or any available part of the issue, for resale to the public.

all or choice: At auction, describing the offering of goods in a lot to be sold either as a whole lot or by the piece.

all or none: 1. A commitment by new securities issue underwriters to sell the entire issue within stated time limits or void the issue, then returning all funds received to the issue's buyers.   **2.** An instruction from principal to broker, that the entire purchase requested be consummated or no purchase be made, thus specifically prohibiting a partial purchase.

allotment: 1. Distribution according to a plan or set of rules.   **2.** A portion of that which is distributed. Examples include a portion of scarce commodities distributed by government in time of emergency; or a portion of a new securities issue sold to a firm by an underwriting syndicate.

alteration: An object which has been modified, in construction, use, or both; also the process of modification.

altered check: A check that has undergone unauthorized change after issuance, usually by addition or erasure, so that such matters as payees, amounts, and dates have been materially altered.

alternative cost: See opportunity cost.

alternative order: An order specifying that a broker take one of two or more alternative courses of action, depending upon circumstances; most often occurring as a buy at one price or sell at another set of instructions.

amalgamation: See consolidation.

American Bankers Association (ABA): The largest national organization of commercial banks, and one of the oldest trade associations in the United States. It is involved in legislative representation of the banking industry, professional development programs, development of industry standards, and publishing in banking areas.

American Depositary Receipt (ADR): Receipts issued by American banks in place of foreign stocks held in trust by those banks. Relatively few foreign stocks are directly traded in the United States, but instead become tradable through the device of the depositary receipt.

American Institute of Banking (AIB): Professional development arm of the American Bankers Association; awards professional certificates and publishes texts and other materials.

American Stock Exchange (ASE): The second largest United States stock exchange. Formerly called the Curb Exchange, it originated as an outdoor securities market.

American Stock Exchange Index: A set of indexes, including a common stock index measuring price changes of common stocks and warrants traded on the American Stock Exchange, an index measuring the breadth of those price changes in terms of the number of stocks experiencing them, and a price-earnings ratio index for stocks listed on this Exchange.

amortization: **1.** The reduction and ultimate wiping out of any amount over a specified period, as in retirement of a mortgage debt through installment repayments that include both interest and principal until the full debt is repaid. **2.** The process of writing off the premium on a bond bought above par. **3.** The reduction and ultimate wiping out of the stated value of a fixed asset over a specified period, including all forms of depreciation, write-offs, and depletion of assets of limited life; of special tax significance in the form of accelerated depreciation.

amortization schedule: 1. A table showing the mathematics of amortization, as the obligation or asset is gradually reduced and eliminated.   **2.** A table showing the mathematics of amortization as the premium paid on a bond is gradually reduced.

amortized loan: A loan repaid in equal installments over the life of the plan, each payment containing both interest and principal repayment; interest is high and principal repayment low at the start of the period, with principal repayment high and interest low toward the end of the period. Home mortgage loans are usually made on this basis.

Amtorg: The foreign trading agency of the Soviet Union, with branches in many countries; an acronym for its Russian name.

annual audit: A thorough examination of a firm's books and records for a year's activities, usually conducted by outside accountants.

annualize: 1. To derive an annual rate from partial figures. For example, under certain conditions costs incurred in one month can be multiplied by twelve to get a projected annual rate of expenditure.   **2.** In taxation, to compute for tax purposes when operations are taxable for only part of a year, as in change from a fiscal to a calendar year on a one-time basis.

annual report: A formal report of a firm's operating results for the year and its year-end financial condition, containing a balance sheet, operating statement, auditor's report, and often other financial materials and management comments; submitted by the board of directors to the firm's stockholders and often to other interested parties.

annuitant: One who has the right to receive an annuity.

annuity: A sum paid periodically in equal installments to annuitants under terms of an insurance policy or bequest. It is usually a form of retirement insurance, in which the insured buys an insurance policy, making periodic premium payments, a single lump sum, or some combination of both: then on maturity of the policy the insured receives payments in one of several alternative payment modes. In the recently introduced variable annuity, an insured may receive payment in shares of an annuity fund that varies with the fortunes of the securities in which it is invested.

antedate: To date a document earlier than the real date on which it is executed, as in dating a gift earlier than the actual date of its giving to qualify for favorable, and often illegal, tax treatment.

anticipation: 1. Any expectation of change; generally used to describe the impact of events and reactions to them on stock market fluctuations, consumer buying patterns, and other economic trends. **2.** In accounting, recording costs and revenues before they actually occur, as in recording all proceeds from a multi-year magazine subscription as if they had already been received, even though payment is yearly.

anticipation factor: The idea that the economic expectations of those in a marketplace to some extent influence marketplace activities, becoming self-fulfilling prophecies; for example, that widespread expectation of market decline on the part of investors can be and often is a substantial factor leading to market decline.

anticipatory breach: A breach of contract occurring before other parties have obligations to perform under the terms of that contract, such as a direct statement of intent not to perform, or bankruptcy clearly making it impossible to perform.

antidumping tariff: An import duty levied to prevent dumping, which is the sale of manufactured goods at export prices far lower than those charged in the country of manufacture; the duty, levied by importing countries, is the difference between the normal home market and the export market price. Such tariffs are often the subject of considerable international dispute, with importing countries charging that exporters dump to create unfair competition with home-produced goods, while exporting countries charge importers have unfair and exclusionary protective tariffs.

antiquarian: One who is expert in some aspect of antiquities; most commonly used in relation to those involved in the purchase and sale of collectible books.

antiquary: One who is expert in antiquities, other than books.

antique: In investment terms, an old collectible, usually a collectible more than 100 years old, the worth of which stems in large part from its age and condition, as well as from current collecting tastes and value estimates. Works of art, except for those of great antiquity, are usually measured by their value as art, rather than as antiques. Some of those dealing in collectibles often erroneously call quite recent items antiques, in an attempt to enhance the desirability of the goods they are selling.

antiquing: 1. The process of shopping for antiques and other collectibles. **2.** The process of making something look like an antique, when that is not really so.

antiquity: 1. The age of an object, described by date or period. **2.** Generally describing all periods before the European Middle Ages, but so general a term as to be often applied to periods of high culture in other parts of the world coincident with the Middle Ages.

antitrust statutes: Laws aimed at curbing and reversing the spread of monopolies, monopolistic practices, and all practices and actions that function as restraints to free trade and the development of free markets. The Federal Trade Commission is charged with enforcement; the main laws are the Sherman Antitrust Act of 1890, the Clayton Antitrust Act of 1914, the Federal Trade Commission Act of 1914, the Robinson-Patman Act of 1936, and the Celler Act of 1950.

a piece of the action: Part of the risk and opportunity; for example, part of the entrepreneurial investment in a new business, a part ownership in a racehorse, or a participation in a new real estate investment.

apportionment: Any proportional division; examples include the allotment of shares among buyers who have oversubscribed a new securities issue; the division of revenues and expenditures between principal and interest in estate administration; the charging of current costs over several periods in accounting, relating costs to benefits; or the division of a tax levied among those who must pay it, according to rules developed by the taxing authority.

appraisal: The development of a formal estimate of value of any real or personal property, usually by an appraiser and in writing; also refers to the document so produced.

appraiser: One who sets value on properties for a wide variety of legal, taxing and transacting purposes, who is generally recognized as an expert in the kinds of properties being appraised, and who often possesses such credentials as a course of study, professional certification, and professional society membership.

appreciation: 1. An increase in the market price of a security. **2.** An increase in the value of any property. **3.** An increase in the value of a fixed asset over its book value.

appreciation potential: The likelihood that an investment will increase in value, and the probable size of that increase; always an estimate.

arbitrage: The practice of buying something in one market and simultaneously selling it in another or the same market, with the aim of taking advantage of price differences existing at the moment of purchase and sale. The usual subjects of arbitrage are currencies, currency futures, securities, precious metals, and other such commodities. For example, the British pound may be selling in Paris at $1.80 and in Tokyo at $1.81. An arbitrageur who buys a large quantity of pounds in Paris at $1.80 and simultaneously sells a large number of pounds in Tokyo at $1.81 can make a substantial profit.

arbitrageur: See arbitrage.

arm's length: Describing a transaction engaged in by parties who are absolutely independent of each other as regards the transaction.

For example, wholly unrelated buyers and sellers can deal with each other at arm's length.

arrears: Debts such as installment payments, rent, and bond interest, which are owing and past due but unpaid on their normal and acceptable payment dates. Occasionally used to describe debts which are due, but not yet overdue.

arrival draft: A bill for goods shipped. The shipment's originator sends the bill and shipping documents directly to a collecting bank, where they arrive before the shipment itself arrives. When the shipment arrives, the bill must be paid before the shipping document will be released by the collecting bank to the shipper, so that the delivery cannot be completed without the bill being paid.

ascribed to: See attributed to.

ASE: See American Stock Exchange.

Asian Development Bank: An international bank composed of many Asian and non-Asian nations, including the United States. Formed to spur economic development in the Far East, it provides loans and technical assistance to both governments and private companies.

as is: Describing a sale made without any express or implied warranty; usually describes merchandise for sale, and does not always bar recovery under United States consumer protection laws.

asking price: The price at which anything is offered for sale; usually used in real estate and other substantial transactions to mean that the price being asked is negotiable, rather than firm.

assessable stock: Stock on which calls may be made for additional funds on the occurrence of such corporate financial difficulties as insolvency and potential bankruptcy; most stock is non-assessable.

assessed value: The value placed on real and personal property by government for property tax purposes.

assessment: 1. An amount levied by such companies as banks, insurance companies, and stock companies on shareholders and other parties holding some form of ownership interest to compensate for such matters as unanticipated losses and impaired capital positions.   **2.** A tax on real property, whether a recurring tax or a special tax for a single property-related purpose, such as sewers or sidewalks.   **3.** The process of determining the assessed valuation of property as a basis for a tax to be levied.

asset: 1. Any owned item that can be converted into cash. In the widest sense, anything of value.   **2.** In accounting, any source of wealth that can produce future value for its owner, including both tangible and intangible items, such as real property and cash.

assignee: One to whom legal rights belonging to a contracting party have been transferred, as in the transfer of rights to collect a debt, receive purchased property, or publish a book.

assignment: The act of transferring legal rights belonging to a contracting party to some other party.

assignor: One who possesses legal rights arising from a contract and transfers those rights to some other party. The assignor may be a party to the original contract or a previous assignee who is transferring the rights once again.

assumed liability: A liability taken over from another, as when a company takes over assets and liabilities of an acquiring company in a corporate merger.

at market: An instruction by a securities buyer or seller to a broker to buy or sell immediately at the best available price, rather than at a specific price.

at or better: An instruction by a securities buyer or seller to a broker to buy or sell at or higher than a specified price.

at sight: Describing a negotiable instrument, such as a bank draft, on which payment is due immediately on presentation.

attachment: A court order authorizing seizure by legal authorities of property belonging to the defendant in a legal action. The seized property may be physically seized and held safe, as with cash, paintings, and other small portable items; may be held in place with a lien against its sale, as with realty; or may be frozen, as with a bank account with the defendant unable to draw upon it. If the defendant loses the lawsuit, the attached property may then be used to satisfy damages and expenses.

attest: 1. To affirm, verbally or in writing, the truth of a statement or the existence of a fact.   **2.** To witness, and to sign a statement that verifies the signing of a document by another.   **3.** To certify that a document copy is genuine; usually done by a court officer licensed to fulfill this function.   **4.** To offer a professional opinion supporting stated facts and opinions, as when an accountant verifies a financial statement.

attestation: The formal and written witnessing of a document's signing by another, at the request of the other.

at the close: An instruction by a securities buyer or seller to a broker to buy or sell at the best available price near the closing of the market for the day.

at the opening: An instruction by a securities buyer or seller to a broker to buy or sell at the best available price at the opening of the market for the day.

attorney in fact: A status conferred by the signing of a valid power of attorney, by which one empowers another to act as his or her attorney for purposes specified in the document.

attorney of record: That attorney on record, in the documents relating to a specific case, as representing a party in that case, and to whom service of process and other communications are to be directed.

attributed to: An identification indicating uncertainty as to the originator of an object; often encountered when works have previously been identified as having been created by specific artists and that identification has later come into substantial question.

attribution: A claim or identification as to the maker of an object.

auction: Any sale to two or more potential buyers in which those buyers bid against each other, with whatever is being sold going to the highest bidder.

auction bookkeeper: One who records transactions on behalf of the auctioneer during the course of an auction.

auctioneer: One who conducts an auction, offering goods for sale, taking bids, and ultimately selling to the highest bidder.

audit: To examine and substantiate the accuracy, completeness, and internal consistency of books of account and the transactions recorded in them by one professionally qualified to do so. Also refers to the examination and substantiation process.

auditor: See audit.

auditor's report: A report issued by auditors on completion of their audit of company financial statements; such reports are usually brief, standard, and in language generally acceptable to the accounting profession.

audit period: The period covered by an audit, usually a year.

audit standards: Those standards for conducting audits that are acceptable to the accounting profession, as set forth by its professional associations and, to an increasing extent, as interpreted by courts and regulatory bodies.

audit trail: In accounting records and computer systems, references from entries back to the source materials from which the entries were generated; used in a wide variety of applications, including tax examinations.

audit year: The kind of year being examined for auditing purposes—fiscal or calendar.

authentic: As claimed. To call a lamp an "authentic" Tiffany is no different than calling it a Tiffany; the term is always redundant, a claim of honesty which need not be made by the honest. The term is sometimes used by experts to distinguish an original from a restored or altered piece.

authorized capital stock: The amount of capital stock a corporation is authorized to issue, as specified in its articles of corporation. A corporation may issue less, but may not issue more, than its authorized amount of capital stock without amending its certificate of incorporation.

authorized shares: See authorized capital stock.

automated clearing house (ACH): An interbank facility, clearing bank transactions for member banks through a central automatic data processing system.

automated tellers: Machines that take the place of human tellers, handling a wide variety of bank functions formerly performed by humans, such as cash receipts and disbursals.

automatic stabilizers: Economic factors built into the economy that are thought to exert counter-pressures on both inflation and recession, therefore tending to smooth out the boom-and-bust features of the business cycle; examples include social security, unemployment insurance and welfare payments.

automatic teller: See automated tellers.

autonomous investment: In economics, an investment made for reasons stemming from the nature of the investment itself, rather than being in any way directly tied to current or near-term anticipated economic conditions.

available assets: Any unencumbered assets available for general business purposes.

available cash: Cash in hand and in the bank, minus outstanding checks, that can be used for general business purposes.

avails: See net proceeds.

average: 1. An arithmetic mean, found by adding two or more items and dividing their sum by the number of items.   **2.** In the securities markets, an average of a series of stocks; several such averages are generally cited as barometers of securities market health, including the Dow Jones Industrial, Standard and Poor's, New York Stock Exchange, and the New York Times averages and indexes.   **3.** Any number expressing the center or typifying a set of numbers of which it is part, such as a median, weighted average, or moving average.

average balance: The amount of deposits maintained in a bank by one using bank-extended credit, with the deposits expressed as a percentage of credit in use. An average of $5,000 in outstanding loans coupled with an average of $1,000 in deposits for the same period would result in a 20% average balance.

average cost: In inventory valuation, the total cost of all salable or usable items in the group of items being measured divided by the number of such items.

average life: The projected useful life of a group of depreciating assets, taken together and weighted for relative original costs.

averaging: An investment technique, consisting of buying the same securities at successively lower prices as a stock goes down or "averaging down," or of buying the same securities at successively higher prices as prices go up or "averaging up." By lessening the risks involved by spreading purchases over a range of prices, averaging is thought to be a mode of insurance against wide stock price fluctuations.

B

baby bond: A bond originally valued at $1000 or less, sometimes at as little as $10; calculated by issuers to appeal to very small investors. These bonds are not routinely accepted for sale or as collateral by banks and brokers, requiring specific agreement to handle.

back: To place oneself behind a plan or project, materially, as in financing a project; by word, as in speaking for a political candidate; or both.

backdating: To date a document earlier than its actual date of execution; for example, the dating of contributions as if they were given on December 31 of one year, rather than on January 2 of the next year, in an attempt to evade timely income tax payments on the money given.

backdoor financing: The means by which a Federal agency raises money for operations other than by direct appropriation, as in the issuance of bonds under general authority previously granted by the legislature or by direct borrowing from the treasury under previously granted authority.

backdoor listing: A stock exchange listing occurring due to the acquisition of a listed company by an unlisted company, with the acquiring company then also acquiring listing; sometimes occurring when the acquiring company would not otherwise have been eligible for listing.

back office: The business handling operations of a securities brokerage firm, including such functions as the execution of trades and the handling of customer accounts.

back spread: In arbitrage, a smaller than normal difference in price in two or more markets on the currencies, securities, or commodities being traded. For example, if the normal price difference between the New York and Tokyo prices of a given stock is $2, and the difference becomes $1, the back spread is $1; then the arbitrageur who buys and sells the stock at the same time in both markets, may make a profit on the transactions.

back taxes: Taxes previously due, and now overdue and unpaid; for example, property taxes due which may ultimately result in forced sale by government to satisfy those taxes.

backwardation: See inverted market.

bad debt: An uncollectible debt. Businesses often hold reserves against such uncollectibles; commercial banks are required by law to hold minimum bad debt reserves against possible loan losses.

bad delivery: In stock sales, a physical transfer of the stock sold which does not conform to stock exchange rules; the defects in delivery must be corrected for the transfer to be completed.

bad faith: Intent to deceive or defraud, usually in relation to a contract; often applied to the state of mind of one committing a willful breach of contract, beyond honest mistake or simple negligence.

bad title: Title that is so defective or otherwise encumbered that it cannot be transferred.

baht: The main currency unit of Thailand, bearing the same relationship to Thailand's national currency system as does the dollar to the United States currency system.

bailee: One who holds property for another, and returns that property after specified purposes are accomplished, as in the instances of a broker, bank, or freight shipper.

bailment: The delivery of property to be held in trust by one for another, and the creation of an express or implied contractual relationship between owner and bailee, in such areas as banking, transporting, warehousing, and rental-purchase agreements.

bailor: One who entrusts property to another for the accomplishment of specific purposes, and to whom that property is to be returned after those purposes are accomplished.

balance: 1. The plus or minus total in an account after all debits and credits have been added and subtracted within that account. **2.** The amount needed to equalize credits and debits in an account. **3.** To equalize credits and debits in an account.

balanced budget: A budget with equal income and expenditures for a given period; the stated but unmet goal of the United States government for most of this century.

balanced fund: A kind of mutual fund that invests in several kinds of securities, including both stocks and bonds, in contrast to some other kinds of mutual funds that focus on specific kinds of securities investments, such as growth stocks or municipal bonds.

balance due: That sum still due and unpaid on a debt obligation; usually an installment debt obligation or one on which a partial payment has been made, to be followed by full payment.

balance of indebtedness: The balance of all amounts owed between a country and the rest of the world in a period. If all amounts owed by a country and its citizens are smaller than the amounts owed to them by the rest of the world, the country is an international creditor; if the reverse, an international debtor.

balance of payments: The balance of all transactions between a country and the rest of the world in a period, including individual, business, institutional, and governmental transactions. It consists of the current account, which includes all exports and imports of goods and services; the capital account, which includes all exports and imports of investment capital; and the gold account, which includes all financial reserves of any kind exported or imported to bring total exports and imports into balance.

balance of trade: The balance of all merchandise transactions between a country and the rest of the world in a period; a major element in the balance of payments. More merchandise exports than imports give a country a favorable balance of trade; more imports than exports are an unfavorable balance of trade.

balance sheet: A financial statement, indicating the financial condition of a business or other organization as of a specific time, including all assets, liabilities and ownership equities. Balance sheets vary in size and the amount of detail included, from the closely detailed statements of some small businesses to the summary statements of major corporations.

balloon: An item of value, such as a common stock or limited edition, that is so far overpriced in relation to its underlying value that some form of manipulation is suspected.

bank: 1. Any organization lending, handling, holding, investing, or otherwise servicing money and other instruments of and claims to value; includes commercial, savings, mortgage and investment banks, savings and loan associations, trust companies, credit unions, and government banks of several kinds. **2.** To place money or other instruments of value in the hands of a banking organization for saving or holding purposes.

bank account: Money deposited in a bank for saving or holding. In a checking account the money is payable on demand; in a savings account, payable on notice to the bank of intent to withdraw funds, a requirement that is generally waived by the bank; in a time deposit, sometimes called a longterm savings account, payable at a stated time after deposit has been made.

bank charter: See articles of association.

bank check: A check by a bank drawn on itself; usually used by bank customers as a means of cashless payment or in transferring funds.

bank credit: 1. Credit available from banks as bank loans and investments grow, as federally regulated by current monetary policies and reserve requirements.   **2.** Credit to the bank account of a borrower, now available for the borrower's use.

bank discount: See discount.

bank draft: A check to a specific payee drawn by a bank on its own funds on deposit with another bank. For example, a bill rendered in Swiss francs to an American may be paid by a bank draft purchased in the United States by the American, sent to Switzerland and cashed there with a correspondent bank of the American bank that issued the bank draft.

banker's acceptance: A negotiable time draft or bill of exchange traded in money markets. These instruments usually originate in international trade, resulting from export or import transactions in which a bank accepts an obligation to pay the seller if the buyer defaults; they also originate in domestic shipping transactions and in the storage of staples in the United States and abroad.

banker's bank: 1. A large, centrally located bank having a large volume of transactions with smaller banks.   **2.** A central bank, such as a Federal Reserve Bank or the Bank of England.

bank examination: 1. A thorough and formal official inspection of a bank's financial condition and related affairs, as required by applicable banking laws. National banks are inspected at least twice yearly by Federal bank examiners; most states require twice yearly inspections of state banks by state bank examiners. Examinations may be conducted more than twice yearly as required by regulating authorities; may sift any aspect of bank activities; and may go beyond legal compliance questions into any aspect of bank management.   **2.** Inspection of the bank's financial condition and related affairs by the bank's own internal auditing staff.

bank examiners: Those empowered to examine any and all aspects of banking activity within their jurisdiction pursuant to law.

bank failure: The temporary or permanent closing of a bank because it is unable to meet the withdrawal demands of its depositors; such failure may be "hidden," when the failing bank is taken over by another bank that is able to meet depositor's demands. After the widespread bank failures following the stock market crash of 1929, a combination of regulation and Federal deposit insurance have served to minimize depositor losses from bank failure.

Bank for International Settlements: A European international banking organization, in which many European central banks are stockholders; functions as agent and handles international transactions for several supra-national European financial and administrative organizations, such as the European Payments Union and the International Monetary Fund.

bank holding company: Any company owning a controlling interest in one or more banks. Such companies are regulated by applicable Federal laws; they may and often do engage in non-banking activities under conditions specified by law and the regulating authorities.

bank holiday: Any day on which the banks are closed by law or official proclamation in a given jurisdiction.

banking law: The body of laws, regulations, administrative decisions, and court cases that form the legal framework within which the banking industry operates.

bank money: Money held in bank checking accounts as demand deposits; this is the most common form of money.

bank money order: A money order sold by banks, usually for a somewhat smaller fee than a postal money order. It is a kind of cashier's check, and a negotiable instrument that may be signed by many successive endorsers.

bank moratorium: See moratorium.

bank note: A form of currency, issued by a bank and backed by that bank's promise to pay the bearer of the note on demand. In the United States today, the only bank issuer of such currency is the Federal Reserve System, operating as a national bank.

bank of issue: Any bank that has the power to issue bank notes; such central banks as the Federal Reserve Banks, the Bank of Canada and the Bank of England are banks of issue.

bank reserve: The amount of money banks are required by law to hold as a reserve against possible depositor demands, composed of vault cash on hand and currency reserves on deposit with a Federal Reserve Bank. These legal reserves are expressed as a percentage of deposits. In banking practice, primary reserves are vault cash, Federal Reserve deposits, and demand deposits in correspondent banks; secondary reserves are highly marketable short-term securities supplementing the bank's more liquid assets.

bank run: Unusually heavy withdrawals by depositors, due to a loss of confidence in the bank's ability to satisfy those demands, often leading to a crisis of bank liquidity and bank failure.

bankrupt: Describing a corporation or individual who has been declared to be in a state of bankruptcy by court proceeding. Often used more loosely to describe a person or firm that is insolvent, whether or not so declared by the courts; used even more generally, describes something of no further value, such as a bankrupt policy.

bankruptcy: The condition of a debtor who has been declared insolvent by court proceeding, and whose financial affairs are being administered by the court through a receiver or trustee. Bankruptcy may be voluntary, when applied for and granted to an insolvent debtor by the court, or may be involuntary, when petitioned for by creditors and granted by the court. Businesses and individuals going into voluntary bankruptcy often use the court as a shield against their creditors while they attempt to solve their financial difficulties.

Banks for Cooperatives: A Federal lending agency established by the Farm Credit Act of 1933, consisting of a central bank and twelve district banks that loan money to farm cooperatives.

bank statement: 1. The balance sheet of a bank, issued periodically, covering assets, liabilities, and net worth. **2.** A statement as to the condition of a depositor's account, usually sent to a depositor monthly.

bar chart: A graph that uses horizontal bars or vertical columns to compare several items in terms of one or two characteristics, or to show the differing proportion of components in several items; widely used in statistical reports for popular consumption and for financial summaries; also called a histogram.

bargain: 1. A contract or agreement, as in to strike a bargain. **2.** To negotiate a contract or agreement. **3.** Anything bought or sold at a price significantly below what it would normally get in its market.

bargain counter: A securities industry term for a market in which a wide range of securities are for sale at prices considerably below the underlying value of the securities themselves; often widely used in a period of stock market decline.

bargain hunter: 1. A securities industry term describing a buyer who looks and waits for bargain counter securities, then buys as low as thought possible; often widely encountered in a period of stock market decline. **2.** Anyone searching for a bargain in any market.

barter: To trade goods and services directly, without the use of money or any other medium of exchange.

base building: Describing a period in which a securities market or single security is beginning to rebuild strength in preparation for a general upward trend after a period of decline; characterized by small price movements and increasing trading volume.

base period: The time period chosen to serve as a yardstick for measuring changes. In business, usually a year chosen against which to measure changes in economic data. For example, choosing 1979 as a base period for a price index would mean that 1979 would be set at a given value of 100. If prices rose 15% in 1980 in relation to the 1979 prices, the 1980 price index would be 115.

basic commodities: Commodities defined by United States law as ''basic,'' and therefore required by law to be price-supported or eligible for loans and payments, including corn, cotton, mohair, peanuts, rice, tobacco, wheat and wool.

basic cost: The total price paid by the purchaser who first buys an item for use. For example, the buyer of a new car incurs a basic cost, which is incurred only once in the life of an item; the cost to a later buyer on resale is not a basic cost.

basis: 1. In Federal tax law, the cost of property to a taxpayer and therefore the figure used for computing both depreciation and gains.   **2.** The rate of interest paid on bonds and other debt securities.   **3.** The current annual rate of return on stocks, expressed as the relation of current dividends to current market prices.   **4.** In commodity trading, the difference between spot and future prices.

basis point: One hundredth of one percent; used to express changes in the yields of stocks and bonds. Bond yields often change only slightly, and must be expressed in fractions of a percent.

bear: One who feels that an entire market, or one or more securities or commodities traded in that market, will fall, and sells accordingly; the opposite of bull. Bears often sell when they think the market is falling or about to fall; they sell short, that is, selling unowned or borrowed stocks or commodities, and hoping to profit by sales at higher prices covered by purchases later at expected lower prices.

bearer: One who has physical possession of negotiable instruments, such as notes, bills and bonds. If such instruments are payable to their bearer, that is if ownership is transferred by a mere change of physical possession, then the bearer is in law the owner of those negotiable instruments. For other types of instruments, the bearer is not necessarily the owner at law.

bearer bond: A bond payable to its bearer, carrying coupons that are clipped and presented to the bond issuer for interest payments. A bearer bond can be transferred without endorsement by simple transfer of physical possession.

bear market: A market in which prices drop over a long enough period of time to indicate a downward trend; normally used to describe trends measured in months or years, rather than short-term swings, no matter how sharp the downward swing or how heavy the volume traded.

bear raid: Strong short selling by bears, tending to force the market down so that they will profit by buying to cover their short sales at lower prices. The securities laws prohibit attempted downward manipulation of the market through such devices as the pooling of funds with intent to manipulate and the spreading of false rumors to drive prices down.

below par: Below listed or par value. Any stock selling for less than its listed value is selling below par.

below the line: Unusual items, such as major one-time costs and revenues, which are shown separately on accounting statements. Such items are described as ''below the line,'' while customary items are ''above the line.''

benchmark: A reference point, from which calculations and predictions stem; for example, a major court decision, providing a basis for evaluating probable future court decisions on closely equivalent matters.

beneficial interest: The right to benefits flowing from an insurance policy, a will, or a contract.

beneficiary: One who is legally entitled to benefit from a will, trust, insurance policy, or contract. A beneficiary may benefit from property legally held by another, as in many trusts, or may hold ownership of the property, as in a lump sum payment of all proceeds of a life insurance policy to survivors.

bequest: A gift of personal property conveyed by the terms of a will; in contrast a willed gift of real property is called a devise.

best efforts: In the issue of new securities, a commitment by the investment banking organization or group handling the new issue to sell the securities as an agent of the issuing party, rather than as underwriter of the entire issue. While an underwriter buys the entire issue, pays the issuer a fixed price, and takes possession of the securities, a best efforts seller acts as agent, does not take possession, and returns unsold securities to their issuer. New securities issues sold ''best efforts'' will often provide that unless a specified minimum portion of the issue is sold, the new issue will be withdrawn and the investors' money will be refunded.

bid: 1. An offer to buy immediately at a specific rate.   **2.** In the securities markets, as offer to buy at a specific price, which, if accepted by a seller, becomes a firm transaction.

bid and asked: The price quotation on a stock, ''bid'' being the price at which the stock is wanted and ''asked'' the price at which it is offered for sale.

bidding up: Raising a bid for a security or commodity before a previous bid has been accepted; occurs when a market or single investment vehicle is thought to be about to move up rapidly.

bid pulling: In auctions, an auctioneer's slow bid closing technique, aimed at getting the highest possible bid for an item being auctioned, by delaying the close of bidding as long as possible so that any wavering prospective bidder may have a chance to put in a higher bid.

Big Board: A popular term for the New York Stock Exchange.

big business: In popular usage, the largest privately held enterprises in the country, taken as a group.

Big Steel: In popular usage, the United States Steel Corporation.

bilateral trade: Trade proceeding between two nations functioning as major trading partners, and wholly or largely excluding other nations. In practice, such trade is usually a one-way arrangement, with a dominant nation free to trade with many other nations and a subservient nation forced to confine its trade to the dominant nation, to its great economic disadvantage; a standard colonial arrangement.

bill: 1. A written, formal statement of specifics. Some of the many kinds of bills important in commerce are the bill of exchange, bill of lading, and bill of sale. **2.** A list of charges, as in an invoice for goods and services. **3.** A piece of paper money, such as a dollar bill.

bill of credit: A written request to extend credit, and a guarantee of the credit extended, usually directed to correspondent banks abroad on behalf of a traveler.

bill of exchange: A written, unconditional order from one party instructing a second party to pay a specific amount of money to a third party. The order may be to pay on demand or at a specified future time.

bills-only trading: The policy of a government's central bank, such as the Federal Reserve System, in trading only the short-term securities of its own government; in the United States, part of Federal manipulation of money and credit, through partial control of commercial bank reserves available for lending.

binder: A relatively small "good faith" payment by buyer to seller in a real estate or insurance transaction; usually returnable if the transaction is not consummated.

black light: A fluorescent light that makes it possible to examine collectible and antique objects and find most kinds of alterations and repair; a key means of determining authenticity and often therefore value.

black market: Any marketplace in which something is traded contrary to law; an illegal marketplace. Black markets exist throughout the world in many commercial and financial areas, ranging from the illegal sale of meat in countries where meat is rationed to illegal trading of currency in countries where such trading is restricted or prohibited.

black money: Money or other stores of value gained illegally, such as the proceeds of bribery, embezzlement, and drug dealing.

Black Tuesday: October 29, 1929, the day of the stock market crash which preceded the Great Depression of the 1930's.

blank check: 1. A check signed by its maker but with key information, such as payee or amount, omitted. **2.** A colloquial expression of the delegation of virtually unlimited responsibility or agency to another, as in "He has a blank check" to do something.

blanket bond: See fidelity bond.

blanket insurance policy: An insurance policy covering a group of related items, rather than a single item. Buildings and their contents are often covered by blanket policies, as are such related items as a fleet of company cars.

blanket mortgage: A mortgage loan secured by more than one property, and which encumbers all properties so mortgaged. The mortgagee must pay back the entire amount of the mortgage before any of the properties are mortgage-free.

blind entry: An entry into accounting records that simply states the amount of the entry, but that is unsupported by additional information, explanation, or documentation.

blind pool partnership: In real estate investment, a limited partnership in which none of the assets to be acquired by the partnership are known to the investor at the time of purchase of the limited partnership interest.

blind trust: A popular term for an arrangement whereby a person places some or all financial affairs in trust, beyond that person's personal control; often an attempt by a public official to avoid charges of a conflict of interest.

block: In the securities markets, a large number of shares of a single security traded as a group, as in the purchase or sale of a thousand shares of the common stock of American Telephone and Telegraph by a single buyer or seller.

blocked account: A bank account or a store of money or credit that has been restricted by the country in which it is located, so that it cannot be drawn upon for use in other countries. Such blocked bank accounts are often also "frozen," that is held where they are, with any kind of use prohibited.

blocked exchange: A government policy that allows only specified kinds of foreign exchange transactions. This kind of exchange restriction is usually part of attempts to control current or potential balance of payments and international currency valuations problems.

block trader: In the securities industry, a trader who specializes or is largely engaged in the purchase and sale of substantial blocks of securities, working as a direct broker with buyers and sellers, and bypassing the organized stock markets. Large institutional traders, such as banks and mutual funds, work directly with block traders.

blowoff: A period of extremely heavy securities buying at the top of a rising market; almost always followed by a sharp, though sometimes brief, price break.

blue chip: A common stock that is highly esteemed as an investment, for its relative safety, consistent earnings, consistent dividend payout, and strong future prospects; often applied to the thirty industrials used in the Dow Jones Industrials average; but can refer to many other stocks as well.

blue sky: Statements unsupported by facts or contrary to facts, and made with intent to deceive or defraud; "That has a lot of blue sky in it," is a common reaction to what is perceived as an over-imaginative sales approach.

Blue Sky laws: State securities laws aimed at the regulation of many aspects of securities industries practice and procedure, from the issuance of new securities to day-to-day procedures in the industry, with particular attention to questions of fraud and deceptive practices.

board: 1. In popular usage, the board of directors of an organization. **2.** In the securities industry, the device by which securities prices are posted in a brokerage office; usually no longer a board but an electronic data processing display terminal.

board lot: The standard minimum lot traded on a stock exchange, usually set by the rules of that exchange. For example, the New York Stock Exchange sets 100 shares as the standard lot of common shares traded, with a relatively small number of specific exceptions. Lots of less than 100 shares are called "odd lots."

board of directors: A group elected by a corporation's stockholders as the chief policy-making body of the corporation. The board of directors is responsible to the stockholders for the overall direction and control of the corporation and usually selects all major corporate officers.

Board of Governors: See Federal Reserve System.

board of trade: 1. An organization composed of member businesses, usually in a geographical area, which promotes group business and community interests. **2.** A name adopted by some commodity exchanges, as in the Chicago Board of Trade.

board room: 1. In the securities industry, a room set aside by brokers for customers, in which the latest quotations are posted.   **2.** A room set aside by companies for meetings of the Board of Directors. In general usage, the term has come to mean any room set aside for formal meetings, including management, staff, and training meetings of all kinds.

bogus: Describing that which is counterfeit or otherwise false, such as counterfeit money and other financial instruments.

boiler plate: A popular term for all standard clauses in legal documents, such as contracts and wills; sometimes used more loosely to describe any conventional often-encountered body of language.

boiler room: In the securities industry, any firm that uses high pressure selling tactics to deceptively and often fraudulently sell securities. Sales are usually made by phone out of minimally equipped offices, using techniques that are specifically prohibited by the securities laws.

bolivar: The main currency unit of Venezuela, bearing the same relationship to Venezuela's national currency system as does the dollar to the United States currency system.

bona fide: 1. In good faith; applied to one who contracts, holds, buys, or sells, innocent of any knowledge or intent that could be construed as bad faith or fraudulent intent.   **2.** A popular term for guarantees of good faith, as when one party to an agreement wants to see the other party's "bona fides" before proceeding to agreement.

bond: 1. An interest-bearing debt instrument issued by a government or a corporation, which promises to pay specific sums at named times, with interest usually paid in installments and principal paid in a lump sum.   **2.** An instrument pledging one as surety for another, as when a bonding company issues a surety bond to cover work to be performed by a contractor, or a bail bondsman issues a bond pledging payment of bail set in a criminal proceeding.   **3.** Any stipulated amount that must be paid by a specified date.   **4.**

Describing taxable goods held pending payment of taxes or duties; such goods are described as being held "in bond."

bond circular: An advertisement offering bonds for sale, which fully describes the nature of the bonds being offered and any conditions attached to the offer; usually placed by banks, bond brokers, and bond underwriting syndicates.

bond discount: The difference between the face amount of a bond, or kind of bond, and any lower price at which it is actually sold.

bond dividend: A dividend issued by a corporation to its stockholders in the form of corporate bonds.

bonded debt: The amount of debt being carried by an entity, as indicated by the total amount of bonds outstanding.

bonded warehouse: A government-licensed warehouse that holds taxable goods pending payment of customs duties and other taxes due.

bond fund: 1. A mutual fund specializing in bond trading.   **2.** A special fund set up by government to handle the proceeds of a bond issue.

bondholder: The owner of a bond and therefore the one to whom payment is owed. Ownership is evidenced by either the simple holding of bearer bonds or being the named owner of registered bonds.

bond house: A securities firm engaged in buying, selling, and underwriting bonds, sometimes exclusively and sometimes in conjunction with other securities industry activities.

bonding company: A company in the business of providing surety bonds.

bond market: A general term for all markets in which bonds are traded, including both stock exchanges listing bonds traded on those exchanges and the major over-the-counter transactions occurring between institutions.

bond premium: The difference between the face amount of a bond, or kind of bond, and any higher price at which it is actually sold.

bond ratings: Evaluation systems established by private companies to assess the investment quality or relative risks of bonds offered for sale. Moody's and Standard and Poor's are the two main bond risk evaluators. The Moody's system rates on a scale from Aaa to C; the Standard and Poor's scale runs from AAA to D.

bonus: 1. Anything freely given over and above what is due under the terms of a contractual relationship, as in stock given to officers of a corporation by its board of directors, or a Christmas bonus given to employees.   **2.** In commercial contracts, sometimes used to describe premium payments, the addition of a fixed sum to be paid by one party to another on top of normal contract terms. For example, a lender in a tight money market may add a "point" to a mortgage loan, forcing the borrower to pay one extra percent of the entire amount loaned, payable immediately upon execution of the loan agreement, out of the proceeds of the loan, or even earlier, refundable to the borrower if the loan is not made.

bonus stock: Common stock given as a bonus to buyers of bonds or preferred stock, often in company start-up situations as extra payments to promoters and other "insiders." This practice is either prohibited or severely restricted in most states.

book: 1. To enter a transaction into a book of account.   **2.** In the securities industry, a trading specialist's order book.   **3.** A shorthand term for book value.

book of account: Any record that is part of an accounting system, including both transaction records in permanent form and supporting papers, such as memoranda and invoices.

book of original entry: Any journal or other record of the day-to-day transactions of a business, kept in permanent form and serving as a source of entries into an accounting system.

book value: 1. The net assets of a business, derived by subtracting all liabilities from all assets. The book value of a share of common stock consists of net assets minus the value of all preferred stock outstanding divided by the number of shares of common stock outstanding.   **2.** The net value of an asset, or a kind of asset, as carried on the books of account of a business entity, such as the book value of a company car.

boom: A period of strong and sustained ecoomic growth; usually applied to an entire economy, but sometimes used to describe a company or section of the economy.

boom and bust: Describing the unrestrained operation of the business cycle; for example, the boom of the 1920's, followed by the bust that was the Great Depression of the 1930's.

bootstrapping: The generation of activity and development of business with limited means, depending for growth upon resources generated by the business.

borrowing: The process of getting a loan from others with a promise to repay, usually within a certain period at a specified rate of interest.

bottleneck inflation: Price rises in all or part of an economy caused by substantial and usually unanticipated increases in demand or decreases in supply for one product or a small group of products.

bottom: In the securities industry, that time during a substantial stock prices swing in which average stock prices are lowest. During the course of such a swing, many successive estimates are made as to when the market has "touched bottom;" when estimates must be revised to conform with current realities observers often say "the bottom has dropped out of the market."

bottom line: The net of profit or loss; use of the term has expanded to include any result thought to be final, or to refer generally to the financial result of any endeavor, whether or not it is subject to accounting procedures. It is sometimes used as synonymous with "ultimate result."

bottom out: To reach the lowest price range after a period of steep securities price declines, anticipating a reversal of price trends and the start of an upward move; always an estimate.

bought in: Describing merchandise unsold at auction because no bidder reached its reserve, or minimum asking price.

bourgeoisie: 1. In French, middle class. **2.** In Marxist theory, a term for the ruling or capitalist class, as distinguished from the proletariat or working class.

bourse: 1. The French stock exchange. **2.** European stock exchanges generally, with the exception of those located in the English-speaking countries.

branch bank: The local office of a bank headquartered elsewhere. Branches of banks range widely in size and the scope of the functions performed. A large commercial banking branch may cover the whole spectrum of commercial bank functions and handle as much banking business as the home office, while a very small branch of a commercial bank, savings bank, or savings and loan association may be little more than a single room with a drive-in window.

branch banking: A system of banking authorized by law, by which banks are enabled to have a home office and many branch offices. In the United States, banks have limited ability to branch, being confined to states, metropolitan areas, cities, and in some instances to single home office installations, with only foreign branch operations unrestricted. In many other countries, banks are national, can branch without restriction, and therefore in some instances have thousands of branches.

breach of contract: Failure by a contracting party to do or allow to be done something that is required by the terms of the contract; or clear renunciation of the contract before it goes into effect. Such failure or renunciation can lead to invalidation of the contract and to the assessment of damages.

break: In the securities markets, a very sharp downturn in prices, often following a period of relatively narrow price movement.

break even: To conclude any commercial transaction with neither profit or loss; often used narrowly, to describe only the money factors in the transaction, failing to take into account many very real costs, such as overhead.

break-even analysis: An analysis of expense and revenue factors, often expressed graphically, aimed at determining at what cost and price points a product, product line, or company break even. Because break-even charts indicate alternate break-even points as cost and price assumptions are changed, this kind of analysis is especially useful in profitability studies, new product proposal evaluation, pricing, and in a large number of corporate planning applications.

break-even chart: A chart used to represent graphically the results of break-even analyses.

break-even point: The intersection of costs and prices in a break-even analysis. In planning, break-even points change as assumptions change; in profitability studies the actual break-even point of a product, product line, or company is a crucial success indicator.

breakout: A market price move past a level that had been thought by investors and their advisors likely to hold relatively firm, whether on the way up or down in price.

Bretton Woods Agreement: An agreement stemming from the 44-nation conference held in Bretton Woods, New Hampshire in July, 1944, under which the International Monetary Fund and the Bank of Reconstruction and Development were established.

broad market: In the securities industry, a market in which trading is very active and many kinds of shares or commodities are traded; used to describe wide and heavy volume, without reference to upward or downward trends in market prices.

broken lot: A group of items for sale in a smaller than usual lot. For example, if a retailer may normally buy from a wholesaler by the dozen, any lot of less than a dozen offered by the wholesaler is a broken lot. In the securities industry, broken lots are called, "odd lots."

broker: One engaged in the business of bringing buyers and sellers together for a fee, who acts as a limited agent for purposes of purchase or sale. A broker acts in another's name, as distinguished from commission merchants or factors, who act in their own names, buying and selling goods belonging to others. A broker is an agent, as distinguished from a middleman, who brings parties together, but not as agent for any of them. There are many kinds of specialist brokers, including stock, insurance, real estate, commodities, collectibles, ship, money, and mortgage brokers.

brokerage: 1. Fees to brokers for transactions arranged between buyers and sellers; such fees may take many forms, including percentage commissions, fixed fees per transaction, and a wide variety of special arrangements in specific situations.   **2.** A business run by a broker or brokers.

broker-dealer: See dealer.

broker's loan: A loan made by a bank to a securities broker or dealer to finance securities carried, underwritten, and purchased for customer margin accounts, the securities acting as collateral for the loan.

bubble: An investment that may or may not be intrinsically and dangerously speculative, but which becomes so as irrational buying pushes it higher and higher, far beyond the real value of its underlying assets. At some point in every bubble, speculative confidence weakens, actual or adverse facts begin to be asserted and panic selling begins as "the bubble bursts."

bucket shop: A fraudulent stock brokerage operation, which either takes customer orders and money, does not execute the orders, keeps the money, folds and disappears very quickly; or takes customer orders and money and does not execute the orders in a timely way to the detriment of the customer and the advantage of the bucket shop operators.

budget: 1. Any formal estimate of future income and costs. A budget is a primary financial planning tool for public and private purposes. The operating budget, usually prepared from year to year, functions as both a forecasting device and performance yardstick; the capital budget functions to forecast expenses and consequent capital needs. **2.** To estimate future income and to attempt to establish a spending plan that conforms with income estimates.

budgetary variance: The amount that actual income and expense differ from the estimates made for budget purposes.

budgeting: The formal process of developing a budget. In business organizations, budget development is often a process involving a series of formal estimates made by every responsible member of management, the working of those estimates into coherent company-wide forecasts, a series of refining and reworking steps, and ultimately the production of the budget as a primary working tool for all of management.

budget period: The time covered by a budget. Operating budgets are normally developed on an annual basis, with results stated monthly and the budget reviewed quarterly, annually, or at any time variances from forecasts cause management to undertake a special review. The period of a capital budget varies with the projects budgeted.

building and loan association: An early form of and name for what has become the savings and loan association. As early "building associations" began to focus more and more on the savings function, the general name for this kind of banking organization changed as well.

built-in stabilizer: Any integral portion of an economic structure that tends to smooth out the "boom-or-bust" tendencies of the business cycle, including such features as unemployment compensation, social security and private pension payments, welfare payments, price supports, and tuition assistance plans. Built-in stabilizers are to be distinguished from such potential stabilizers as money supply control, which depends on conscious acts of manipulation.

bulge: In the securities markets, any relatively small, unanticipated, and short-lived increase in the general level of securities prices.

bulk sale: The sale of most or all of the assets or stock of a business, to avoid creditors or as part of a bankruptcy proceeding. Such sales to avoid creditors are prohibited by law.

bull: One who feels that an entire market, or one or more securities or commodities traded in that market, will rise, and acts accordingly; the opposite of bear. Bulls often buy when they think the market is rising or about to rise, and optimistically hold on when the market is falling.

bullion: Gold and silver in any form other than coins, and available for coinage. Bullion may be in bars, ingots, lumps, or nuggets; may be of ore or refined; and may be refined and put to other non-coinage uses, such as dishes or jewelry. In international markets, gold and silver are usually encountered in standard bars of minimum specified fineness or quality.

bullion dealer: A private person or organization buying and selling gold or silver bullion.

bullion value: The value of a coin as measured by the market value of its gold or silver content at current market prices, treating the coin as if it were a commodity.

bull market: A market in which prices rise over a long enough period of time to indicate an upward trend; normally used to describe trends measured in months or years, rather than to describe short-term swings, no matter how sharp the move upward or how heavy the volume traded.

Bulk Sales Act: A kind of statute aimed at the prohibition of secret bulk sales of assets or stock by businesses to avoid the claims of creditors.

Bureau of International Commerce: A Federal agency responsible for assisting the American business community in a wide variety of international matters, including exporting and licensing, and for representing the United States Government in dealing with international trading authorities.

Bureau of Printing and Engraving: A bureau of the Treasury Department, responsible for the total production of all currency and other financial printing, and a wide variety of other items for the United States Government.

business: 1. Any gainful activity. The gain sought is generally commercial or financial, but the term is so broad that it includes activities engaged in for personal development and emotional gain.   **2.** An organization engaged in any form of commerce.   **3.** An amount of trade engaged in, as in "Total business for the day was $1,000."

business activity: The general level of business transactions within an economy, taking into account such indicators as the number of transactions, their total value, employment and loans.

business barometers: See economic indicators.

business combination: Any fusing of two or more businesses into one, however achieved. Such combinations may take the form of acquisitions by one of others; of consolidations forming new businesses; of purchases; or of mergers of interest.

business cycle: A widely observed general tendency of the United States and other similar economies to alternate periods of economic prosperity and depression, boom and bust. In recent decades the intensity of cyclical swings has generally been thought to have diminished; causes of cycles and variations in their intensity are the subject of considerable theoretical speculation.

business environment: A complex of social, political and economic factors surrounding a business, and impinging on its ability to operate. Such factors as government regulations, taxes, local zoning restrictions, consumerism, and local union activity are elements that combine to create a business environment.

business failure: A firm that ceases doing business primarily because of inability to meet its obligations. Failure may be involuntary, as in bankruptcies, foreclosures, assignments, and attachments; or it may be voluntary, as in cessation of business leaving unpaid debts or making an agreement to pay part of creditor's claims.

business firm: An organization doing business for profit, and organized as a corporation, partnership or individual proprietorship.

business forecasting: Attempting to predict future business trends and events through the use of a considerable variety of analytical approaches and tools. Forecasting usually involves the use of statistical techniques, often featuring mathematical models and computerized analyses. Business forecasting is far from precise, and invariably includes political and social analyses and a good deal of speculation.

business indicators: See economic indicators.

business law: See commercial law.

business panics: See panics.

business paper: Notes or trade acceptances used as payment for merchandise, instead of cash or checks; synonymous with "trade paper."

business risk: For credit and investment purposes, an estimate of the skills and performance of management, of such marketplace factors as relative prices and the strength of competition, and of the over-all conduct of and prospects for the business.

business situs: A legal determination as to where a business is located for tax purposes, more popularly referred to as "doing business at."

business trust: See Massachusetts Trust.

bust: A deep, major, protracted downward swing in the business cycle; an economic depression. There have been several substantial downward swings in the business cycle since 1945, but the last generally recognized "bust" was the Great Depression of the 1930s.

buy back offer: A bid by a dealer in collectibles or antiques to a recent purchaser to repurchase itens, usually at some sort of premium to the purchaser.

buyer's market: Any market in which supply exceeds demand, giving buyers leverage over sellers in such areas as prices, quality guarantees, and delivery timing.

buying on margin: See margin.

buy order: An order from a securities or commodities purchaser to one purchasing on his or her behalf, such as a bank or broker, to buy under specified conditions and at specified prices. Unless otherwise stated, such orders are normally good only as of the day placed, and must be replaced on subsequent days if not then consummated.

buyout: 1. A purchase of controlling ownership in a business organization. **2.** A purchase of any entire stock of goods for sale.

buy outright: To buy on a cash basis, therefore taking full title to that which has been purchased on conclusion of the sale. In the securities industry, buying for cash, rather than on margin.

C

c. or C: See circa.

ca: See circa.

cable rate: The rate charged by a bank for sending money abroad via cable or other electronic means. The purchaser of the bank draft being transmitted pays the cost of the cable plus a somewhat higher rate than would be charged for a check, reflecting cable handling costs plus the issuing bank's loss of interest on the funds so quickly transmitted, which, if transmitted by check, would take as long as several weeks to clear.

cable transfer: A means of sending money abroad quickly by cable or other electronic means, through a bank or other transmitting agency.

call: 1. An option to buy a specific amount of stock at a fixed price and within a specified time. The option buyer is speculating—buying an option for a set amount now and hoping that the stock will rise more than the amount paid within the period covered by the option. If the stock does rise the option buyer may profit greatly by exercising the option, buying the stock, and then immediately reselling it. But if the stock goes down, the option buyer will lose some or all of the money spent for the option. The opposite of a "call" is a "put." **2.** A demand for payment of the balance due on a purchase of capital stock. **3.** A repurchase of outstanding preferred stocks or bonds by a corporation, if authorized by the terms of the issue.

callable bond: A bond that may be redeemed by its issuer at any time before maturity, usually with a premium payment to the bond-holder at the time of redemption. The "callable" feature of the bond is specified by the terms of the issue, often on the face of the bond itself.

call loan: A demand loan, which either lender or borrower may terminate at will and without notice. In the securities industry, it is a standard form of loan from bank to stockbroker, amounting to a special line of credit on which interest is computed daily at that day's rate.

call money: Money lent by banks on which repayment may be demanded at any time and without notice.

call premium: The amount of the premium payment due a bond-holder when a callable bond is redeemed before maturity by its issuer, as specified by the terms of the bond issue. That amount may vary with redemption date, the premium diminishing as the bond matures.

cancellation: 1. The legal termination of an instrument or agreement on maturity or completion, such as termination of an insurance policy pursuant to the terms of the contract, whether before or at the end of the term covered by the contract, or the retirement of a debt instrument upon payment in full. **2.** The termination of an order for goods or services, often prior to fulfillment of that order.

cancelled check: A check which has been drawn against a bank account, paid by the bank holding that account; marked, perforated or otherwise voided; and returned to its maker. Cancelled checks serve as evidence that banks have cashed them and that bills have been paid; they also provide hard evidence for use in tax and accounting audits.

capacity: 1. The ability of a business to produce goods and services with its present physical equipment. Usually stated as full theoretical capacity, it differs from practical full capacity, which takes into account unavoidable production losses caused by such factors as machine breakdowns and worker absences.   **2.** In extractive industries, the amount of material that can be extracted in a given period by present equipment, such as the amount of coal a mine or oil a well can produce in twenty-four hours.   **3.** The amount of freight a carrier can carry, as the weight of freight a truck can bear or the volume of goods a boxcar can take.   **4.** A synonym for "business risk."

capital: 1. Any kind of tangible wealth that is or can be used to produce more wealth. In this sense, money invested to start a business is capital. Intangibles, such as the good reputation of one starting a business, are often loosely called capital, but the term is then stretched so far as to make it lose its useful meaning.   **2.** The net worth of a business.   **3.** Amounts invested by shareholders in a business, called "paid-in" capital.

capital account: 1. An account or group of accounts indicating ownership equities. They are designated proprietorship, partnership, or capital stock accounts, depending on the business form of organization.   **2.** Any fixed asset account.

capital appropriation: A sum authorized for capital expenditure by the policy making group of a business organization, usually the board of directors.

capital asset: Any asset held and used for the production of goods and services, including fixed assets, such as land, plant, raw materials sources, and reserves; investments in owned and affiliated companies; and some long term intangibles, such as patents.

capital budget: A budget or part of a budget which handles the acquiring and financing of capital assets. Capital budgets may be developed by private organizations or governments; may be short term or long term; and may be financed out of current revenues or debt instruments or both.

capital coefficient: The amount of new capital investment needed to produce one new unit of output capacity. The figure can be derived for a whole economy or any portion of an economy, and it varies widely from enterprise to enterprise and industry to industry. For example, the capital coefficient, or the amount of new investment, needed in the oil refining industry, which requires heavy plant expenditure to increase capacity and employs relatively few people, is much larger than the capital coefficient of the garment industry, which requires relatively small plant expenditure to increase capacity and employs a great many people.

capital costs: An estimate of what the money tied up in inventories might earn if applied to other investments. For example, if $1,000 tied up in inventory might earn $80 per year, the capital cost of carrying that much inventory for one year would be $80.

capital expenditure: 1. An expenditure to acquire capital assets.   **2.** In accounting, an expenditure which wholly or mainly benefits future accounting periods rather than the current period.

capital flight: See flight of capital.

capital flow: The movement of funds in and out of an enterprise, as recorded in a cash flow statement.

capital formation: In an economy, the total net new private investment in capital assets, derived by totalling gross capital assets investments and subtracting depreciation and other relevant deductions. The rate of capital formation is an important long range indicator of the future health of any economy.

capital gains: The profits realized from a sale or exchange of capital assets, usually securities or realty. Long term capital gains are given preferred treatment for tax purposes, since they are taxed at substantially lower rates than short term gains, which are treated as ordinary income for income tax purposes.

capital goods: Capital in the form of fixed assets used to produce goods, such as plant, equipment and rolling stock. The term is used to describe the assets themselves, rather than the amount or kinds of funds used to acquire them.

capital-intensive: Any kind of business or economic unit requiring large amounts of capital investment relative to the number of people employed in it. For example, the nuclear industry requires far more investment per employee than the garment industry. The nuclear industry is then described as capital-intensive, while the garment industry is described as the opposite—labor-intensive.

capital investment: See capital expenditure.

capitalism: An economic system characterized by private ownership of capital and investment of that capital in the means of production and other wealth-producing ways. Private ownership and the pursuit of profit are essential features of capitalism. In many countries, economies mix public and private ownership, but where a major private sector controls substantial industries, capitalism can be said to exist.

capital issues: The stocks and bonds issued by corporations and governments to finance the purchase of capital assets or to permanently increase the pool of working capital funds. In modern corporate practice, some long term notes and lines of credit also function as part of the long term fund pool, though they are treated differently than stocks and bonds for accounting purposes.

capitalization: The total value of a corporation's stocks, bonds and surpluses. The term includes stocks, normally carried at par rather than market values, and bonds and debentures carried at their face values, but does not include other debts, such as bank loans.

capitalize: To carry forward capital expenditures for accounting purposes. Investments in the acquisition of capital assets then appear as expenditures in future profit and loss statements, and are associated then with any benefits derived from those assets.

capitalized value: The current value of assets that will yield future earnings, derived by projecting both anticipated earnings and interest on the money invested as if it had been borrowed forward over the life of the asset.

capitalized expense: An expense charged to a capital asset account which would normally be charged to a current account and would appear on the current profit and loss statement; for example, tax and interest payments on a plant being built but not yet in operation.

capital market: The long term debt obligations market, dealing in long term loans and bonds, with the proceeds of the obligations normally used to finance the purchase of capital assets. The distinction between long and short term loan markets tends to blur in modern practice, as most major lending institutions engage in both long and short term financing, with financing "packages" often including loans in several forms and of varying durations.

capital movements: The movement of capital, both government and private, between countries, including long and short term loans, credits, deposits, and any other form in which capital can move. The total of all such capital movements forms the capital account portion of a country's balance of payments.

capital-output ratio: See capital coefficient.

capital requirements: The minimum amount of capital a securities or commodities exchange member must have at all times, net and unencumbered by current calls upon it; a sum determined by the rules of each exchange with minimum capital rules.

capital restructuring: See recapitalization.

capital spending: See capital expenditure.

capital stock: The ownership stock in a business, representing the equity held by its owners. Not all of the capital stock need be distributed; some may be held in the business. Sometimes stock issued and outstanding is bought back, wholly or in part, by a business.

capital sum: The principal of an investment plus any sums that have been added to that principal but not yet accounted for as income.

capital surplus: See paid-in surplus.

capital turnover: The speed with which the net worth of a business turns over relative to that business' sales in a given period; usually a period generally accepted and used as a basis of comparison by those in that industry. For example, a business with net worh of $2,-000,000 and sales of $4,000,000 in a year experiences capital turnover of 2:1 in that year. Each industry has its own optimum and average turnover rates, and those considering the extension of credit to a business take capital turnover into account in assessing the health of a business, with relatively slow turnover an indication of possible problems.

captive company: A company entirely owned by another company, and organized for the purpose of providing a particular kind of service or performing a certain kind of function for the owning company; for example, the Western Electric Company, which provides telephone equipment for American Telephone and Telegraph, or a real estate company that functions solely to hold and manage parent company installations.

captive item: An item that is both produced and used by a single firm. For example, telephone equipment is both manufactured and used by American Telephone and Telegraph through its Western Electric Company subsidiary.

captive market: A market that has little real choice as to which seller to buy from; for example, the market for electric power, which is substantially dominated by one supplier in each area.

captive shop: See captive company.

carry: To extend credit to a customer beyond normal practice. For example, a supplier, who normally requires payment within sixty days after delivery of goods and will cut off credit arrangements if a payment is not made, may decide to extend credit and deliver more goods to help a customer through a cash flow problem; a bank may carry a borrower by extending a loan for the same reason.

carrybacks: For business income tax purposes, those current operating losses that can be used to offset profits from preceding years, thereby diminishing taxes for those years.

carryforwards: For business income tax purposes, those current operating losses that cannot be absorbed as carrybacks to diminish taxes on income of previous years, but can be used as deductions carrying over and thrown forward into succeeding years.

carrying charge: Any normal and repeated charge stemming from asset ownership, such as interest charged by brokers on margin accounts and charges for warehousing goods.

carrying cost: The cost of holding an asset, such as inventory or equipment, for a given period, including both actual costs, such as maintenance and warehousing, and opportunity costs, such as the interest that might have been earned at current rates on money tied up in inventory and spent in warehousing.

carrying value: See book value.

carry overs: See carry backs and carry forwards.

cartel: **1.** A group of business entities functioning as a monopoly. **2.** A group of companies or countries functioning together to control all or a substantial part of a world market. A recent example is the Organization of Petroleum Exporting Countries.

cash: **1.** Money in any form that can be directly and immediately used as legal tender, including paper money and coins. **2.** For accounting purposes, anything immediately usable or almost immediately convertible into legal tender, including paper money, coins, checks, net bank balances, and some other negotiable instruments. **3.** To turn a negotiable instrument of any kind into cash as in cashing a bond.

cash and carry: A way of doing business that requires the buyer to pay cash immediately for goods and to carry away the goods bought. Cash and carry is often used in private sales, auctions, and cut price sales conducted by businesses.

cash assets: Assets that are either in ready cash form, such as currency and coins on hand, or that can be easily turned into cash while continuing business as usual, such as bank deposits and trade acceptances.

cash basis: An accounting method that records and keeps books on the basis of when cash is received and spent, rather than accruing income and expenditures. While most individuals operate on a cash basis, most businesses are on an accrual basis.

cashbook: A book in which cash transactions are recorded.

cash budget: An income and expenditure estimate based solely upon cash receipts and cash spent for a certain period. In a cash budget, nothing is accrued or in any way deferred.

cash customer: One who pays for purchases in cash. "Cash" in this sense is used broadly, and includes currency, coins, checks, negotiable money orders, and other readily negotiable instruments.

cash dividend: A dividend paid in cash. Most dividends are paid in cash, although some are paid in stocks, bonds, or other forms.

cash equivalent: What something would be worth if immediately converted into cash. The term is normally encountered in a sale or exchange in which items that are paid for in ways other than money are valued by the transacting parties at agreed-upon levels.

cash flow: The movement of cash into, through, and out of an entity. Cash flow may be traced for an individual or a major corporation; for a single product or a line of products or services.

cash flow statement: A statement accounting for the movement of cash through an entity during a specific period.

cashier: 1. One who directly handles and records receipts and expenditures for a business. **2.** In banking, an officer in charge of the bank's funds, who is directly responsible for all disbursements and must personally authorize them.

cashier's check: A bank's check, signed by a cashier of the bank, and functioning as a direct obligation of the bank. Cashier's checks are issued for many purposes, including deposit transfers, bill payments, and loans.

cash in transit: Cash in motion to or from an entity which at a given moment, has not yet been received or expended and which therefore does not appear on the entity's books as a receipt or expenditure.

cash machine: A machine for dispensing cash, used by banks as a mechanical means of handling depositor transactions, often in hours when banks are closed.

cash market: A market in which commodities are sold for immediate delivery in return for a cash payment.

cash on delivery (C.O.D.): The payment terms of a purchase in which buyer and seller agree that payment will be made in cash immediately upon delivery and acceptance of the goods, with completion of delivery contingent upon cash payment.

cash price: The price of goods or services when payment is made either on delivery or within a specified period thereafter. Normally, cash prices assume payment within 30 days of delivery.

cash rich: Describing a company holding a relative large amount of cash or easily convertible-to-cash assets for a company of its size and kind of business.

cash sale: 1. A sale paid for immediately in cash, either at the point of sale or on delivery, as in most non-credit retail stores. **2.** A sale paid for soon after delivery, often within a specified 30 day period, as in many industrial sales.

cash statement: A periodic statement of cash flow for specific, usually short periods, such as days or weeks. The statement shows cash balances on hand at the beginning of the period, cash in and out during the period, and the balance on hand at the close of the period.

cash surrender value: The amount an insurance policy holder or other contracting party can recover upon cancellation of a contract. The term is most often applied to ''whole'' or ''straight-line'' life insurance policies, which incorporate both death insurance and savings features, and is the net of previously paid premiums plus interest minus sums actually paid for the insurance portion of the policy and certain other deductions.

casualty insurance: A now somewhat outdated term, generally describing all the kinds of insurance other than life, fire and marine insurance; now covered by multiple line companies, writing all property insurance, including fire and casualty.

cats and dogs: In the securities industry, a colloquial term for highly speculative and thoroughly unpromising securities; securities that may have seemed promising once, but are now seen to be very nearly worthless.

caveat emptor: Latin for ''let the buyer beware,'' an underlying theme in commercial transactions of all kinds. This maxim places the burden of prudence on the buyer, except for specified warranties or misrepresentations made by the seller. To some extent, consumer oriented statutes and court decisions have redistributed burdens in this area, resulting in the creation of a large number of implied warranties binding on sellers, so that ''caveat emptor'' now has rather limited significance.

caveat venditor: Latin for ''let the seller beware,'' placing the burden of truthful representation on the seller. Short of specific and wilful misrepresentation, ''caveat emptor'' has been the far stronger maxim in the marketplace; but recent legislative and judicial trends have created a large number of implied warranties binding upon sellers, which to some extent have changed the balance between ''caveat venditor'' and ''caveat emptor.''

CBOE: Chicago Board Options Exchange. See Chicago Board of Trade.

CBOT: See Chicago Board of Trade.

CD: See certificate of deposit.

cease and desist order: An order issued by an administrative body with quasi-legal powers, such as the Federal Trade Commission or the National Labor Relations Board, demanding that a particular activity, such as an allegedly unfair trade or labor practice, be stopped.

ceiling price: The maximum price that may legally be charged on an item covered by government-imposed price controls.

celebrity auction: An auction of items owned by or associated with people of celebrity status, such as athletes, movie stars, people holding great wealth, and major politicians.

census: A collection of quantitative data for a given area of inquiry, such as a government count of population and its characteristics or of types of business and their characteristics within an industry, a local area, or the entire country. The Bureau of the Census conducts massive and continuing censuses, touching on every aspect of business activity.

central bank: A bank funded by and representing a national government, responsible for the development and execution of national money and credit policies and for the health of the nation's banking system. In the United States, the Federal Reserve System functions as a central bank through twelve regional banks and its Board of Governors; in most other industrial countries the central bank is a single bank, such as the Bank of England and the Bank of Canada.

centralized planning: In fully planned economies, government control through an agency of the state, of all major economic functions. In mixed economies, a tendency toward central planning of some major economic functions.

certificate: A document stating that something has been done or complied with. The document is usually issued by an established public or private institution, such as a government agency or a college, though in the widest sense a "certificate" may be issued by any person or organization for any purpose not specifically covered by existing law.

certificate of beneficial interest: An ownership share in a Massachusetts, or business, trust.

certificate of deposit: A receipt for a bank deposit, in certificate rather than passbook form. Time certificates of deposit are payable either on a specific date or after passage of a specific amount of time, can bear interest, and are therefore widely used by companies and institutions as short term investment vehicles. They are also negotiable and widely traded as short term paper in the money markets. However, demand certificates of deposit are payable at any time on endorsement and therefore are not available as money market instruments.

certificate of indebtedness: The short term promissory note of a corporation or institution, unsecured by specific property but generally interpreted as carrying the same obligation as a bond. There is some question about whether it operates as a lien prior to the liens of general creditors or whether it is merely an unsecured promissory note that is no more than equal to the claims of other general creditors.

certified check: A check drawn on a depositor's account which a bank endorses and accepts, usually on the face of the check, after first setting aside enough of the depositor's funds to cover the check. The check then becomes a bank obligation, backed by the full resources of the bank, and short of bank failure will be paid if properly endorsed on presentation. Certified checks are widely used as payment in transactions requiring sure immediate payment of large amounts of money and immediate passage of title, as in many securities and real estate transactions.

cestui que trust: One who holds a beneficial interest in a trust, but not legal title to that trust, as a beneficiary who gets money distributed by a trustee. See trustee.

CFTC: See Commodity Futures Trading Commission.

chain banking: The ownership of three or more banks by one person or a group acting as one in terms of mutual interests and joint policies.

chairman of the board: The head of a corporation's policy making body, the board of directors. The chairman of the board can be the most powerful person in the corporation, but such factors as ownership equities and the realities of operating control must be taken into account.

charge-off: See write-off.

chartist: In the securities industry, one who wholly or in large part believes that current and future market fluctuations can largely be predicted on the basis of previous fluctuations, as graphically represented in charts. Many securities analysts, traders, and investment advisory services subscribe to this view.

chattel: Any personal property, except for freehold title to real estate, including both movable and fixed items of property. For example, clothing, dogs, automobiles, and real estate leases are chattels, while wholly owned real estate is not.

chattel mortgage: A mortgage loan using chattels, such as vehicles and paintings, as security for the loan. If there is default on repayment of the loan, the chattels become the property of the lender. Chattel mortgages are substantially similar to real estate mortgages.

cheap money: See easy money.

check: A draft or order drawn on funds belonging to the drawer and on deposit with a banking organization. Checks are payable on demand.

checking account: A bank account holding credit balances against which a depositor may draw checks. Although there have traditionally been sharp differences between checking and savings accounts, those differences have in recent years tended to diminish. For example, checks may now be drawn against balances in savings accounts, in some states, and checking accounts sometimes pay interest on deposit balances.

Chicago Board of Trade (CBOT): A major commodities trading exchange, handling large quantities of both current cash and futures trades in corn, wheat, soybeans, oats, and associated materials; an affiliated organization is the Chicago Board Options Exchange, (CBOE), which handles a very large volume of options trades.

Chicago Board Options Exchange (CBOE): See Chicago Board of Trade.

Chicago Mercantile Exchange: A major commodities trading exchange, handling large quantities of both current cash and futures trades in many dairy, meat, and natural resources items.

choice: Describing the condition of antiques or collectibles; a claim that an item is one of the best of its type.

Christmas club: A special purpose savings account, stressing the regular deposit of specified sums, usually each week for fifty weeks a year, to be withdrawn at the end of the year and used for Christmas expenses.

churning: In the securities industry, the unethical and sometimes illegal practice of turning over customer accounts faster than necessary for the customer's investment purposes, in order to create brokerage commissions.

circa: Approximately as of a given date or period; usually encountered as describing the origin and age of collectibles and antiques and often abbreviated as ca, c., or C.

circle of: See school of.

circulating capital: That portion of a business' capital that is invested in current and continuously working assets, such as materials and labor.

class action: An action at law brought by one or more on behalf of a larger number, all alleged by those bringing the class action as being commonly interested and commonly damaged. The class action has been a widely used form of complaint in suits brought against businesses and institutions by such groups as consumers and stockholders.

clean bill of exchange: An undocumented bill of exchange; that is, one unaccompanied by such documents as bills of lading.

clean credit: A letter of credit without significant qualifications placed on the issuing bank's commitment to pay when presented with an undocumented bill drawn on that letter of credit.

clean hands: In law, the equity-derived concept that a party seeking redress or relief come into court untainted by fraud, dishonesty, or other attitudes or actions that discredit motives as to the matter at issue.

clear: 1. In law, entirely free of any kind of ambiguity, limitation, or encumbrance, as in ownership of a property "free and clear." **2.** To complete a financial transaction, most often as in the collection of a check that has been passed through a bank clearing house.

clearance: The settlement of financial transactions, through the physical transfer of financial instruments; usually operating through a clearing house.

clearing: The process of consummating a financial transaction, through the physical transfer of instruments of value between sellers and buyers, including any necessary accounting and record keeping.

clearing house: A voluntary association of banks or brokers, acting to settle transactions between its members on a daily basis.

climax: In securities and commodities markets, a very large volume of buying or selling at the top or bottom of a protracted rise or decline in the general level of market prices.

close: 1. The end of the trading day in a securities or commodities market. Many commodities trades are executed and securities prices quoted "at the close." **2.** In accounting, the process of closing the books of a business at the end of a given accounting period.

close corporation: See closely held corporation.

closed account: An account that was once active, but that now no longer exists, except for record keeping purposes, having been closed by final withdrawals of deposits, as from a bank account, or of securities and cash, as from a securities or commodities brokerage account; or an account that has been ended by action of bank or broker, as for insolvency or inadequate margin.

closed end investment company: An investment company owned by a limited number of stockholders and with an initially fixed amount of capital, which invests in other companies for the benefit of its stockholders. Investment company shares may not be redeemed by their holders as can mutual funds shares by their shareholders, but they are often traded on stock exchanges.

closed end mortgage: A mortgage specifying that no further money can be borrowed on the property being mortgaged. Some bonds carry the same limitation.

closed out: A margin account sold out by a broker when a customer has failed to raise necessary additional margin.

closely held corporation: A company that is owned by a small number of people, all or most of whom are directly involved in the conduct of the business, with very little of its stock in the hands of outsiders.

closing: 1. The consummation of a real estate transaction, in which buyer and seller exchange purchase price and deed and title passes. **2.** In accounting, the process of closing the books at the end of an accounting period.

closing costs: The costs attendant to the closing of a real estate transaction, such as title insurance, lawyer's fees, and recording fees.

closing date: In accounting, the date the books of account are closed for accounting purposes, and the date of preparation of all financial statements derived from the books of account.

closing entries: In accounting, a series of entries closing the books as of the end of an accounting period, which serve to balance the books and prepare them to be the basis for preparation of the financial statements.

closing price: The price of a security listed on an exchange as of the end of the trading day on that exchange.

cloud on title: A potential threat to a clear title. Such claims as tax liens, mortgages, and prior judgments may cloud title and must be settled before the title can be conveyed unencumbered.

COD: See cash on delivery.

coin: 1. A piece of metal stamped by government and used as a form of money. In very few United States coins now in use is the underlying value of the metal in the coin worth more than a small fraction of the stated value of the coin. **2.** To process metal into coins.

coinage: The physical production of coins by government at a government mint.

coincident indicator: An economic indicator that moves at about the same time as the economy moves, in contrast to leading or lagging indicators that move earlier or later; examples are current retail sales, personal income, and industrial production.

collateral: Security for a loan, in the form of real or personal property belonging to the borrower which is formally pledged to the lender, and which can become the property of the lender upon default on the loan. Collateral is property of determinable value that can be fairly readily sold and converted into cash, such as securities, real estate, savings account passbooks, and commodities.

collateralize: To provide collateral as security for a loan. A loan is described as "collateralized" when it has been so secured.

collateral loan: A loan secured by collateral, usually applied to a short term loan in which the collateral security is physically held by the creditor.

collateral trust bonds: Bonds secured by other bonds and sometimes stocks of the issuing company. The securing bonds and stocks are placed in trust as collateral for the bonds being issued.

collateral value: The value of assets pledged as collateral for a loan. In setting collateral value lenders will consider such factors as the collateral's current market value, its stability, and its convertibility into cash.

collectibility: The likelihood that an item, by its nature, will become the kind of item that will be collected; usually an item of modest intrinsic value and limited supply, and one posing difficulties for the potential counterfeiter.

collectible: 1. Any item, whatever its age, that is acquired, held, and traded, and for which a market of any kind, formal or informal, has developed. In the widest sense, the term embraces antiques and works of art, as well as such well-defined collecting areas as stamps, comic books, and many kinds of glass. **2.** A balance due, which a creditor is legally justified in collecting from a debtor.

collect on delivery: See cash on delivery.

collector-dealer: One who both collects for personal purposes and also buys and sells as a dealer to others.

collusion: A secret agreement by two or more parties to commit fraud or other illegal actions against others.

co-maker: One who signs a debt instrument with others and is therefore responsible for repayment, often without being in any way a recipient of the money borrowed.

combination: Any formal or informal joining of individuals for common purposes. In business, any joining of business organizations, including such formal joinings as mergers and consolidations and such informal joinings as pools, trusts, syndicates, and interlocking directorates.

combination in restraint of trade: Any business combination prohibited by law. The phrase is the language of the basic United States anti-trust statute, the Sherman Act of 1890, and refers to such combinations as trusts, pools, cartels, discriminatory freight rate arrangements, and interlocking directorates.

COMECON: See Council For Mutual Economic Assistance.

commemorative: An item made to celebrate the occurrence of an event; for example, a stamp issue to honor a national figure.

commerce: Any and all trade and commercial intercourse between individuals, organizations, peoples, and governments. The term is so wide as to be used synonymously with "business" and "trade."

commercial bank: A bank primarily in the business of holding demand deposits and making business loans. Commercial banks have many other functions, however, including a wide variety of consumer loans, trust functions, finance and securities industry service and selling functions, and a large number of services usually described as "full service banking." Commercial banking is the major form of banking in the United States.

commercial credit: Credit customarily extended by lenders to businesses, to satisfy fluctuating and seasonal cash needs, finance inventories, and satisfy other short term cash needs.

commercial credit company: A company in the business of lending money to other companies using the borrowers' accounts receivable as collateral, or of buying those accounts receivable at a discount and collecting them.

commercial law: A very wide and imprecise term generally used to describe all matters in the law relating to commerce, trade, and the people and organizations engaged in them.

commercial paper: 1. All short term, negotiable debt instruments issued by businesses, including all bills, notes, and acceptances arising from the normal conduct of business.   **2.** Short term notes issued by large, well-established and well-regarded businesses, usually in the $100,000 to $1,000,000 range. Such notes are traded in the money markets, rated by private rating organizations as to their degree of investment safety, and often provide short term, relatively low-cost financing to their issuers.

commercial property: Property classified as usable for commercial purposes, and so zoned by local zoning authorities; such property may be used for residential purposes as well.

commingling: Mixing funds, as when the administrator of several estates mixes funds owned by those estates and his or her own private funds as well; often accompanied by illegal misuse of the funds held in trust.

commission: A sum paid by a principal to one acting in some sort of representative capacity. Commissions are usually figured as a percentage of the transaction consummated. Both independent representatives, such as real estate brokers, and employees, such as salespeople, are often compensated on a commission basis.

commission agent: An independent businessperson or company, selling goods for another on a commission basis.

commodity: Any item which may be traded, broadly including every item of value. In a somewhat narrower sense, any one of a considerable group of materials and products traded on commodities exchanges.

commodity agreement: An international arrangement between producers to control production and prices of a commodity.

Commodity Credit Corporation: The bureau of the United States Department of Agriculture responsible for a wide range of farm-support aids, including cash payments, crop purchases, loans to farmers, the management of farm surpluses, and the encouragement of domestic consumption and foreign trade in agricultural commodities.

commodity exchange: A market for the sale and exchange of commodity futures contracts and current or spot cash commodities contracts. United States commodity exchanges trade a wide range of agricultural, agriculture-related, and natural resource contracts, such as pork bellies, cotton, wool, soybeans, corn, wheat, gold, silver, lumber, coffee and rubber.

commodity futures: Contracts between buyers and sellers specifying the prices, terms, and delivery locations of commodities that are to be delivered at some stated future time. These contracts are some of the instruments of value that are traded on "futures" markets.

Commodity Futures Trading Commission (CFTC): A Federal agency responsible for the regulation of United States trading in commodity futures, including the setting up of the machinery of regulation.

commodity paper: Negotiable bills of exchange payable on sight or demand, and backed by the value of staple commodities, properly stored and insured, as evidenced by appropriate shipping or storage documents, such as bills of lading.

commodity price index: Any price index that measures the average price of a group of commodities, including both current or spot prices and futures prices. Both the United States Government and private sources, as well as including commodities in wider price indexes publish such current and future indexes.

common-law trust: See Massachusetts Trust.

Common Market: The European Economic Community, a partial economic union of most of the nations of western Europe, organized to stimulate trade and production and to help provide the economic basis for a wider European political and economic union.

common stock: An ownership share in a corporation, in the form of capital stock which is neither preferred nor in any way limited, and therefore fully shares the risks and opportunities created by corporate operations. It is the standard form of stock ownership in American corporations.

common trust fund: A fund administered by a bank or other trust investment organization which pools the funds of two or more individual trusts and manages the pooled funds as one. The aim is to gain the flexibility and leverage offered by the larger pool of funds, while cutting administrative costs.

Communications Satellite Corporation (COMSAT): A privately owned United States communications company, owning and carrying responsibility for operation of all United States commercial communications satellite operations.

company: 1. A very broad term, meaning any business entity, including corporations, partnerships, and sole proprietorships. **2.** A group joining together to pursue common interests for profit.

comparative advantage: The ability of a country or of any other economic unit to produce an item at less cost than another country or economic unit. For example, if the Japanese television industry can produce television sets of comparable quality cheaper than American industry can, the Japanese industry has the comparative advantage.

compensating balance: An amount kept on deposit by a borrower, in a non-interest-bearing regular account in a bank holding active loans to that borrower. Many commercial banks informally but very firmly require that borrowers keep deposits of approximately 20% of the amounts currently borrowed on deposit. As the deposits do not bear interest, the loans in fact cost considerably more than they seem. For example, $100 borrowed at a simple interest of 12% costs $12 in interest. But if $20 must be kept on deposit, $12 in interest is being paid on 80 usable dollars, a real interest rate of 15%, or 20% more than it seems.

compensatory tariff: A tariff levied on imported goods to equal taxes levied within a country on the same kinds of goods manufactured domestically, or to compensate for taxes levied on imports used to make domestic goods.

composite demand: The total demand from all sources for a product or service. For example, the composite demand for legal services includes many kinds of public and private demands, only part of which are met by lawyers in private practice.

composition: 1. An arrangement between a debtor and all creditors to satisfy the entire body of debt outstanding for less than the totals due and on a pro rated basis. For example, a debtor owing a total of $10,000 to five creditors, composed of four $1,000 debts and one $6,000 debt might reach an agreement to repay on a 50% basis, and then repay each of the $1,000 debts at $500 and the $6,000 debt at $3,000. Composition is a common-law arrangement between debtor and creditors, arrived at voluntarily and not as part of a bankruptcy settlement.

composition in bankruptcy: Substantially the same arrangement as composition (above), but arrived at by operation of law in pursuit of a settlement of outstanding debts during bankruptcy.

compound entry: In accounting, a single entry that combines three or more elements; often used to record a series of related transactions, clarifying the nature of those related transactions as a single complex transaction.

compound interest: A system of computing and paying interest that takes the original sum on which interest is to be computed, adds simple interest, and then uses the resulting amount as the basis for the next computation of interest. For example, payment of compound interest on $100 for two years at 5% per year would result in a first year interest payment of $5. With the $5 added to the original $100, second year interest would be 5% of $105, or $5.25.

compound tariff: A customs duty that combines both an ad valorem tax, in which a percentage is added to the value of the imported item, and a specific tax, such as $10 per set for imported television sets.

computerized analysis: Any analytical function or set of functions that is computer-assisted; for example, an analysis of stock trends that is done with the assistance of a computer rather than hand-computed.

COMSAT: See Communications Satellite Corporation.

condition: The physical state of an antique or collectible, compared to its presumed original state, reflecting whether it needs or has experienced repair or restoration.

condominium: A housing unit, usually an apartment in a multiple occupancy building, which is separately owned, just as if it were a single family house standing alone. It may be purchased, sold, mortgaged; and in all other ways handled as any other wholly-owned building. Condominium owners also own a share of communally used elements, such as land or land lease, lobbies, basements, stairs, roof, heating, and cooling systems.

confirmation: A document expressly validating a previously made oral or in some other way voidable purchase, agreement, or contract. For example, a telephoned order for goods must often be followed by a written confirmation, signed by the ordering party.

confirmed credit: Credit that cannot be withdrawn or altered in any way, usually in the form of a letter of credit.

conglomerate: A large, diversified organization, doing business in a number of more or less unrelated areas. A conglomerate usually acquires many of the unrelated portions of its operations, instead of developing them from the kinds of business it originally conducted.

An example is the International Telephone and Telegraph Corporation, which does business in dozens of areas unrelated to its communications activities.

connoisseur: One thought by others to be knowledgeable in a field and to be capable of understanding, evaluating, and appreciating high quality work in that field; very much a subjective classification.

conservative: Describing an investment or investment choice that is aimed at safety more than at quick profit; for example, a Federal Government debt obligation rather than a volatile common stock.

conservator: 1. A court-appointed administrator of the affairs of one who has been judged mentally incompetent, that function terminating on the death of the incompetent. **2.** One professionally engaged in the physical care and restoration of antiques and collectibles.

consignment: See on consignment.

consolidated balance sheet: A balance sheet covering a parent company and all its subsidiary companies as a single business or ganization.

consolidation: The joining of two or more business organizations into a single succeeding organization, with the previous organizations ceasing to exist.

consortium: A group of large companies participating in a joint venture; most often applied to international ventures involving the development and exploitation of the resources of less developed nations.

constant-dollar value: The value of an item as if the dollar had constant value, neither inflating or deflating. This is done by adopting a given year as a base year and figuring the values of items as if the dollars used to buy them purchased as much as they did in the base year. For example, a car purchased in 1980 for $8,000 may be worth $4,000 in "1970 dollars," if the dollar's purchasing power is 50% of what it was in 1970.

consumer credit: Any credit used by consumers for purchases; includes such short term sources of credit as installment purchases, credit cards, bank loans for consumer purchases such as automobile and general purpose personal loans, finance company loans, and revolving credit or overdraft loans.

consumer debt: See consumer credit.

consumer finance company: See finance company.

consumer goods: Goods used directly by consumers, as distinct from goods used by businesses to produce other goods for business or personal use. Only end products consumed by individuals are consumer goods.

Consumer Price Index (CPI): A national monthly index generated by the United States Bureau of Labor Statistics, which compares a weighted average of prices with the same weighted average for a previous year selected as a base year. It is a basic measure of increases in the cost of living, and was formerly called the "cost of living index."

contingency reserve: In accounting, a reserve kept to meet possible and unspecified liabilities. It is composed of funds in no way encumbered by any other claims or allocations.

contingent liability: A liabiliy which does not now exist, but will come into being if some now-perceived event occurs; contingent liabilities are potential, not probable. When considered probable, they become contingent but real, and are treated as real in accounting statements.

contingent profit: A possible but not certain profit, which may be realized if a perceived event occurs.

continued bonds: Bonds that are not redeemed when mature, but instead are carried on as interest-bearing obligations, though not necessarily at the same rate of interest.

continuous audit: In accounting, an audit that is carried on, at least in part, throughout the audit period, rather than entirely during a relatively short time at the end of the audit period.

contract: 1. In commodities trading, a legally binding agreement in which two or more parties, for adequate consideration, agree to buy or sell now or in the future, commodities or the future right to own commodities; the contract itself then becomes an instrument of value capable of being traded upon an organized commodity exchange. **2.** In general, a legal agreement in which two or more parties, for adequate consideration, make and accept promises to do or not to do specified things. Also the written record of that agreement, agreed to and signed by the parties.

contraction: An imprecise euphemism for a recession or depression as in a "contraction of economic activity."

contrary market: A market moving other than expected by the vast majority of trading professionals in that market, who have guessed wrong as to the next market trend.

contributed capital: The money invested in a firm by its owners, including both money invested in capital stock and money they later put into the firm for operating purposes.

contribution: 1. A share payment made to accomplish a purpose, as in a contribution to capital or to payment of any joint obligation. **2.** For tax purposes, any gift which is defined by law and regulations as tax-free.

controllable cost: 1. A cost that can literally be controlled by management, usually within limits set by production and distribution requirements. **2.** A synonym for variable cost.

controlled account: In the securities industry, a trading account that is controlled by someone other than the owner of that account.

controlled company: A company that is under the control of another company, such as a subsidiary.

controlled price: See ceiling price.

controlling interest: That percentage of ownership of the common stock of a company which enables one or more stockholders to secure effective control over the operations of the company. The percentage necessary for control varies from 51% of some closely held companies to less than 10% of some very large and widely held companies.

conversion: 1. The act of exchanging one instrument of value for another, as in conversion from paper money to the precious metal, usually gold, backing that money or a conversion from bonds or preferred stock to common stock by the terms of a stock issue. **2.** The unauthorized taking of another's property, whether by direct physical taking or by an action which in law can be construed as unauthorized taking.

conversion price: The specific price at which a security, usually a preferred stock or bond, can be converted to the common stock of the issuer.

conversion ratio: The number of shares of one kind of security that can be exchanged for shares of another kind of security issued by the same corporation, under the terms of a convertible debt issue; for example, the number of shares of common stock that will be exchanged for a single convertible bond if and when the holder of the bond chooses to convert it into that common stock.

convertible: A bond or stock that may be exchanged for a specified number of shares of the common stock of the same corporation at a specified price, as defined by the corporation on issue of that instrument; the convertible shareholder may or may not choose to exercise that conversion privilege. Both bonds and preferred stocks may be issued carrying such conversion privileges attached.

convertible bond: See convertible.

convertible preferred stock: See convertible.

conveyance: The transfer of legal title to land and the document transferring that title. The term has developed a much wider meaning as well, and is now used to describe any transfer of title to real or personal property.

cooperative: A form of business in which a group of individuals or firms jointly organize some aspects of production or consumption. Producers may jointly buy equipment and supplies, as in a farm cooperative, or may sell their products together, as in a milk producers' cooperative. Consumers may buy food together and sometimes resell it at a profit to cooperative members, as in a food cooperative.

cooperative apartment: A form of conditional apartment ownership, in which a tenant in a multiple occupancy building owns a share in the building, holds an open-end lease on the apartment occupied, and shares on a pro rata basis with other tenants the total cost of running the building. The tenants are stockholders in the building, in contrast to condominium owners, who own their portions of their dwellings.

corner: In the securities and commodities markets, to obtain enough control of the available stores of a commodity or outstanding shares of a stock to be able to control price and supply. Although cornering was a commonly employed competitive technique in the last century, it is seldom encountered now because federal and state laws and regulations substantially preclude its use.

corporate bond: See bond.

corporate income tax: A tax levied by government on corporate profits. Corporate income taxes are graduated according to taxable income, as are personal income taxes.

corporation: A business entity created under law, which functions in all ways as an individual under law and is regarded as an individual in the eyes of the law. Corporations may be formed by a single individual or by an unlimited number of individuals joining together as stockholders. In the main, the liability of stockholders for the actions of the corporation is limited to the resources of the corporation, so that in the event of bankruptcy stockholders may lose only the value of their ownership interests; in contrast the individual proprietor and partners' liability is personal and unlimited.

correspondent bank: A bank maintaining a direct relationship with another, holding deposits and performing services for the other. In United States banking, the use of correspondent banks is widespread, with large banks in major cities, and especially those in New York City, performing a wide variety of services for less centrally located banks and holding substantial deposits from those banks.

co-signer: See co-maker.

cost: 1. The price to be paid for anything, whatever medium of exchange is used for payment.   **2.** In economics, the amounts committed to pay for the factors of production, including all expenses necessary for production.   **3.** To determine what something will cost, applying all necessary expense factors, as in "to cost out" an item.

cost basis: In accounting, the valuation of assets based upon their original cost minus any depreciation and without allowance for the addition of intangible factors, such as goodwill or developing antique value.

cost-benefit analysis: In planning, the weighing of projected costs and possible benefits of incurring those costs against alternative costs and benefits. The process may be informal, as it often is in very small companies, or formal and involved, depending on the resources and skills available for planning purposes. In some very large companies, cost-benefit analysis is a highly complex, computer-oriented process.

cost control: A general term embracing all those management techniques aimed at keeping costs to a minimum while still maintaining current quality and quantity standards.

cost depletion: See depletion allowance.

cost effectiveness: An evaluation of whether or not to do something based on the cost-benefit relationship resulting from the move.

cost escalation: See escalation.

cost of goods purchased: The total cost incurred for goods purchased, including prices paid, transportation charges, receiving costs, storage, and all associated overhead and in-plant costs.

cost of living: The level of expenditure necessary to maintain a current standard of living for families and individuals, as measured against previously necessary levels of expenditure. The Consumer Price Index, formerly called the Cost of Living Index, is a major United States cost of living indicator.

cost of living index: See Consumer Price Index.

cost of possession: See carrying cost.

cost of production: All costs associated with producing goods, including overhead, labor and materials. In manufacturing, the analysis and proper allocation of production costs is central to the pricing process.

cost of reproduction: An estimate of the cost of replacing present assets, usually buildings and equipment, at current cost levels, and as they were when completed.

cost of sales: The total costs associated with goods sold, as measured in accounting periods. In manufacturing, it is synonymous with the cost of production.

cost or market: Sometimes expressed "cost or market, whichever is lower," this is a method of inventory valuation that takes into account any decreases in the market value of inventory items. For example. pocket calculators in inventory during the nineteen seventies often were marked down in evaluating inventory, as newer, more effective, and much less expensive calculators reached the market.

cost out: See cost.

cost-price squeeze: A situation in which sellers are trapped between rising costs of production and sales on the one hand and marketplace resistance to price increases on the other, resulting in an erosion of their profits.

cost-push inflation: A type of inflation, caused largely by a wage-price spiral, that consists of upward pressure on the cost of production caused by wage increases, followed by price increases, then further wage increases and so on.

Council For Mutual Economic Assistance (COMECON): An Eastern European economic equivalent of the European Common Market.

counter check: A blank check available at a bank for the convenience of depositors who do not have their own checks with them. They must be cashed in person at the bank in which they are issued.

counterfeit: False, simulated, or imitating the genuine. The term often refers to bills and coins issued illegally by forgers, but is also used to refer to many other imitation articles of value.

country bank: A bank located in an "undesignated" city under Federal Reserve Board rules, which therefore can carry somewhat smaller legal reserves than banks located in designated Federal Reserve cities.

coupon bonds: Negotiable bonds payable to their bearer, carrying interest certificates or coupons which are clipped when mature and presented to the issuer of the bonds for payment. Coupon bonds need not be endorsed, either at passage of title in them or at the presentation of clipped coupons for payment.

cover: 1. In insurance, for an insurer to assume certain kinds of risks and potential liabilities when issuing an insurance policy, such as specified medical and surgical costs in a health insurance policy.   **2.** In the securities markets, for a short seller to complete or cover short sales by buying stock.

coverage: See cover.

CPI: See Consumer Price Index.

Crash: The 1929 United States stock market collapse, which triggered the Great Depression of the 1930's.

credit: 1. The ability to secure goods and services now with a promise to pay later. Credit comes in many forms and from many sources, including both moneylenders and producers. It may be granted on the basis of a simple promise to pay, as in most routine commercial transactions between buyers and sellers, or may be granted only if completely covered by collateral, as with most home mortgages.   **2.** In accounting, an entry on the right side of an account recording the reduction or elimination of an asset or expense, or the addition to or creation of a liability, net worth, or revenue item. In double-entry bookkeeping, each credit is accompanied by a debit entry to a balancing account, so that the books always reflect the current relationship between assets and liabilities.

credit approval: The granting of credit to a purchaser or borrower by a seller or lender; for example, approval of credit for an appliance purchase by a retail store manager or approval of an individual line of credit by a bank branch manager.

credit balance: In general, the excess of credits over debits in any account, as in banking, where the excess of credits over debits in a depositor's account indicates that the depositor has funds currently on deposit. When an account shows a debit balance, the depositor either has an overdraft in the account or is using an overdraft privilege or line of credit.

credit control: Controls over national money and credit policies, credit and money supplies, and interest rates, vested in the Federal Reserve System and its Board of Governors, which affects the quantity and cost of credit available to private borrowers throughout the country, and can strongly influence and direction of the national economy.

credit instrument: A document evidencing debt, including all paper instruments other than paper money and coins. In a certain sense, even paper money and coins issued by a government solely on the basis of its full faith and credit, as in the United States, are credit instruments. The most widely used of all credit instruments is the check, accounting for well over 90% of all commercial transactions in the United States.

credit investigation: Any investigation of the potential creditworthiness of one seeking credit entered into by a lender, seller, or one acting for a lender or seller, including the use of credit bureaus and direct checking of such matters as bank references supplied by the potential creditor.

credit investigator: One who is employed by a lender to gather information about the credit-worthiness of a potential borrower. Credit investigators may be employees of a lending institution or of a private organization serving lending institutions.

credit line: An overdraft privilege granted by a lending institution, allowing a customer to borrow sums within a stated range without treating each loan as a new loan, requiring separate approvals and documents from the lender. Credit lines are often stated in fixed sums, such as $50,000 credit line at the bank, but are in fact somewhat variable, depending on the borrower's bank balances, business and personal status, interest rates, and general economic conditions.

credit money: In economics, the concept that lending institutions create money when they grant credit to borrowers because money loaned does not really exist until the credit granted is used.

creditor: One to whom money is due. In the widest sense, one who has the right to collect anything of value from anyone for any reason, including the right to collect from another as a result of a legal proceeding.

creditor nation: A nation whose people and institutions have larger total investments outside their country than the total of all foreign investment inside their country.

credit rating: An assessment of the credit-worthiness of a business or individual made by private organizations, such as Dun and Bradstreet, specializing in the gathering and evaluation of credit information. A credit rating may be expressed on a scale, such as A to D, or may be expressed in evaluative comments.

credit report: A report made by a credit investigator or bureau on the creditworthiness of one seeking credit.

credit risk: The degree of exposure to risk faced by a lender with respect to a specific customer, as in an evaluation of a not-very-credit-worthy firm as a "high" credit risk.

credit standing: See credit rating.

creditworthiness: An estimate made by a lender as to how likely a potential borrower will be to pay back a requested loan. Lenders will base estimates on such factors as available collateral, the character of the credit applicant, the capital available to that applicant, presumed capacity to repay based upon such factors as current income and future prospects, and general economic conditions as of the time of application for credit.

creeping inflation: A slow inflation rate, about 2-3% per year. Creeping inflation is thought to be stoppable or reversible by some economists and government officials. The average rate of inflation has been far higher than 2-3% since World War II, however, so the term has lost most its precise original meaning.

crown: The main currency unit of Czechoslovakia, bearing the same relationship to Czechoslovakia's national currency as does the dollar to the United States currency system.

cruziero: The main currency of Brazil, bearing the same relationship to Brazil's national currency as does the dollar to the United States currency system.

cum dividend: A stock which is transferred with a dividend declared, but not yet paid, which is payable to its new owner. In contrast, stock sold "ex-dividend" is sold without the right to collect such a dividend.

cum rights: A stock which is transferred with rights to buy newly issued stock at prices somewhat lower than subscription prices attached, which may be exercised by its new owner.

cumulative dividends: Dividends due but unpaid on cumulative preferred stock that is entitled to fixed dividends and is in arrears. Cumulative dividends are paid out of corporate earnings before dividends are issued to common stockholders.

cumulative preferred stock: Preferred stock that is entitled to receive fixed dividends for a specific period if justified by corporate earnings, and that accumulate; these accumulated dividends must be paid before common stock holders receive dividends on their stock.

curb exchange: Any market in which trading takes place outdoors, as trading on the sidewalk or curb. The American Stock Exchange originated as one of many such curb exchanges, and was formally named the Curb Exchange for many years.

currency: All paper money and coins acceptable as legal tender, but not including negotiable paper, such as checks, even if it is freely transferrable from bearer to bearer. Currency is often used synonymously with paper money, but the term does include coins.

currency swap: A currency exchange between two countries at an agreed upon rate of exchange, usually to help stabilize international currency values.

current account: An open account between buyer and seller, through which normal transactions flow, with payments due in the normal course of business and without any special billing or settlement terms specified between the parties.

current assets: Those assets that are held in cash or are relatively easy to convert into cash, including such items as collectibles, short term investments, and inventory. They are normally convertible into cash within one year, but for accounting purposes some assets that take longer than a year to convert may still be classified as current.

current expense: A normal operating expense chargeable to an accounting period, as contrasted to extraordinary and nonrecurring expenses.

current income: Income attributable to an accounting period, normally as distinguished from cash receipts, which may or may not be treated as income in the accounting period in which they are received.

current liability: Any debt which is due and payable within a specified short period, usually one year, including both short term debts and longer term debts maturing and payable within the period.

current ratio: The ratio of current assets to current liabilities. It is a key indicator of the current health of any business, and is carefully noted by investment analysts and potential lenders. A current ratio of $2 in current assets to $1 in current liabilities is minimally acceptable for credit-securing purposes in almost all businesses, with somewhat lower ratios acceptable in some instances.

current return: See current yield.

current yield: The relationship between the dividends paid in a year on a stock and its current market price. For example, a stock which paid $1 in dividends last year and is now selling at $10 has a current yield of 10:1, with a selling price 10 times the dividends paid.

customer's man: In the securities industry, a woman or man who represents a securities firm in handling customers' buy and sell orders. This somewhat out-of-date term has now been largely replaced by the synonymous "registered representative," or "account executive."

customs duties: Taxes levied by a country on imports and, in the United States, collected by the Customs Service.

customs union: A trading union between two or more countries, which establishes common levies on imports from all other countries and eliminates all or most taxes on imports and exports passing between the countries in the union. The European Common Market is such a customs union.

cycle: Any repeated sequence of events. A cycle can be measured by the passage of time, as in the twenty-four hours of a day; by the passage of events, as in the events comprising the "business cycle;" or by both time and events, as in the start-to-finish time of a closely timed, sequenced production cycle.

cyclical industry: An industry that is particularly sensitive to economic upswings and downturns caused by the operation of the business cycle. For example. the travel industry, because it depends to a significant degree on the spending of discretionary income, which tends to dry up in periods of economic downturn, is more cyclical than the grain industry.

cyclical stocks: Stocks whose market values tend to move in fairly direct response to the ups and down of the business cycle, rising quickly in periods of prosperity and dropping equally quickly in periods of recession or depression; for example, the stocks of companies producing mainly such consumer goods as appliances and clothing.

D

daily average contract volume: The average number of options contracts in force during a single day's session on a specific options exchange.

daily high: The high point reached by a stock or a market on a given day on a specific exchange.

daily low: The low point reached by a stock or a market on a given day on a specific exchange.

daily trading limit: See trading limit.

daily trading range: See trading limit.

date of issue: The date on which an instrument of obligation, such as an insurance policy, or bond or other debt instrument, becomes operative. The instrument bears that date rather than the date on which the instrument is executed or any other date.

day loans: Unsecured loans to stockbrokers made by lending institutions at the start of the business day, and for that day only, as a means of supplying working cash for that day. The loan is in the form of a line of credit for the day, to be used by the borrower as transactions necessitate, and as secured by the collateral resulting from the securities transactions themselves as they occur.

day order: In the securities markets, a customer buy or sell order that must be consummated on the day it is placed. If not so consummated, it is automatically nullified at the end of that business day.

days of grace: See grace period.

deal: In general, an agreement. Deals range from contracts with full legal force to verbal agreements wih little or no legal force, intended to lead to contracts. Deals may lead to development of a single contract or of a number of legal instruments which together embody the agreements reached.

dealer: Any person or organization buying or selling goods and services who takes title to whatever is bought and passes title on whatever is sold, as distinct from brokers and agents, who represent and deal with buyers and sellers but do not take or pass title. Dealers are sometimes also brokers or agents, as in the securities industry, where many securities dealers buy and sell for themselves through their own accounts while, acting as brokers, they also transact business for their customers.

dealer discount: The difference between the retail selling price and the price paid by a dealer.

debasement: In business or finance, a reduction in the value of metal used in coins, especially as regards the value as metal of the precious metals used in coinage. The term has also come to be used loosely as describing erosion in the value of currencies caused by inflationary processes.

debenture: Any long term debt instrument issued by a company or institution, secured only by the general assets of the issuer. Debentures are usually issued as bonds, primarily by corporations and governments. They are therefore only as good as their issuer's ability to meet the debt obligations they create.

debenture bonds: Unsecured debt obligations issued by governments and corporations backed only by their promise to pay, and only as good as the repayment ability of their issuers.

debit: In accounting, an entry on the left side of an account, recording addition or creation of an asset or expense, or the subtraction or elimination of a liability, net worth or revenue item.

debit balance: A debit amount left in any account, as in a credit account showing an amount still owed by buyer to seller or a bank account with a minus balance, showing money owed to the bank by the customer.

debt: A fixed sum owed by one to another, payable now, and collectible at law by the creditor. In a somewhat wider sense, all debts owed by one to all others, as in a "national debt." The term is also loosely used to describe any obligation, however unenforceable, as in the "moral debt," or "debt to society."

debt ceiling: See debt limit.

debt limit: The maximum lawful debt which may be incurred by any government. Debt limits are set by law, and for sovereign states may be revised by law, as in the instance of the United States, which has often raised its own debt limit. Most states need state constitutional amendments to raise their own debt limits, but in fact are at least as much influenced by bond market considerations as by statutory constraints. Most municipalities need state approval for debt limit changes.

debt monetization: The issuance of new debt obligations by government to pay existing debts, and therefore the expansion of money supply; for example, the issuance of new short-term United States Government securities, providing a larger money supply and consequent expansion of credit available in the economy; a primary cause of inflation.

debtor: One who is legally responsible for the payment of debt, however that debt was incurred. One liable for payment of a judgment is just as much a debtor as one responsible for repayment of a loan.

debtor nation: A nation whose people and institutions have smaller total investments outside their country than the total of all foreign investments inside their country.

debt service: The amounts a debtor must pay a creditor to keep a debt currently paid up, including due and payable interest payments and principal repayments. Debt service often also refers to the total of all such payments due on all debts by a single debtor in a specified period.

deceased account: A bank account held in the name of someone who is deceased. A bank must freeze such an account on notification of the death of the accountholder, pending legal process leading to the close of the account and payment of the sums in it as directed by a court after probate.

decimal coinage: The organization of a nation's coinage system on a decimal basis, with a base of 10. The United States has a decimal coinage system.

declining balance method of depreciation: A method of figuring depreciation by applying a fixed percentage to each year's balance, which remains after the previous year's depreciation.

deductible: In taxation, any expense item that serves as a subtraction from taxable income.

deduction: See deductible.

de facto: Literally, "in fact." Often used to describe the realities of a situation, as distinct from its appearance or legalities. For example, a "de facto" government may be in actual possession of state power, but may not have been accorded legal or "de jure" status.

defalcation: The misappropriation or other illegal use of funds by one in a position of fiduciary trust. The term is normally used in relation to corporate or government officials who have so abused their trust.

default: Failure to do a legally required act, and subsequent liability for the resulting consequences. For example, failure to make payment on a loan may make a debtor liable for immediate payment of the entire loan amount, or a corporate bond default may force a corporation into bankruptcy. Failure to defend an action at law may result in a judgment by default, in favor of the plaintiff.

defensive investment: An investment aimed primarily at the conservation of capital, rather than at its aggressive growth. For example, an investor during a prolonged downward turn in common stock prices may sharply limit common stock investments and turn to less volatile and probably considerably safer investments, giving up the possibilities of aggressive capital growth inherent in common stocks for slower-growing, capital-conserving defensive investments.

deferral: Any item of expense or revenue that should be carried forward for accounting purposes so that it is attributed to the period in which the benefits stemming from the expense are received or the revenue is earned.

deferred charge: A charge that by its nature should be spread, all or in part, over future accounting periods rather than be treated as a current operating expense. For example, research and development costs are often properly spread over future years, with little or no charges expended into the current period.

deferred contract: A futures contract that specifies delivery three months or more after current purchase; as the delivery date comes closer, the contract becomes a "nearby" contract, due for delivery in the near-term.

deferred credit: See deferred revenue.

deferred delivery contract: A contract to purchase goods in which one party pays consideration due and the other takes delivery at some future time. While under many circumstances this is a normal commercial arrangement, the device has been widely used to defraud the unwary, in such areas as precious metal sales to small investors.

deferred dividend: A dividend that has been announced but on which payment has been postponed, either until a specific future date or until the occurrence of a specifically stated event.

deferred income: See deferred revenue.

deferred revenue: Advance payment received but not actually yet earned, and therefore for accounting purposes held for attribution to the period in which it is earned.

deferred tax: A tax that will result from current income and transactions at some later date beyond the current taxing period; for example, money earned in a current year and accrued in a profit-sharing plan, which will be taxable only when the money in that plan is paid out.

deficiency: 1. An amount claimed by a taxing authority over what a taxpayer has actually paid. **2.** In accounting, the amount by which liabilities exceed assets, which normally must be balanced by capital contributions to avoid insolvency.

deficit: The amount of deficiency, or excess of liabilities over assets, at a specified time, as at the end of an accounting period. In a much wider sense, the term is used as a synonym for "loss," and is often used to describe a process rather than a fixed sum at a specific time, as in "We are running at a deficit."

deficit financing: Government spending in excess of income, year after year on a long term basis, with a corresponding very large and continuous increase in the national debt. It is most often used as a term of opprobrium by critics charging excessive government spending.

deflation: A sustained drop in the general price level of goods and services: the opposite of inflation. The last substantial deflation in the United States was the Great Depression following the stock market crash of 1929.

deflationary gap: A theory that deflation is wholly or largely caused by a relatively large proportion of saving in an economy, resulting in too little investment spending to fuel economic growth and substantially full employment.

delayed delivery: A securities trading arrangement in which the parties understand that physical delivery of the securities traded will be delayed, and waive for a specified time the normal provision that delivery must be timely or the transaction will be voided.

delayed opening: Holding off the official opening of trading in a stock on an exchange by arrangement between the specialist and the exchange, in order to help smooth out possible sharp price fluctuations that might be caused by an unusual accummulation of buy or sell orders overnight, or by the placement of a large single block on the market overnight, by developing counter-balancing orders between the opening of the exchange and the opening of trading in that stock.

delisting: The dropping of a stock from the list of those traded by a stock exchange. To be listed, and thus traded, stocks must meet a number of rules set up by a stock exchange, usually including minimum earnings, company size, numbers of stockholders, and shares of stock held by the public. When a stock ceases to meet these minimum qualifications for listing, a stock exchange may delist it.

delivery: 1. The physical giving over of possession of instruments or articles of value, in fulfillment of contractual obligations, such as the passing of stocks, bonds, and spot or immediately deliverable commodities to their new owners, or the passing of possession under futures contracts at those future dates specified in the contracts. **2.** The legal transfer of possession of real or personal property. The transfer of possession may be by means of physical delivery or by means of an instrument of control, such as a bill of sale or deed; it may be absolute or conditional, actual or constructive. **3.** In commercial transactions, the actual physical delivery of purchased goods to their buyer, as specified by contract or common practice.

delivery point: The place at which commodities are to be physically delivered, under the terms of a commodities futures contract.

delivery price: The price specified in advance in a commodities futures contract, to be paid on delivery.

demand: 1. In law, the claiming of a specific right, asserted to be an absolute right under law, as in the demand for withdrawal of a demand deposit.   **2.** In economics, the total of wants for a product, service, or body of products and services.

demand curve: A graph showing the varying relationship between demand and price, often used in pricing new products, to determine optimum price levels.

demand deposit: A bank deposit that may be claimed by the depositor without notice, either in the form of checks drawn upon it or by outright withdrawal of the deposited amounts. Legally, many such deposits may be held for up to 30 days, but practically they are almost always recoverable on demand, except in some instances of bank failure.

demand loan: A loan that has no fixed date of termination, but may be terminated at any time by either lender or borrower.

demand pull inflation: An inflationary spiral, with strong demand for goods and services, resulting in increased business and credit expansion, increased money supply, and still higher prices.

demonetization: Discontinuance of the use of a substance as legal tender, such as the dropping of gold and silver as legal tender.

denationalization: The turning or returning of publicly owned businesses to private ownership.

denomination: The face value of ownership, debt, and currency certificates. While debt instruments and currency are issued in face value certificates, stocks are normally issued in multiple share certificates, such as a certificate for 100 shares; the denomination of a $10 bill being $10.00, and of each share whatever the par value of the single share.

Department of Commerce: A Federal department responsible for all executive branch matters dealing with business and commerce, including a wide range of regulatory, enforcement, administrative, and educational functions.

Department of Housing and Urban Development (HUD): A Federal department responsible for the development and administration of programs aimed at improving the quality and quantity of the nation's housing, with special attention to the needs of the poor and disadvantaged.

Department of Justice (DOJ): A Federal department functioning as the nation's chief executive branch legal arm, carrying substantial prosecuting and regulatory responsibilities.

depletable: Capable of being used up, usually referring to natural resources, such as coal, oil, metal ores and standing timber.

depleted cost: For accounting purposes, the cost that is left after accrued depletion has been subtracted.

depletion: The concept that natural resources can be and are used up over a period of time, and that tax policy and accounting practice must take into account that exhaustion of resources. Also refers to the amount of resources so used up.

depletion allowance: 1. In taxation, the amounts of the deductions from taxes allowed their owners for the using up of natural resources, such as oil, coal, metals and timber. Depletion allowances when occurring, are set by law.   **2.** In accounting, the value reductions set for depletion of specified natural resources.

deposit insurance: Insurance of bank deposits up to certain limits set by law. See also: Federal Deposit Insurance Corporation; Federal Savings and Loan Insurance Corporation.

depository: 1. A person, institution or place used to store anything for value. Also spelled depositary, when referring to a person or institution entrusted.   **2.** A bank authorized to receive and hold government, trust or other bank funds.

deposits: Amounts placed into bank accounts, which are then drawn upon for business or personal use or held for the accretion of interest, and which provide a base for the bank's ability to create credit and make loans.

deposit slip: A record of deposit filled out by a depositor and stamped by a bank which functions both as an entry document for the bank and as a legal and vitally necessary evidence of deposit for the depositor.

depreciable cost: The basis upon which an asset's depreciation will be taken, often the money cost of the asset to its current owner.

depreciation: The lessening in value of an asset due to age and use. Depreciation is an accounting estimate, essential both for avoiding overstatement of an asset's value and for tax accounting purposes. Although its tax significance is similar to that of depletion, it results from use rather than using up. A machine may be fully depreciated for tax and accounting purposes and still be whole and entirely useable, while a stand of timber may shrink year by year as it is used up or depleted.

depreciation reserve: Those valuation amounts set aside for accounting purposes to reflect the depreciation that has accumulated on an asset. Depreciation reserves are accounting estimates, rather than actual reserves.

depression: A long, deep economic crisis, with widespread unemployment and the collapse or near-collapse of major economic institutions. The last depression was the Great Depression of the 1930's. Depressions and recessions are distinguished by the length and depth of the business cycle downturn, with recessions much less severe than depressions.

deregulation: The ending of government regulation of private activities, usually business activities; for example, the ending of government-imposed price controls on a product, such as gasoline.

derived demand: Demands for some products and services that are created by demands for other products and services. For example, demands for automobiles create a very large number of other demands for metals, fuel, accessories and services. In a highly integrated economy, the concept becomes somewhat blurred as an analytical tool.

deutschemark: The main currency unit of West Germany, bearing the same relationhip to West Germany's national currency system as does the dollar to the United States currency system.

devaluation: Redefinition downward of the precious metal content of a country's currency by that country, or of a country's currency in relation to other national currencies. Under conditions of international currency price-fixing, devaluation can be precise; when currencies float freely against each other, backed in a practical sense only by the full faith and credit of the issuing governments, devaluation is a matter of national policy and central bank control operating within a fluid international currency situation.

developing nation: A wide and imprecise term generally describing any nation that is not highly industrialized, often referring to those relatively unindustrialized nations of Asia, Africa and South America thought to be aligned with neither the United States nor the Soviet Union in international power bloc matters. Although often used synonymously with the term "Third World," some highly industrialized unaligned nations, such as Brazil, cannot be properly described as "developing."

development expense: 1. An expense incurred in new product introduction. **2.** Any expense related to advertising and promotion. **3.** A cost directly or indirectly related to the exploration and exploitation of natural resources.

differential costs: Those costs which can be associated with doing or not doing, adding or subtracting from something in being or planned. For example, the cost to make a milkshake without an egg may be 20 cents; with an egg 25 cents. The differential cost of the egg in the milkshake is 5 cents.

dilution: As applied to securities, the lessening of an ownership share's earnings and assets equity, caused by the issuance of more ownership shares without corresponding increases in earnings and assets. Stock dilution can occur in several ways, including new common stock issues and the exercise of stock options and warrants.

diminishing balance method: See declining balance method.

dinar: The main currency unit of several countries, including Yugoslavia, Iraq, Abu Dhabi, Aden, Bahrein, and Algeria, bearing the same relationships to their currency systems as does the dollar to the United States currency system.

direct cost: A cost that can be specifically related to a product, such as labor and materials used in manufacture. The proper identification of direct costs and their control is a major management goal, and the number of unattributable and therefore "indirect" costs is constantly diminishing.

direct investment: The purchase of active ownership interests, whether controlling or substantial minority interests, in other companies, in contrast to the purchase of shares in those companies for non-active investment purposes.

direct overhead: Those overhead costs that can be directly attributed to goods and services produced, and can therefore be accounted for as direct costs, in contrast to those unattributable costs which must be accounted for as indirect costs.

direct placement: The sale of securities directly to a limited number of purchasers, rather than to the general public; for example, the sale of a corporate bond issue to a single bank or a group of banks and other institutions, without resale by them to the public.

dirty float: A currency float, or exchange rate, that does not float freely as against other currencies, with relative currency prices determined by marketplace conditions, but rather is manipulated by government in pursuit of national policy; normally a pejorative term applied to what other governments do, but a most usual practice indulged in directly or indirectly by most governments under most conditions.

disbursement: The immediate actual payment of money by check or cash. Disbursements are cash out, rather than expenditures, and affect cash flow, not profit and loss.

disclosure: Generally, the revealing of previously hidden or private facts about a person or situation. In modern business, the term has also come to mean the legally required process of revealing facts about people and organizations, as in the disclosure requirements surrounding a public stock issue or a corporate political contribution.

discount: 1. Generally, any specific subtraction from a sum due prior to payment. **2.** To make a specific subtraction from a sum before payment. In a wider sense, to evaluate skeptically assertions made by others. **3.** A reduction in price paid, usually but not always in advance of payment, as in a 2% reduction in stated price for payment received within 30 days of billing, or for quantity purchases. **4.** A reduction in the net proceeds of monies loaned, almost always in advance of payment of loan proceeds by lenders to borrowers, as in the subtraction of stated interest of 8% from the proceeds of a $100 loan. The amount of the loan is $100, the proceeds to the borrower are $92, and the borrower pays back $100. **5.** The amount by which a security is selling below its face value, as in a $1,000 bond being sold for $950, with a resulting discount of 5%. **6.** To make advance allowance for anticipated trends and events, as in discounting the impact of projected political events. In this sense, the term is often used in describing securities price fluctuations as stemming from anticipated financial events.

discount broker: A securities broker who offers trading facilities at the lowest possible commission rates, hoping to attract customers with cut rates rather than with brokerage services, which are minimal.

discounted cash flow: The evaluation of cash spent now on capital expenditures in terms of both the cash spent now and an assumed compound interest rate on that cash over the anticipated life of the asset acquired.

discount market: The market for bank and commercial paper of all kinds, composed of all those who buy and sell these kinds of money market instruments.

discount rate: 1. The rate of interest charged by a bank when discounting bank and commercial paper. Discount rates depend on a number of variables, including the kind of instrument being discounted and the market's assessment of the quality of the issue and issuer. **2.** The rate of interest set by Reserve banks on loans to member banks. This rate varies with both economic conditions and government money policy. Raising the discount rate makes money more expensive to borrow, and is thought to be deflationary; lowering it makes money less expensive to borrow and is thought to be inflationary.

discretionary account: A securities account in which a customer grants a broker partial or complete authority to buy and sell securities on behalf of the customer, with the broker controlling such matters as which securities to buy or sell and when, where and at what prices to buy and sell.

discretionary income: Income that need not be committed to mandated expenditures, and that can be used as desired, for spending, saving and investing. The term is usually applied to individual income, with such items as rent, food and debt repayment seen as mandatory and such items as boats, savings accounts and stock purchases seen as discretionary.

discretionary order: See discretionary account.

discretionary spending: Money spent by consumers on goods and services that are not basic necessities, such as money spent on travel and entertainment; but in some areas, as with money spent on home improvements, the line between discretion and necessity can blur.

diseconomy of scale: A theory describing the tendency of costs to rise under certain conditions with increases in the size of enterprises; for example; cost increases caused by the development of bureaucratic overstaffing in some highly centralized private and public enterprises.

dishonor: To refuse to pay the amount due on an instrument presented for payment, as in a bank's refusal to pay a check that has been stopped by its issuer or the nonpayment of any money market instrument by its issuer when due.

disincentives: Incentives aimed at reducing private activity, usually supplied by government; for example, the supplying of government subsidies to agricultural producers for limiting crop production.

disinflation: The arresting of inflation without forcing recession, attempted through a series of governmental economic manipulations. See also: deflation.

disintermediation: The flow of money to those savings vehicles yielding the highest interest, as in the flow of personal savings from savings accounts to government obligations when interest rates are higher on government obligations.

disposable income: That personal income available for consumer spending, savings and investment, consisting of all income minus taxes and other payments to governments.

dissolve: To terminate or cancel. Business organizations of all kinds can be dissolved by legislative, judicial or voluntary action, although some matters may remain open in proprietorships and partnerships. Contracts can be dissolved, as can legal proceedings and restrictions.

distribution: 1. The process of moving goods and services from manufacturer to consumer, including all physical and marketing steps. Altough marketing is sometimes used as a synonym, it is only part of the distribution process. 2. Payments, including dividends, by business organizations to their owners, other than salaries and salary-related sums. 3. In accounting, a synonym for allocation, the assignment of income and expenditures to accounts. 4. In statistics, the mode of spreading related information over a given area. 5. The allocation of the remainder of an estate after all legal costs.

distribution of risk: The spreading of investments among several kinds of investments to provide some protection should one or more investments turn out badly, as in developing an investment portfolio that includes savings, insurance, bonds and common stocks, rather than common stocks alone. Similarly, the spread of a single large loan among several large lenders; and the spread of a large insurance risk among several insurers.

diversification: The development by a company of more than one line of products or businesses; for example, an office machine company's development of a line of related office products, or a company's acquisition of related and unrelated businesses.

divestiture: Disposal of a subsidiary, division or any other substantial portion of a company; normally accomplished by some kind of sale or liquidation, as in the sale of a subsidiary pursuant to pre-trial agreement or court order in an anti-trust prosecution by the federal government.

dividend: A payment of a portion of profits to owners of corporations and other business organizations. Payment is proportional to the amount of equity owned, with the owner of 200 shares getting the same amount of dividends per share as the owner of 100 shares, and therefore twice as much in payments. Payments may be regularly scheduled or exceptional, but each decision to pay dividends is a separate decision made by the organization's governing body.

doing business: Act of conducting business within the geographical bounds of a regulating authority, and therefore becoming subject to the regulatory powers of that authority. The term is used to define several situations, but is most often encountered in taxation, as when a business is adjudged to be doing business for tax purposes in a jurisdiction, and therefore taxable within that jurisdiction.

DOJ: See Department of Justice.

dollar: The main currency unit of the United States, and of several other countries as well, including Australia, Canada, Hong Kong, and Singapore. Dollars used in the several national coinage systems differ in value, and those differences vary with fluctuations in the relative values of national currencies.

dollar bond: A bond wholly denominated in United States dollars, with interest and principal are paid in those dollars. Any bond may be so denominated.

dollar cost averaging: The practice of periodically buying securities with fixed amounts of dollars, as in a monthly investment plan in which an investor buys $200 per month of the same common stock, over a long period, and without regard to whether the stock goes up or down in the short term. The theory behind the practice is that the long term tendency of the stock market is up, and that by purchasing sound stocks steadily, a steady investment profit can be made. As a practical matter, both theory and practice suffer greatly in periods of long term market decline, especially when accompanied by a pronounced inflationary trend and its negative impact on the value of the dollar.

dollar exchange: Bills of exchange and banker's acceptances payable in dollars, although drawn or payable outside the United States.

dollar gap: International currency situation in which dollars outside the United States are in short supply, tending to push the value of the dollar up in relation to the values of other currencies.

dollar glut: International currency situation in which dollars outside the United States are in oversupply, tending to push the value of the dollar down in relation to the value of other currencies.

dollar shortage: See dollar gap.

domestic: Of a home or domicile. In business, the term usually refers to the original and legal domicile of transactions and legal entities.

domestic corporation: A corporation chartered in a state and therefore described as domestic to that state.

domestic product: A product produced in a particular place, such as a state or nation, and therefore described as domestic to that place.

domicile: That place which in law is regarded as the main place of residence of an individual or business entity. Corporations are domiciled where chartered, but for some regulatory and other legal purposes may be considered domiciled in other locations.

donated stock: Capital stock given back to a corporation by its stockholders, without consideration. It is often stock originally issued to early shareholders in payment for start-up services rendered, now returned to the corporation for new financing purposes.

donated surplus: Surplus resulting from contributions of property to a corporation by its stockholders, including both real and personal property, cash and stock, usually as a means of supplying needed additional capital to the corporation.

dormant account: A financial account, usually a bank account, that has little or no activity for a protracted period, and usually very small balances on deposit.

double bottom: Describing the movement of market down to nearly its most recent substantial bottom twice within a short period, without going through the level of that recent bottom to new, even lower price levels.

double digit inflation: A rate of inflation of 10% or more per year.

double option: See straddle.

double taxation: A term widely used to describe alleged double taxation of corporate earnings, once through corporate income tax and again through taxation of corporate dividends paid out of after-tax earnings to stockholders.

double top: The opposite of double bottom. See double bottom.

Dow Jones averages: Three United States stock price averages—industrial, transportation and utilities—which are widely quoted as indicating the general rise or fall of stock market prices. The best known of the three averages, and the one most often cited, is the

Dow Jones industrial average, composed of thirty well known and highly regarded common stocks. Although other averages are also quoted, such as the Standard and Poor's Composite Index and the New York Stock Exchange Common Stock Index, the Dow Jones averages continue to command the widest popular and securities trade attention.

down tick: A securities trade made at a lower price than the last such transaction.

Dow theory: A popular stock market price forecasting theory based on the movement of the Dow Jones industrial and transportation averages. This theory attempts to predict general stock market price movements by interpreting parallel upward and downward movements of these two averages past stated price support points.

drachma: The main currency unit of Greece, bearing the same relationship to Greece's national currency system as does the dollar to the United States currency system.

draft: A bill of exchange, called a draft in domestic commercial and securities transactions, in which a buyer pays a seller for goods received with a call upon the buyer's bank for the agreed upon sum. The buyer, or drawer, makes a draft, instructing the bank, or drawee, to pay the sum to the seller, or payee.

drawee: The person or company upon which demand for payment of a draft is made, usually a bank responding to the draft of one of its clients.

drawer: A person or company making a draft, usually upon its bank, for payment of a sum to anyone.

dry hole: A well drilled in pursuit of oil or natural gas that produces neither.

dual listing: The listing of a security on two or more exchanges; many securities are so listed.

due bill: See IOU.

due date: The date on which any debt becomes payable, as in the maturity date of a bond or note.

dummy: In business, one who substitutes for another in a business situation, such as a dummy stockholder, who holds a stock actually belonging to another, to shield the identity of the real owner, or a dummy corporation, holding property really belonging to another.

dumping: 1. The sale of large quantities of goods in foreign markets at prices lower than those being charged in the producing country's home markets, usually in an attempt to undersell similar goods produced in those foreign markets. **2.** The sale of large quantities of securities in the securities markets at whatever price can be secured, with little or no regard for the adverse effects of the sale on the prices of the securities being sold.

durable goods: Goods purchased for personal consumption that normally last some years, such as major household appliances and automobiles.

Dutch auction: A backwards auction, with the seller quoting an asking price, and moving backward in stages until reaching someone who will bid at the then-current asking price, that bidder then buying.

dutiable goods: Goods on which import or export duties are by law imposed.

duty: See tariff.

duty free: Imports that are by law free of customs duty payment obligations.

E

earning power: The amount of earnings an asset is thought likely to return at present levels of price, volume, and profitability. When used in regard to securities, the term is usually synonymous with yield.

earnings: The profits of a business enterprise.

earnings acceleration: An increase in a company's rate of earnings as compared with comparable recent previous periods.

earnings deceleration: A decrease in a company's rate of earnings as compared with comparable recent previous periods.

earnings growth: Any increase in earnings as compared with recent periods, often as compared with the most recent period; to be distinguished from an increase in the rate of earnings growth, as a company may experience larger earnings, but on an even larger revenue base, resulting in an actual decrease in the rate of earnings.

earnings per share: The net earnings of each share of outstanding common stock of a company, arrived at by subtracting taxes and preferred stock dividends from earnings, and then dividing the resulting net earnings by the number of outstanding shares of common stock of the company. For example, if earnings are $100, and taxes are $40, net after-tax earnings are $60. If preferred stock dividends are $10, net earnings for figuring earnings per share become $50. If there are 50 shares, earnings per share are $1.

earnings statement: See income statement.

easy money: An economic condition in which a nation's money supply is expanding, and credit is easy to obtain. In the United States, a period of easy money results in large part from federal manipulation of the amount and cost of money available for commercial bank reserves and, therefore, for bank credit available to potential borrowers. In addition to federal credit control, other factors, such as the condition of the international money market, also affect available money supplies.

econometrics: A branch of economic theory and practice that uses mathematics, and especially statistical analysis, as its main means of measuring, analyzing, and forecasting economic matters. As an aid to decision making, econometrics relies heavily on modern computer capabilities to set up and follow alternate mathematical models to possible future conclusions.

economic: 1. Relating in any way to the economy. **2.** Relating in any way to the study of economics. **3.** The most efficient and least costly way of handling an economic matter.

economic activity: All activity that is primarily concerned with the generation and distribution of goods and services.

economic forecast: A description of anticipated economic trends for any future period, usually focusing on such matters as expected growth in national product, employment, business investment levels, retail sales, prices, wages, profits, and other key indicators of the future health of the economy.

economic growth: The growth and maturation of an economy, usually measured by growth in average productivity per worker, the development of increasingly complex and sophisticated means of production and supporting structures, and Gross National Product.

economic indicators: A series of economic factors which, taken together, are used in attempts to measure the economy's tendency to cyclical movement. Major indicators, such as wages, prices, profits, and investments, and scores of less important indicators, are tracked, weighted, placed in composite indexes, and used as much of the raw material of economic forecasting.

economic life: See service life.

economic planning: The organization of production and distribution by government. Often referring to totally planned economies, in which all major industry is controlled by the state, the term is also widely used in describing mixed economies, in which some major economic functions and sometimes industries are controlled by the state. In the United States and other major industrial countries, money supply control and manipulation is an example of economic planning, as is the use of taxing policy.

economics: That branch of the social sciences that deals with the organization and operation of the economic system and with the entire economic side of life, with primary emphasis on the production, distribution, and consumption of goods and services.

economic sanctions: Punitive economic actions taken by one government against another in pursuit of political goals, as in the refusal of one government to export strategic goods to another while a dispute is in progress between the two governments.

economic unit: A single entity operating for common economic purposes. Working individuals, families, wholly or in part, that pool their income and expenditures, and organized businesses, ranging from the sole proprietorship to the conglomerate, are all considered economic units.

economy: 1. The economic life and structure of a specified geographical area; usually applied to a city, country, region, state or nation. **2.** The prudent and efficient use of resources and material.

economy of scale: The theory that unit costs tend to decline as the size of the producing unit and the amount of production grow. In modern American practice, economies of scale have often seemed to be overbalanced by major efficiency and operating problems, resulting in attempts to limit the size of producing organizations and facilities through decentralization.

ECSC: See European Coal and Steel Community.

edge: Advantage, such as one tenth of a point in arbitrage or in options trading.

EEC: European Economic Community. See Common Market.

effective date: The date on which an agreement goes into effect, as specified by contract, purchase order, insurance policy, or other specifying document.

effective rate: 1. The real as distinct from the quoted rates of interest paid on borrowings, as in a bank's quoted 8% interest rate that is a real 12% rate on a personal loan. **2.** The real as distinct from the quoted yield on investments, figuring the yield as a percentage of market value, rather than as a percentage of face value.

EFTA: See European Free Trade Association.

EFTS: See Electronic Funds Transfer System.

either/or order: See alternative order.

elasticity of demand: Changes in the demand for a product or service, as a result of price changes relative to other products or services. Such changes occur mainly in areas of buying discretion, rather than in areas of necessity. However, demand for seeming necessities can sharply diminish, as in the instances of gasoline and coffee.

elasticity of supply: Changes in the supply of a product or service, as a result of price changes relative to other prices or services. Under some conditions, producers will supply more products and services to take advantage of higher prices.

electronic calculator: Any modern calculating machine that has little or no memory; the line between calculator and computer has virtually disappeared with the advent of small personal computers and minicomputers of all kinds.

electronic data processing (EDP): The recording and processing of data by electronic means, using computers and computer-related machines, materials, and techniques. EDP is by far the widest use to which computers are put.

Electronic Funds Transfer System (EFTS): A centralized system for handling financial arrangements for transactions in decentralized locations, such as for sales made at local branch stores around the country.

eleemosynary: Connected in some way with charity and charitable organizations.

eleemosynary corporation: A not-for-profit corporation organized for charitable purposes.

elevator receipt: See warehouse receipt.

eligible investment: See legal investment list.

eligible paper: Commercial paper, consisting of notes, bills of exchange, and acceptances that will be rediscounted by Federal Reserve banks on submission by member banks, and subject to Federal Reserve requirements as to form, maturity, kinds of transactions generating the paper, and total amount relative to current bank capital.

embargo: Any formal ban imposed on trade, including action by government and by private organizations. Most often, it is a ban on international trade imposed for national policy reasons by one government on the products or carriers of another government, with the scope of the ban ranging from a single product to a total ban on all products and carriers.

embezzlement: The fraudulent taking of valuables by one acting in a fiduciary capacity for their owner. The valuables taken may be in any form, including cash and all other kinds of property; the embezzler may be in any position of fiduciary trust, including employees such as bank tellers and company treasurers, public officials, agents, and representatives.

EMS: See European Monetary System.

endorse: 1. To sign a document, such as a check, bill of exchange, or other negotiable instrument, and thereby make passage of title possible.   **2.** To publicly approve of someone or something, as in recommendation of a product.

endorsee: One to whom an endorsement and delivery are made.

endorsement: The actual signature of the owner of a document, making that document negotiable and passage of title possible. That signature must be on the document or otherwise attached to the document. Where the endorsement is to a specific entity, both signature and the delivery of the signed instrument to the one specified is required for the transaction to be completed; where the endorsement is in blank, as on a bearer bond, only delivery is needed.

endorser: See endorse.

energy stocks: The stocks of companies primarily engaged in energy producing or energy related businesses, such as oil, coal, and solar energy companies.

enterprise: A business of any size, usually of some complexity. The term is sometimes used more widely, to describe any organized form of endeavor.

entrepeneur: One who undertakes the conception and development of a new business enterprise, doing whatever is necessary to make the enterprise go, and taking ultimate responsibility for every aspect of development, from financing to distribution; and who takes major risks and can reasonably expect a major share of any profits.

ephemera: Antiques and collectibles that were originally intended for short term use, such as comic books and fragile consumer goods.

equilibrium: That theoretical point at which a firm is most profitable.

equipment trust bonds: Certificates issued by companies buying heavy equipment, such as railroad cars, that in essence are mortgages on the equipment which are then sold to lenders. The lender can foreclose the mortgage for nonpayment; the company has the equipment with very little capital investment.

equipment trust certificate: See equipment trust bonds.

equities: A popular synonym for securities.

equity: 1. The money value of that which is owned, arrived at by subtracting all that is owed from the value of the ownership to arrive at a net ownership value figure. Some examples are: the value of real property minus all mortgages and other borrowings; the market value of stocks in a margin account minus the borrowings in the account; and the value of all outstanding common and preferred stock in a corporation. In some instances, as in determining the value of stock in a margin account, the ownership value can be easily determined at any time, as both market value and borrowings are firm figures. But often, as in attempting to determine a homeowner's equity in a mortgaged home, equity is only an estimate because the market value of the home is only an estimate until the home is sold. **2.** The concept of fairness and justice applied to that portion of the English common law relating to the rights and duties of individuals. Once administered through a separate system of courts, called chancery courts, cases involving matters of equity are now handled within the regular court system.

equity financing: A stock issue, in which a corporation sells a piece of its ownership to others to raise money, as distinct from raising money by borrowing.

erratic market: A market characterized by securities prices that move in no well-defined direction, up or down, with considerable price fluctuation within short time periods.

escrow: The holding by a third party of something of value which is the subject of a contract or proceeding between two other parties, until that contract or proceeding has been consummated. A deed evidencing ownership of real property being sold is often so held by a bank until the entire transaction has been cleared and recorded, as is a payment on a contract pending completion.

escudo: The main currency unit of several countries, including Portugal, Chile and Angola, bearing the same relationship to the currency systems of those countries as does the dollar to the United States currency system.

estate: 1. Any and all individual ownership or interest and the total of all ownerships and interests in real or personal property, including absolute, conditional, and contingent interests. In economic and legal senses, the term describes anything owned on which a monetary value can ultimately be placed. **2.** The sum of all such individual ownerships and interests remaining after death.

estate sale: The sale at auction or at fixed prices of assets consisting of antiques and collectibles residing in an estate, to turn those assets into cash.

estate tax: An excise tax upon the entire estate of the deceased.

Eurocurrency: Strong currencies held on deposit in banks in other countries and used as sources of financing by a wide variety of borrowers throughout the world. As long as American dollars, backed by American gold, were regarded as key reserves throughout the world, they were the prime source of such financing; in recent years, other currencies have increasingly been used as well, and the financing mode in this portion of the money market has become international.

Eurodollars: American dollars held on deposit in banks abroad, serving as a basis for financing throughout the world; a form which has been replaced by the Eurocurrency market, which includes American dollars and several other harder currencies.

European Coal and Steel Community (ECSC): A predecessor to, and now effectively an agency of, the Common Market; it develops joint international policies in the area of coal and steel, and finances its activities through international taxes on coal and steel production in the member countries.

European Commission: The main administrative organization of the Common Market, developing budgets and proposals for legislative action and holding substantial regulatory power in several economic areas affecting commerce in and between the member states of the Common Market.

European Court of Justice: An international court operating within the Common Market and responsible for interpreting and enforcing the policies and regulations of the Common Market. By international agreement, it has supranational powers in some economic areas, as defined by the 1957 Treaty of Rome.

European Economic Community (EEC): See Common Market.

European Free Trade Association (EFTA): A group of European countries outside the European Common Market, and including Austria, Finland, Iceland, Norway, Portugal, Sweden, and Switzerland, organized as a free trade area, and having special trading arrangements with the European Common Market.

European Investment Bank: An international bank and agency of the Common Market, charged with the development of financing policies and plans, including both grants and loans, which will benefit the members of the Common Market, especially the less developed member nations.

European Monetary System (EMS): The monetary control system of the European Common Market, which ties together the currencies of most national governments in the Common Market as against all other world currencies, functioning so as to adjust Common Market currencies to each other within a relatively narrow range, with the whole currency group therefore moving together in world currency markets.

European Parliament: An institution of the Common Market, consisting of a consultative assembly with representation from all the member countries of the Common Market.

even lot: See round lot.

excess loan: A loan granted by a bank that is larger than allowed by statute or banking regulation; therefore an illegal loan, and one for which the bank's directors may be held liable in the event of default.

excess profits tax: A special tax set on corporate profits, beyond normal corporate tax rates, in circumstances in which those profits are exceptionally high due to national circumstances, especially war.

excess reserves: The amount of reserve funds held by a bank above legal requirements. Bank reserves are a percentage of deposits, and a bank may lend only those funds beyond its legal reserve. But it may hold excess reserves, above the legal limit, for a wide variety of reasons, including current economic conditions and specific bank policies.

exchange: 1. A specific market place, in which instruments of ownership, such as stocks and bonds are bought, sold, and traded. **2.** A market place transaction, in which valuables are bought, sold, and traded, as in the sale of a single orange or ten thousand shares of a common stock.

exchange controls: Wide-ranging governmental restrictions on the free international exchange of foreign currencies within its own borders, aimed at stabilizing the international price of its own currency.

exchange depreciation: A fall in the value of a currency as measured against other currencies, whether by market action, governmental manipulation, or both.

exchange rate: The rate at which one currency can be exchanged for another at any given time, as in a dollar being exchangeable for half a British pound or two Japanese yen at a given moment of a given day, with the pound and yen directly exchangeable with each other as well. Exchange rates, regulated by international agreement for many years following World War II, became unregulated in the late 1970's, with currencies floating freely and continuously seeking new values in relation to each other after that.

Exchequer: 1. The British treasury, a central account into which all national income is paid and from which all national expenditures are drawn. **2.** The British Government's treasury department, generally performing the same kinds of financial administrative, taxing, and handling functions as the United States Treasury Department.

excise tax: A tax on two quite different kinds of activities: sales of goods and intangible privileges. It is usually described as a single kind of tax on the privilege of selling those goods and exercising those privileges. Excise taxes are levied either as a percentage of the selling price or a fixed amount per item sold, on a wide variety of goods, including such necessities as gasoline and such luxuries as handbags. They are also levied on a wide variety of privileges, such as franchises and licenses.

ex-dividend: Describing stock on which a dividend has been declared but not yet paid and which is then sold, with the declared dividend going to the seller rather than to the buyer, reflected in a somewhat lower selling price. Stock exchange rules normally define the length of the period after dividend declaration and before delivery of stock sold ex-dividend during which the stock will be so treated, and also provide for sales on a cash basis, with the dividend going to the purchaser.

Eximbank: See Export-Import Bank of the United States.

expanding economy: An economic system experiencing a period of growth, usually but not always accompanied by prosperity for most of those living in that economy, and in contrast to contraction, which is relative decline of an economy.

expenditure: The act of spending to acquire an asset or to pay a debt; also the amount so spent.

expense: 1. A cost incurred in the course of doing business and attributable to the business done. **2.** A present operating cost. **3.** Outlays attributed to accounting periods, as determined by accounting systems and conventions used and by company objectives and financial management techniques.

expiration date: In securities trading, the date on which such possibly valuable privileges as rights and options expire. Beyond that date, they have lost their value.

Export-Import Bank (Eximbank): A United States bank functioning to stimulate United States international trade by a wide-ranging program of loans, guarantees, and insurance to domestic and foreign exporters and importers, as a major supplement to private financing available for these purposes.

export quota: A limitation placed by government on the kind and quantities of goods that may be shipped by its exporters. Such quotas normally serve either home industry protective purposes or more directly political national purposes, as in restrictions on the export of strategic materials.

exports: 1. Goods made in one country, sold, and shipped abroad for use in other countries. **2.** To send those goods abroad. **3.** Popularly, all goods and services originating in one geographic unit and sold for use in another. States are described as exporting goods abroad and to one another. Consulting services are sometimes described as being exported abroad.

exposure: 1. A very general measure of the risks involved in taking any course of action, and in business with special emphasis on money risks. **2.** The amount that is at risk by an insurer on an insurance policy, usually measured by the maximum amount of insurance that may have to be paid in claims on that policy under conditions of maximum possible liability.

ex-rights: A stock on which rights have been declared but not yet issued, and which is then sold without those rights attached.

extended bonds: Bonds that come to maturity and on which the face value is not paid but held by the issuer, with interest payments instead continued and the original backing of the bonds unchanged. Issuers desiring to extend their bonds must offer to do so and have that offer accepted by their bondholders.

external audit: An independent audit conducted by auditors not directly employed by the organization being audited; an outside audit.

external debt: The total of all public and private debts owed by a country and its citizens to all other countries and their citizens.

extractive industry: An industry that takes its materials from nature, as in the mining of coal, iron, and gold, and the drilling and taking of oil and natural gas.

extra dividend: A dividend that is declared by a corporation to be higher than the normal dividend paid, and that may not be repeated, as distinct from a corporate decision to move to a higher normal dividend rate.

extraordinary depreciation: Depreciation far beyond that ordinarily to be expected, caused by such unusual matters as protracted cold or precipitation, extraordinary use factors, and unanticipated obsolescence, but not including such property loss matters as fire, flood, and theft.

extraordinary expense: A very unusual and often entirely unanticipated expense, which must be taken into account separately for financial statement purposes, rather than being placed in with and to some extent therefore distorting normal expenses.

ex-warrants: Describing a stock that is traded without warrants attached, when those warrants have been exercised by a previous owner of the stock.

F

face value: The amount stamped, printed, or otherwise affixed on an instrument of value, indicating its stated value when issued or at maturity. Coins, currency, notes, bonds, stocks, insurance policies, and other such instruments have such face values, with bonds and insurance policies carrying stated values as of their maturity dates, and stocks carrying par values that often have no real relation to their market values.

facsimile: A reproduction, usually referring to a careful, virtually identical work, rather than to a photocopy.

factor: 1. One who buys accounts receivable from a manufacturer, pays the manufacturer at a discounted rate for them, and then assumes all risks and makes and keeps all collections of those accounts receivable. In many instances factors have also become lenders and suppliers of working capital in ways that go beyond their original factoring roles. **2.** A consignment agent, possessing control over the goods being sold, collecting commissions on sales, and remitting sales revenue minus those commissions to the goods' owners.

factors of production: The main elements involved in production, in orthodox economics normally described as land, labor, capital, and entrepreneurial contribution, though theorists disagree as to the inclusion of entrepreneurial contribution as a main element of production.

factory of: See school of.

fails: The failures of brokers to deliver physically and in timely fashion securities that have been transferred to other brokers. Each such failure of delivery is a single fail; the aggregate of such fails at any given moment is the fails level in the securities industry or some segment of it.

failures: Those businesses that do not survive, going out of business voluntarily or involuntarily, solvent or in bankruptcy.

fair market value: The trading price of anything, at which a willing and informed seller and buyer will or would trade, and without either party possessing extraordinary trading leverage. The term is used widely in setting values for tax assessment and judicial purposes.

fair return: A theory and series of formulas developed by regulatory bodies and the courts to determine what rates of profit should be allowed to companies in highly regulated industries such as telephone, power supplying utilities, and railroads.

fair trade: The concept that producers, distributors, and retailers should be allowed to set minimum prices on their goods. Formerly supported by a series of statutes in many states, setting minimum prices on a wide range of goods, it is now mainly prohibited since repeal of federal laws that had barred application of the anti-trust statutes to this form of collusive price fixing.

family business: A business controlled by the members of a single family; examples range from a "Mom and Pop" corner grocery store to a corporation in which a controlling interest, though not necessarily a majority shareholding, is owned by a single family.

Fannie Mae: See Federal National Mortgage Association.

Farm Credit Administration (FCA): A Federal agency charged with the responsibility for administering a wide range of credit alternatives for American farmers, organized into a cooperative farm credit system that includes Federal land banks, Federal land bank associations, intermediate credit banks, production credit associations, and banks for cooperatives.

Farmers Home Administration: An agency of the Department of Agriculture, which loans money on favorable terms to farmers who might otherwise find affordable credit difficult or impossible to secure. Loans are available for a wide variety of purposes, including home and land ownership, operating expenses, and special projects.

favorable balance of trade: See balance of trade.

FCA: See Farm Credit Administration.

FCIC: See Federal Crop Insurance Corporation.

FDIC: See Federal Deposit Insurance Corporation.

Fed: A popular term for Federal Reserve Board. See Federal Reserve System.

Federal Advisory Council: A purely advisory organization attached to the Federal Reserve System, consisting of one member, often a banker, selected by each of the twelve Federal Bank boards of directors.

Federal budget: The fiscal year budget of the United States, running from July 1 to June 30, and detailing all anticipated income and expenditures.

Federal Crop Insurance Corporation (FCIC): A Federal agency, part of the Department of Agriculture, responsible for a national system of federally funded insurance against crop losses due to natural and unavoidable causes, such as weather and insects, rather than such avoidable causes as market conditions and uncompetitive work practices.

Federal debt: See national debt.

Federal Deposit Insurance Corporation (FDIC): An independent Federal agency that insures individual deposits up to certain limits in all national banks and in all state banks that are part of the Federal Reserve System, as well as in those other banks which apply for such insurance. The FDIC has substantial regulatory and supervisory powers as well.

Federal funds: Funds held by Federal Reserve member banks in excess of funds needed to comply with legal reserve requirements. These funds are traded among member banks on a short term basis, allowing those banks with more-than-necessary reserve funds to loan them on a day-to-day basis to banks with less-than-required reserve funds. The sum of those trades comprise the "Federal funds market." Although banks with reserve fund needs may also borrow from the Federal Reserve, funds may be available in the Federal funds market at less than the Fed's discount rate, and banks that have borrowed up to their legal limit from the Fed find that market a useful source of short term funds.

Federal funds rates: The rates of interest paid on Federal debt obligations, and especially the various rates of interest paid on United States Treasury bills.

Federal Home Loan Bank System: A federally organized and administered banking system, consisting of twelve regional Federal Home Loan Banks that supply credit reserves to all savings and loan associations, which must by law be members of the system, and to other lending institutions, including savings banks and insurance companies, engaged in home mortgage lending.

Federal Housing Administration (FHA): A Federal agency, part of the Department of Housing and Urban Development, responsible for a wide variety of mortgage and loan insurance functions covering all the forms of residential housing.

Federal intermediate credit banks: Part of the farm credit system administered by the Farm Credit Administration, consisting of twelve banks engaged in providing reserves for and lending to those institutions and organizations that lend directly to farmers.

Federal land banks: Part of the farm credit system administered by the Farm Credit Administration, consisting of twelve Federal land banks, that make long term mortgage loans at favorable rates and for a wide variety of purposes to the members of some hundreds of land bank associations throughout the country.

Federal mortgage insurance: A federally funded program which insures private lenders against losses stemming from some kinds of mortgage and housing loans. Administered by the Department of Housing and Urban Development, the program is intended to encourage lower down payments and interest rates and the availability of loan money to those of relatively modest means.

Federal National Mortgage Association (Fannie Mae): A federally sponsored private corporation which buys, sells, and otherwise deals in government insured or guaranteed mortgages to help provide liquidity in the secondary market for home mortgages and therefore a greater availability of mortgage money for borrowers.

Federal Reserve Bank: One of the twelve central Federal banks, each operating in one of the twelve Federal Reserve Districts in the United States.

Federal Reserve Board of Governors: The chief policy making body of the Federal Reserve System, composed of seven Presidentially-appointed, Senate-approved members, each serving seven years, and with terms expiring at different times to assure continuity within the Board. It is an independent body, with major power to influence the direction of the United States through its control of money and credit policies, tools which it openly and consciously uses to influence national and international economic trends.

Federal Reserve credit: The total of all Federal Reserve Bank credit outstanding, including government securities, loans to commercial banks, and checks outstanding; the base of the credit system of the United States, and a key government instrument of money and credit manipulation in pursuit of national purposes. As that credit outstanding increases, so does commercial bank lending power, at a multiple of that increase, fueling both economic activity and the tendency toward inflation; as it decreases, lending ability decreases and economic activity tends to diminish.

Federal Reserve System (Fed): The United States Federal banking system, operating as a central money and credit control organization and as a system of twelve regional banks implementing the policies of the central Board of Governors. One of the world's major banking systems, it has substantial impact on national and international economic events and trends.

Federal savings and loan association: A savings and loan association whose main business is home mortgage lending, and which is chartered and regulated by the Federal Home Loan Bank Board.

Federal Savings and Loan Insurance Corporation (FSLIC): A Federal agency, responsible for providing insurance on deposits in savings and loan associations. All Federal savings and loan association deposits are by law insured up to certain limits; state savings and loan associations may apply for such insurance coverage.

Federal Trade Commission (FTC): An independent Federal agency, responsible for enforcing and interpreting anti-trust laws and a wide range of other laws relating to unfair competition, consumer protection, deceptive practices, and other matters affecting free and fair competition. The FTC is the main Federal trade regulatory body and has an extremely wide mandate.

Feds: A popular term for Federal officers, applied loosely to all Federal law enforcement officers.

fee simple: An absolute, unconditional ownership of land or other estate, which belongs to its holder during his or her lifetime and then passes to its inheritors.

FHA: See Federal Housing Administration.

fiat money: Money that is backed by the faith and credit of its issuing government, rather than by any store of value, such as gold and silver. All United States paper currency and all currently issued coins are fiat money.

fiduciary: One who has a relationship of trust, including one holding specific and legal status as a trustee of any kind. A fiduciary may be an executor or administrator of an estate, as well as anyone holding any position of trust, as does a banker, lawyer, or company treasurer.

fiduciary accounting: A body of accounting practice relating to property being held by legally recognized fiduciaries, such as executors, administrators, and trustees.

fiduciary capacity: A relationship in which trust of an agent acting in money and property matters is central to the relationship between the parties. The fiduciary has a position of trust, either defined as such by the very nature of that position, as with trustees and executors, or capable of being so construed by law, as with lawyers, bankers, and corporate financial officers.

fiduciary money: See fiat money.

field warehousing loan: See warehouse receipt loan.

fifo: See first in, first out.

finance: 1. To raise and supply money for any purpose, as in securing of funds needed by an enterprise by borrowing, by selling shares, or from personal resources.   **2.** The entire field of money, credit, and capital, including theories, practices, and institutions.

finance bill: A bankers' bill of exchange, drawn on a bank in one country by a bank in another country, usually unsecured by anything other than the full faith and credit of the bank drawing the bill, and functioning as an advance of funds by one bank to another.

finance company: A company mainly in the business of making loans to individuals, businesses, or both, such as a personal finance company, specializing in loans to individuals, or a sales finance company, specializing in the buying and collecting of business accounts receivable.

financial accounting: A body of accounting practice concerned with matters relating to the financial side of a business, including income, expenditures, assets, and liabilities.

financial expense: A business expense directly attributable to financing, as are mortgage and bond interest payments.

financial futures: Contracts between buyers and sellers specifying the prices and terms of financial instruments that are to be delivered at some future time, such as treasury bills and other United States Government securities. These contracts are instruments of value that are traded in "futures" markets.

financial position: The financial situation of a company or individual, as evidenced by current financial statements.

financial statement: Any formal statement that indicates the current financial position of a company or individual, such as a balance sheet, profit and loss statement, flow of funds statement, or any other summary document helping to illuminate that financial position, and including any supporting material.

financier: One who finances a business operated by others; usually one whose main business is the use of substantial sums of money to finance large businesses run by others, whether those sums are loaned or are venture capital.

finder: One who brings the parties to a financial transaction together, whose role in so doing is recognized by those parties, and who is in some way compensated by them for that role.

finder's fee: A fee paid to a finder by one or more of the parties to a financial transaction. Such fees are usually highly negotiable as between parties and finders and are often paid as a matter of practice rather than of contract.

fineness: The proportion of pure metal in a coin or ingot, usually referring to precious metals. For example, the degree of fineness of a "silver" coin may be 40%, with the coin composed 40% of silver and 60% of other metals; or a gold bar may be 100% fine, consisting of pure gold.

firm order: An order that has taken on the nature of an enforceable contract, either by a writing between purchaser and seller, or by generally accepted industry practice, such as a telephone order for which adequate evidence of placement exists.

firm price: A price that is non-negotiable or minimally negotiable; normally found in a seller's market, in which demand is considerably in excess of supply.

first in, first out (fifo): 1. An inventory evaluation method, which assumes that material being currently used is always the earliest purchased such material currently in inventory. Materials used in manufacture are generally costed at less than current replacement costs when this method is used, so profits and therefore taxes paid tend to be higher than when different inventory evaluation conventions such as last in, first out, are adopted. **2.** A queueing model in which each is served in order of arrival, as in those banks where all customers wait in order for the first available teller, rather than having to choose a line which may be delayed by a single lengthy transaction.

first mortgage: A mortgage senior to all other mortgages, in that it is the first loan to be secured by the property mortgaged, and therefore is the first to be paid in the event of sale of the property.

first mortgage bond: A bond secured by a first mortgage on part or all of the property of its issuer, as well as by the issuer's promise to pay.

first preferred stock: See preferred stock.

fiscal: That which refers to or describes financial matters; for example, a fiscal year, which is any twelve month period designated consistently for financial reporting purposes.

fiscal agent: One who is empowered to handle financial matters for another, as with a financial institution that handles some kinds of receipts and expenditures for a corporate client.

fiscal policy: The over-all direction of a national government's spending and taxing policies aimed at accomplishing the current economic, social, and political goals of that government, and significantly affecting such matters as inflation, recession, expansion, and the taking and holding of national power.

fiscal year: 1. For tax purposes, a 12 month period ending with the last day of any month other than December, in contrast to a calendar year, which ends only on the last day of December.   **2.** For accounting purposes, any year-long period, including any 12 month, 52 week, or other set of accounting periods running consecutively and adding up to a year.

fixed assets: Assets that are part of the operating capital of a business, such as land, buildings, machinery and associated tangible production-related items.

fixed charges: Periodic and continuing financial overhead charges that must be paid, and that have no direct relationship to the level of activity of a business, including such charges as rent, interest, and depreciation.

fixed costs: Periodic and continuing operating overhead costs which are not directly and immediately affected by the level of operations, though they may be in the long term. Fixed costs include general administration and indirect labor and materials costs.

fixed income: Income that is set at specified dollar levels, such as the income from social security and from such investments as most bonds and annuities. In periods of inflation, the value of fixed incomes declines, often sharply, as the number of income dollars remains constant and the value of those dollars diminishes. In periods of deflation, however, fixed incomes appreciate in value.

fixed investment trust: An investment company that sells shares to investors and that may invest its assets only in a specified list of securities, usually in predetermined proportions.

fixed liabilities: See long-term liabilities.

fixed overhead: See fixed costs.

flash report: A report on current conditions, based on as much information as is available at the time the report is generated, and to be superseded later by more complete reports based on fuller data. Such reports are often interim operating reports for intra-company use, to be replaced by formal and complete reports at the ends of accounting periods.

flat: Describing the sale of a bond in which the purchaser receives all interest accrued on that bond since the last interest payment date. Most often, bonds are sold "full" and the seller receives that interest.

flea market: A market for goods and collectibles in which a wide range of items is sold, usually from temporary or semi-permanent stalls; very much like a classic bazaar.

fleece: See lamb.

flexible budget: A budget carrying different expenditure levels for different levels of activity, with those alternatives spelled out in the budget from the start of the budgeted period.

flexible tariff: A tariff that can be adjusted at the discretion of its administrators, usually within bounds specified by those legislating the tariff, and sometimes only on occurrence of specific events, such as specified unfavorable trade balances.

flight of capital: The movement of capital, including both long- and short-term investment money, from its home country to other countries offering more favorable conditions, such as higher interest rates, lower taxes and greater safety.

float: 1. In finance, the total value of checks outstanding and un-collected. **2.** To raise money, whether through a securities offering or a loan.

floating capital: Capital that is currently circulating and being used for working purposes rather than being fixed and held for longer term purposes.

floating debt: The total of all current short term debts, expressed in accounting as the current liabilities of a government or business.

floating exchange rate: The variable rate at which currencies can be exchanged with each other, which is the price of each currency as against all other currencies in the absence of governmental intervention into the world currency markets.

floating interest rate: An interest rate that is not fixed, but moves with other money market factors, especially with changes in the prime rate. As a practical matter, most businesses with bank lines of credit have de facto floating interest rates; in recent years, the concept has been formally extended to include such instruments as home mortgages, that previously had only fixed rates.

floating supply: The total amount of a common stock or bond issue that is actually available for purchase and sale at a given time, as distinguished from the amount outstanding, much of which is held for long term investment purposes and therefore is not really available for trading.

floor man: A person who works on the floor of an auction market, handling goods, identifying bids, and helping keep the flow of the auction moving.

floor partner: A securities firm partner who handles transactions for his or her firm on the floor of a securities exchange.

floor trader: A trading exchange member who trades on the floor of the exchange for his or her own account, or one in which he or she holds an interest.

flower bonds: Low denomination United States government bonds formerly widely purchased because of their preferential tax treatment in decedent's estates, hence their popular name; such special tax treatment has now been largely terminated.

flow of funds analysis: A statement of the flow of money through any economic entity, following funds from entry to departure. In business accounting, this analysis results in a cash flow or funds flow statement; in national accounting, the result is a periodic national flow of funds analysis.

fluctuation: The movement of prices in securities and commodities markets, stated in such gradations as points, fractions of points, cents, and dollars.

footnotes: In financial statements, comments keyed to financial items, to explain those items more fully to those reading the statements.

forced loan: A loan which is made by the lender due to the pressure of circumstances, rather than by choice, as in the payment of a customer's overdraft or the extension of an unpaid loan when due.

forced sale: A sale that is made by the seller due to the pressure of circumstances, rather than by choice, as in the sale by a broker of the margined securities of a customer who has inadequate margin to continue holding those securities, the involuntary sale of foreclosed property by law, or the voluntary sale of goods at a loss to raise cash to save a business.

forecast: An estimate of future trends, events and results, such as an estimate of future stock market price trends made by a stock advisory service, or an estimate of its own future sales, costs, and earnings made by a business as part of a report to stockholders.

forecasting: Predicting future business trends and events through the use of various analytical tools, especially mathematical models using computer technology. In a wider sense, any systematic attempt to predict the future, as in weather or crop forecasting.

foreclosure: A legal proceeding, in which the mortgage holder takes possession of property on which mortgage payments are in default. The foreclosed property is normally sold at public auction, with proceeds used to pay the balance due on the mortgage and anything over that paid to the former owner of the property.

foreign bill of exchange: A bill of exchange that is drawn on a drawee in another country and is payable in another country, including a wide variety of financial instruments.

foreign corporation: A corporation whose main domicile is in a jurisdiction other than the one in which a question is being considered. For example, a corporation domiciled in Delaware is a foreign corporation to a court in any other state; a corporation domiciled in Germany is foreign to any United States court.

foreign exchange: The means by which international financial transactions are handled, through the transfer of financial instruments, denominated in several currencies, between buyers and sellers; and the financial instruments themselves.

foreign exchange market: A worldwide market in the currencies of all countries, used for settling international financial obligations, trading in world currencies, and speculating in world currency futures, with participants located in financial institutions of all kinds throughout the world, rather than in a single central location.

foreign exchange rates: The prices of the world's currencies in relation to each other; the rate at which a unit of one currency will be exchanged for units of other currencies. For example, the number of American dollars it takes to buy one British pound expresses the exchange rate between the two currencies.

foreign exchange reserves: The amount of foreign currency and other foreign financial instruments held by a government as reserve against foreign debts.

foreign trade: Trade between public and private parties in two or more countries.

foreign trade zone: See free trade zone.

forfeiture: The loss of money or a right because of failure to fulfill obligations or the performance of illegal acts, as in forfeiture of a bond for nonperformance of a contract.

forint: The main currency unit of Hungary, bearing the same relationship to Hungary's national currency system as does the dollar to the United States currency system.

formula investment plans: Investment plans that provide for specific moves on the part of investors in response to specific securities market behavior, with particular reference to the proportions of common stocks and bonds to be held in investment portfolios.

forward buying: In commodity trading, buying at current prices for future delivery, in anticipation of future advantageous price moves; for example, the purchase of contracts now calling for the future delivery of wheat.

forward exchange: Foreign exchange bought or sold at current prices for future delivery, in anticipation of future advantageous price moves.

forward movement: Any upward trend in the market prices of securities or commodities, and used to characterize price trends of as little as a few hours and as much as several years.

forward selling: In commodity trading, selling at current prices for future delivery, in anticipation of future advantageous price moves; for example, the sale of contracts now calling for the future delivery of wheat.

foundation: A tax-free, non-profit private organization that receives and distributes funds for charitable and other benevolent purposes, such as health research and support for the arts.

founders' shares: Capital stock carrying special privileges issued to founding members of a company in return for their role in the initiation and early promotion of that company.

fractional currency: Any currency denominated in fractions of the main currency unit, as are pence to pounds and cents to dollars. All coins less than $1 in value are fractional currency in the United States.

fractional reserve banking: That system of banking, now in use in the United States and in all other industrial nations, in which banks carry only a relatively small liquid reserve against all deposits, on the theory that all deposits will never be withdrawn at once from all banks in the system.

fractional share: Any portion of stock less than a single share, as occurs in some stock dividend and dividend reinvestment situations.

franc: The main currency unit of several countries, including France, Switzerland, Belgium, and a number of African nations, bearing the same relationship to their national currency systems as does the dollar to the United States currency system.

franchise: 1. An agreement between a business organization—the franchisor—and a retailing organization—the franchisee—, providing the franchisee the right to deal in the franchisor's goods and services. Usually the franchisor provides such supporting mechanisms as financing, marketing, materials procurement, and management help in return for a share of the franchisee's revenues or profits. **2.** The right to perform stated functions, granted by government to a private organization or individual, in such areas of quasi-public and essentially monopolistic operation as power supply, lighting, telephone service, and public transportation.

franchised dealer: A dealer holding a franchise agreement with a producer, usually for a specific length of time and subject to certain terms and conditions involving minimum acceptable volumes of business done by the franchisee and acceptable modes of business behavior.

franchisee: See franchise.

franchise tax: A tax on a corporation's right to do business within a taxing jurisdiction.

franchisor: See franchise.

free enterprise: A theoretical construct, positing the existence of perfectly free competition in all aspects of economic life, with a free marketplace regulating all economic developments. Given the present massive, interconnected, highly regulated, and heavily manipulated world economic system, free enterprise is far more a political slogan than an economic fact.

free market: A market which is in no way controlled or manipulated, but which functions purely in response to supply and demand factors, as in the instance of some securities markets and the markets for some foodstuffs.

free port: A port operating as a free trade zone, where no duties are levied on either imports or exports.

free supply: The physical amount of a commodity available for trading at any given time, arrived at by totaling the world stock and subtracting that which is held by governments; often a considerably misleading figure, as governments do release commodity stocks from time to time, in some cases suddenly adding to the free supply and tending just as suddenly to drive commodity prices and futures down. An example is the United States sale of substantial gold stocks in the early 1970's.

free trade: A theoretical construct, proposing a system of international trade entirely without government-imposed barriers of any kind, such as tariffs, currency restrictions, and political restraints. Like free enterprise, free trade is more a political slogan than a current reality.

free trade area: A group of two or more countries that have agreed to free trade between themselves, eliminating all tariff and other trade barriers between them, while maintaining the ability to set individual trade barriers against other countries.

free trade zone: A duty-free area, often but not always in or near a port city, where no import or export duties are placed on goods bought, sold, or processed.

front end load: Sales and other administrative costs charged against some kinds of investment contracts at the start of a contract period. For example, an investor in a mutual fund may buy a five year plan, want to sell it out after one year, and find that half the payments made during that year have gone to pay front end costs and cannot be retrieved.

front load commissions: See front end load.

frozen account: A bank account on which all transactions have been suspended, usually either by court order to avoid the account holder fleeing with the funds or by administrative order in pursuit of national policy, as in the freezing of the accounts of enemy nationals in time of war.

frozen asset: An asset that has been set aside and held by a legal body, and will not be returned to its owner until that legal body relinquishes it; for example, property held by a court pending the resolution of legal action or the property of aliens that is held by a government during and after a war.

FSLIC: See Federal Savings and Loan Insurance Corporation.

FTC: See Federal Trade Commission.

full: Describing the sale of a bond in which the seller receives all interest accrued since the last interest payment date, as opposed to a "flat" sale where the buyer receives that interest.

full disclosure: See disclosure.

full faith and credit: Describing a promise to pay a contracted debt. If unsupported by collateral, the promise describes a general debt, supported only by the worth of the organization or individual making it.

full service: A company that provides a wide range of services to its customers, including all those main services supplied by any such company in its industry. For instance, a full service department store provides many services a discount department store does not; a full service bank provides a wide range of services to business and individual depositors.

full service banking: See commercial bank.

fundamentalist: One who believes that such basic economic facts as deep economic trends, specific company managements, and the condition of the money market are primary predictive factors in forecasting securities price fluctuations.

fundamentals: See fundamentalist.

funded debt: The total long term debts of a business or government, in the form of such long term debt instruments as bonds and long term notes.

funding: 1. In the widest sense, the securing of money for any purpose, as in the funding of college study through a combination of grants and loans.   **2.** The creation of a pool of reserve funds to pay for future obligations, as in the development of pension funds to pay for future pensions.   **3.** The conversion of short term debts into funded debts, by the creation of long term debt instruments.

funds flow statement: See flow of funds analysis.

futures: Contracts for commodities and other tangibles and intangibles, specifying future delivery or receipt of stated amounts at specific future times, specifying identical quality, quantity, and terms as all other such contracts, and traded on commodities and other futures exchanges according to the rules of those exchanges.

futures contract: See futures.

futures exchange: An organized exchange, on which futures are traded, such as the Chicago Board of Trade (CBOT), on which commodities futures are traded.

futures markets: A group of commodity markets in which futures contracts are traded, organized into several commodities exchanges, such as the Chicago Board of Trade (CBOT). Futures markets also exist in foreign exchange and in some government obligations.

G

gain: The net of any income over costs; in accounting, summed up by the entry "gain or loss." In the widest sense, any advance or profit.

galloping inflation: A popular term for a relatively very high and seemingly almost impossible to control rate of inflation.

gambling: Risk taking with small factual bases, as in the instance of the entrepeneur who moves into a new business on the basis of predicting a new consumer buying pattern, or the investor who speculates on the basis of a "hunch."

GATT: See General Agreement on Tariffs and Trade.

General Agreement on Tariffs and Trade (GATT): An international agreement and administrative organization participated in by most countries, outside the Soviet and Chinese areas of influence, dedicated to the removal of tariff barriers to trade throughout the world.

general fund: A fund that can be used for any normal organizational purposes, rather than being earmarked for use to accomplish specific tasks.

general ledger: The main accounting ledger of a business, containing either detailed or summary information on every aspect of business activities.

general mortgage bonds: Bonds backed by a general mortgage on all company property already subject wholly or partially to existing first mortgages.

general partner: One who shares in all profits and has unlimited liability, in contrast to a limited partner, who has sharply defined shares of profits and limited liability.

gift taxes: Federal and state taxes on the value of property given to others, the gifts being taxable to the recipient and graduated according to the value of the property given.

gilt-edged: High grade and relatively safe securities, usually bonds; a popular term some generations ago, but now rarely used in the United States. In the United Kingdom "gilts" is a popular term for bonds.

Ginnie Mae: See Government National Mortgage Association.

glamour stock: A stock that is very popular with investors in any given period, far beyond its intrinsic value or current prospects, due to widespread expectation that the specific stock or the group of stocks of which it is part will rise in value far more quickly than most other stocks; for example, gambling stocks for a time in the late 1970's, or electronics stocks in the early 1960's.

glut: A market condition in which supply far exceeds demand at current consumption and price levels. Glut is traditionally encountered in agricultural commodity areas, given the wide variance in crop yields from year to year due to factors beyond farmers' control.

GNP: See gross national product.

go-go fund: A popular term for a kind of mutual fund, oriented toward investment in rather speculative common stocks, with the hope of very rapid appreciation.

going concern: A business that is in operation and is expected to continue operations, in contrast to a business that either has not yet started operations or is not expected to continue doing business.

going public: The sale of shares to the general public by a corporation that has been closely held, usually through the issuance of common stock.

gold certificates: United States paper currency fully convertible into gold. Gold certificates are no longer legal tender and were withdrawn after the United States went off the gold standard in 1933.

gold reserve: The amount of gold physically held by a government. Although gold no longer directly backs the world's major currencies, gold reserves are still major elements indirectly supporting national currencies.

gold shares: The stocks of companies primarily engaged in gold mining, in many cases the stocks of South African companies.

gold standard: A monetary system in which gold provides a basic value for a national currency, stated as a unit of currency being worth a specified quantity of gold. Gold standards throughout the world began to be modified and then abandoned during the Great Depression of the 1930s.

go long: To buy stocks long, in anticipation of rising prices. Also see long.

good delivery: Delivery of securities, in ready-to-transfer condition, to be sold or held by a bank or broker.

good-till-cancelled order: An order to buy or sell securities placed with a broker on an "open" basis, to be fulfilled at any time by the broker unless specifically cancelled by the customer who placed the order.

goodwill: The value of a business beyond the total of its tangible assets; normally determinable only on purchase or sale of the business and defined by the price that is paid for the business. It is sometimes, but relatively rarely, treated as an intangible asset and taken into books of account on that basis.

go public: See going public.

go short: To sell stocks short, in anticipation of declining prices. Also see short.

government bill: A general term for any short term government debt obligation, such as a ninety day Treasury note.

government bond: A bond issued by a government or an agency of government. In the United States, the term is reserved to describe United States Federal government debt obligations in the form of bonds.

Government National Mortgage Association (Ginnie Mae): A federally owned and financed corporation administered by the Department of Housing and Urban Development, which finances several kinds of mortgages pursuant to national policy, in relatively high risk areas that might otherwise have difficulty in securing financing; for example, inner city public housing and commercial development projects.

grace period: A period beyond the due date of a debt obligation, in which the creditor allows payment of the debt without penalty to the debtor.

graduated tax: A tax that increases in relative rate as the value of that which is taxed increases. For example, the tax rate on taxable income between $20,001 and $24,000 may be 30%, and then rise to 34% on taxable income between $24,001 and $28,000.

gray knight: In corporate takeover situations, a company that follows an antagonistic bid by a first company attempting takeover with a somewhat higher bid of its own; such a company usually also holds out a more amicable takeover situation to the management and stockholders of the takeover candidate.

gray market: A market in which exhorbitant prices are charged for goods and services, usually those in short supply for some reason. Where those goods and services are being supplied legally, a gray market exists; where illegally, a black market exists.

Great Depression: The worldwide economic depression that began with the United States stock market crash in 1929 and continued in many countries until the beginning of World War II. In the United States, it was deepest between 1929 and 1933, with significant aspects remaining until 1941.

greenback: United States paper currency. A popular term now passing out of the language, it was derived from the color of United States Treasury debt obligations issued by the United States government during the Civil War, which later became recognized as part of the national currency.

Gresham's Law: The observation that "bad money drives out good," attributed to Sir Thomas Gresham, Queen Elizabeth I's Master of the Mint, meaning that when two kinds of money, one of greater intrinsic value than another, are circulated simultaneously at the same face values, the less valuable money will be used, and the more valuable money will go out of circulation due to hoarding, sale at greater than face values, and such illegal devices as melting down the more valuable money for its metal content.

gross: Total before any applicable deductions of any kind, but after any necessary corrections.

gross income: Total income from all sources, before subtracting any applicable deductions or other necessary subtractions, but after any necessary corrections.

gross margin: The remainder, after subtracting direct costs from sales revenue, but before making any other subtractions.

gross national product (GNP): The total market value of all goods and services produced by a nation within a period, usually a year, before any subtractions for depreciation and capital goods consumption.

gross profit: The remainder, after subtracting costs of goods sold, including factory overhead, from net sales.

gross sales: The remainder, after deducting direct sales and excise taxes, cash discounts, and corrections from total sales, but before subtracting returns and allowances.

group banking: The control of a group of banks by a single holding company, which may hold both the banks and other non-bank companies. The holding company has its own structure and personnel, as do each of the banks held.

growth company: See growth stock.

growth fund: A mutual fund oriented primarily to the purchase of the common stocks of companies thought to be growing fast, with stocks therefore thought to be excellent prospects for rapid appreciation.

growth portfolio: A portfolio of securities carried by an investor or investing organization, oriented primarily toward the most rapid appreciation possible consonant with reasonable prudence, rather than oriented toward the production of current income.

growth recession: A recession in which economic growth continues, although at a considerably slower rate than that experienced during periods of prosperity.

growth stock: A popular term describing a common stock which is appreciating in value quickly, and which is thought to reflect the excellent future prospects of its issuing company.

guarantee: 1. A legally binding assurance by one of the obligation of another to a third party, as in the assurance of payment of a loan to another. **2.** A legally binding assurance of product quality, issued in writing to the purchaser of that product; in this era of consumer protection, a guarantee can be implied as well as expressed.

guaranteed bond: A bond issued by one business, which is guaranteed wholly or in part by another, as in the instance of a subsidiary, controlled, or affiliated company bond guaranteed by a parent company.

guarantor: One who makes a legally binding commitment to guarantee payment or performance due from another.

guidelines: General requests by government to private parties asking for voluntary compliance; for example, requests that price and wage increases be kept generally within certain bounds.

guilder: The main currency unit of the Netherlands, bearing the same relationship to the Netherlands national currency system as does the dollar to the United States currency system.

H

hallmark: See mark.

hard loan: An international loan that must be repaid in a currency which is not subject to rapid losses in value, such as those occasioned by inflation in the borrowing country; therefore, usually a loan that must be repaid in the currency of the lending country.

hard money: 1. Coins, rather than paper money.   **2.** Cash or assets that can be quickly converted into cash.

hauler: See picker.

heavy industry: The basic industries, such as metal production, machine tools, mining, and other extractive industries.

heavy market: A securities or commodities market in which prices are falling.

hedge fund: A speculative mutual fund, aiming to make quick profits with a combination of borrowed money and highly leveraged transactions, requiring relatively small cash and carrying relatively high risks.

hedger: A commodities user who makes equal investments simultaneously in cash or spot commodities on the one hand and in futures on the other, in an attempt to minimize the risks stemming from fluctuations in commodities prices, and in some instances to attempt also to profit from those fluctuations.

hedging: An attempt to reduce the risks inherent in a situation or transaction by developing alternate courses of action that minimize the risks, as in the instance of a gambler who places two almost-contradictory bets simultaneously, hoping to alter the over-all odds in his or her favor. In the securities or commodities markets, hedging is the simultaneous execution of present and future transactions in the hope of minimizing risks.

heirloom: An antique or collectible that has unique value to its seller, usually because it has been in the seller's family for several generations; often a term used by sellers in an attempt to enhance the seeming value and condition—and therefore the selling price—of articles offered for sale.

hidden assets: Assets that are not in an accounting sense assets at all, but rather are company advantages to be considered by potential investors and acquirers; for example, a very favorable market position, or a new and promising product or process.

hidden inflation: A reduction in the real value of goods sold, by changing the quantity and quality of the goods supplied and without or with small dollar price increases. Examples are machines that are less well made, reflecting far poorer material and less labor than the same goods in prior years; and packaged foods that come in smaller quantities but larger packages and are adulterated with less expensive and usually far less nutritious ingredients. These very real price increases do not show up in the Consumer Price Index, yet are quite normal features of the American economic landscape.

hidden liabilities: Liabilities that are not in an accounting sense liabilities at all, but rather are company disadvantages to be considered by potential investors and acquirers; for example, an increasingly unfavorable market position, or a product made obsolescent by new developments in its field.

hidden reserves: Assets that are substantially understated in company financial statements, causing company net worth to be understated, as in the instance of regulated utilities which may understate assets in an attempt to hide growth in net worth as part of a strategy aimed at securing rate increases.

hidden tax: A tax on goods that is not separately stated to the buyer at point of purchase; often encountered in the sale and purchase of imported goods at retail, as with the price of an imported television set which includes, but does not separately state, the import duties that have been paid on it.

high finance: A popular way of describing financing functions, implying complex, speculative, and somewhat dishonest financial practices on the part of people and organizations involved in financing activities.

high flyer: A stock that is appreciating in value very quickly, when compared to other stocks in the markets in which it is traded; often but not always a speculative stock, subject to wide price variations.

high grade securities: Securities carrying little risk of loss, such as United States government debt obligations; some state, local, and corporate debt obligations; and the common and preferred stocks of some well established and carefully managed corporations.

high-low index: An index of securities reaching new highs and lows each day, kept as a moving average.

high technology company: A company significantly involved in producing or providing services resulting from the use of complex modern technologies; such as companies in the aerospace, computer, and nuclear energy industries.

histogram: See bar chart.

hoarding: Storing anything that is in short supply, whether for personal use, business use, or resale at anticipated higher scarcity prices. Examples are the storage of gasoline for personal use during a fuel shortage and the storage of metal money during a period of ruinous inflation.

holder: One who by delivery or endorsement lawfully possesses the right to be paid the value of a money instrument.

holder in due course: One who legally holds a money instrument which has been received for value in good faith and timely, and without knowledge of any defect in the lawful right to be paid.

holding company: A company that is primarily in the business of controlling other companies, fully or in part, usually directly owned subsidiaries.

holding the market: Buying to support the market price of a security that otherwise is being sold heavily enough to decline quite substantially; sometimes done by a specialist to help smooth out too-rapid price fluctuations in a stock, and sometimes by such interested parties as major stockholders anxious to support the price of a stock until buying pressure develops naturally.

honor: In finance, to pay or fulfill. For example, a bank honors a check by paying its lawful holder its face amount when it is presented for payment; a contracting party honors a contract by fulfilling it.

horizontal acquisition: The acquisition by one company of other companies doing essentially the same kinds of business as the acquiring company. Such combinations among companies that are significant factors in their industries are often considered by Federal regulatory authorities to be combinations tending to diminish competition, in violation of antitrust laws.

hot issue: A stock in great demand, usually just after original issue, and therefore experiencing a considerable increase in market price.

hot money: 1. Investment capital that is repeatedly moved from one investment vehicle to another, and usually also internationally, seeking the highest possible short-term returns. **2.** Currency illegally acquired, such as the proceeds of a bank robbery or drug smuggling.

house account: 1. A brokerage customer account serviced directly by a securities firm, usually through one of its partners or owners, rather than being assigned to a securities seller employed by the firm.   **2.** A securities firm's own trading account, usually run for and with the funds of partners or owners.

house bid: See absentee bid.

house of issue: That underwriting firm primarily responsible for managing a new securities issue; when an issue is co-managed, the co-managers are all houses of issue for that security.

house picker: See picker.

hush money: Blackmail or bribes paid to try to cover up illegal activities or legal activities the payer does not want known; for example, blackmail paid to cover up embezzlement or to cover up a public official's drinking problem.

hyperinflation: See runaway inflation.

hypothecated stock: Stock that has been used as loan collateral, and which is therefore so encumbered as to be incapable of being traded, as clear title cannot be passed.

hypothecation: The use of pledged collateral to secure a loan. In law, possession of the pledged collateral stays with the owner of the collateral, though the lender has the right to force sale of the collateral to cover default of the loan. In practice, collateral which cannot be delivered, such as a ship, stays with the borrower; collateral which can be delivered, such as securities and warehouse receipts, usually are physically moved to the lender.

I

IDA: See International Development Association.

IDB: See Inter-American Development Bank.

idle capacity: Unused ability to produce on the part of a production facility, measuring the time allocated to production against the time that would be allocated to production if the facility were in full normal use. For example, a steel plant that normally operates seven days a week and 24 hours a day is operating at only two thirds of capacity if it is working seven days a week and 16 hours a day; but an electronic assembly plant normally operating five days a week and 16 hours a day may, for accounting and reporting purposes, be operating at full capacity.

IFC: See International Finance Corporation.

illiquid: Describing a company or individual not in possession of sufficient cash to meet its cash needs and facing difficulty in raising that cash.

IMF: See International Monetary Fund.

imperfect competition: A construct in economics that posits a marketplace in which some sellers can influence such market factors as prices and supplies, in contrast to a marketplace that is in theory entirely free, with supply and demand the sole factors influencing prices.

154

implied trust: See trust.

import credit: See letter of credit.

import duty: A tax levied by a country on products brought into it from abroad.

import license: A license issued by government, authorizing import of goods that are in some way regulated by government. That regulation may be pursuant to public policy favoring some home products by limiting imports of foreign products; may be limiting trade with unfriendly nations; or may be limiting trade in specific goods, such as some drugs.

import quota: A government-imposed limitation on imports of a product or products. That limitation may be on the quantity or the value of goods imported; may apply to some countries and not to others, or to countries unequally; and may set different tax levels on different values and quantities imported.

imports: 1. Goods made in other countries, purchased abroad, and shipped into the buying country. **2.** To procure those goods abroad and bring them into a country. **3.** Popularly, all goods and services originating in one geographic unit and brought into another. States are described as importing goods from other states. Consulting services are sometimes described as being imported from abroad.

imprest fund: A cash fund or bank account maintained for payments that are made in cash, most commonly used as a petty cash fund. A fixed maximum sum is kept in the fund, and, as the fund is depleted, that sum is periodically brought up to maximum.

imputed costs: Costs that are estimated rather than specifically determinable through the generation of accounting information, such as cancelled checks and journal entries. Sometimes such costs are actually incurred, but are difficult to allocate and are therefore spread over several functions on an estimated allocation basis; sometimes such costs are not actual, but are figured as if they had been incurred, such as the foregone interest from other sources that might have been earned on the amount of an owner's investment in a business.

imputed income: Income that is not actual but equivalent to what might have been earned had something been paid for in cash rather than in non-cash equivalents, such as work performed in a family business by family members who are not paid in cash but in such non-cash equivalents as food, housing and clothing.

inactive account: A banking or brokerage account which has few or no transactions and modest balances over a substantial period of time, usually measured in years.

inactive stock: A security that is little traded; rarely carried on any exchange, and hard to trade even in over-the-counter markets, as no one may make a market in the stock.

in-and-out trade: In the securities industry, a quick sale following a securities purchase, usually in the hope of turning a quick profit on the transaction. Speculators often engage in in-and-out trading.

in-and-out trader: One whose pattern of securities trading is marked by a relatively large number of in-and-out trades; usually a speculator.

income: 1. Total business or personal revenue received from all sources, usually within a defined period, such as a month, calendar year, or fiscal year.   **2.** The total increase in net assets achieved by a business in any accounting period.   **3.** In general, any item of determinable value received.

income averaging: As provided for in federal personal income tax law, the ability to lump current income and several previous years' incomes for figuring income tax rates; when current income is much higher than the average income, lower tax rates apply.

income bond: A bond bearing interest that is only payable out of the profits of its issuer, in contrast to bonds that carry interest as an unconditional debt obligation.

income distribution: The spread of a nation's income among its population, indicated by the numbers of people earning or otherwise receiving income at a series of given income levels; used in analyzing changes in the apportionment of a nation's wealth over a period of time and also in comparing patterns of income distribution between countries.

income fund: A mutual fund oriented primarily toward the generation of current income for its holders, rather than toward growth securities.

income portfolio: A portfolio of securities carried by an investor or investing organization, oriented toward the production of current income, rather than toward rapid appreciation with little income.

income property: Real property used by its owner primarily as a source of income; for example, a farm leased to tenants or rental property.

income statement: An accounting statement, summarizing the income, expense, and resultant profit or loss of a business organization for any accounting period; usually issued yearly, often quarterly and monthly as well.

income tax: Any tax based on the income received, usually net, of any defined economic unit, including individuals and both business and non-business organizations. Income taxes are usually graduated with rates rising according to net income. Federal income taxes were levied during the Civil War, starting in 1861, and stopping after the War; modern Federal income taxes date from 1913; state and local income taxes also developed after 1913.

inconvertible: Unable to be exchanged for precious metals, describing money which is backed only by the faith and credit of its issuer, as has been officially true of United States currency since 1971 and unofficially true for some decades earlier.

incorporation: 1. One of the three major forms of business organization, the others being sole proprietorship and partnership, and the form favored by most medium-sized and large businesses, as it provides for limited ownership liability, easy ownership transfer in the form of stock sale, multiple ownership by stockholders, maximum financing flexibility, and a wide variety of other advantages over the other two ownership forms.   **2.** The process of becoming a legal corporation.

increment: Any increase or growth in steps, usually small, rather than continuous.

incremental: 1. In business, describing an increase, usually relatively small, tied to existing business operations, as in the addition of an element that costs little to an existing product line, with both the cost and the additional revenue being thought of as incremental.   **2.** In accounting, marginal, describing a cost that results from the exercise of choices in production or marketing.

indenture: 1. An instrument naming a trustee to act for all holders of a bond issue and stating the amount, form, and conditions involved in the issue.   **2.** A deed owned by two or more parties which states their rights and obligations toward each other regarding the jointly owned property.

index: A measure of such factors as cost and performance, such as the Consumer Price Index and the Dow Jones stock market indexes.

indexing: An investment technique, in a mutual fund or an individual portfolio, that attempts to organize and weigh its holdings so that it will perform much as a specific major stock index performs, such as Dow Jones or Standard and Poor's.

index number: A number designated as a marker within a body of developing statistical information, such as the Consumer Price Index of the United States Government, which gives data from the base year of 1967, an index of 100, and measures changes in the cost of living from that point, with the index having reached 200 during 1978.

indicated yield: An estimate of the income a specific stock will yield during a given period, usually a year; projected by the company itself and by outside analysts on the basis of current and antici-pated results.

indicators: See economic indicators.

indirect cost: A cost that cannot be directly attributed to a specific product made or service performed, but which is attributable to a related function. Indirect costs are usually allocated over several products or services in one or more overhead categories, such as maintenance or administration.

indirect liability: A potential liability, that may become a real lia-bility in the future; for example, the co-signer of a note may become liable if the primary borrower defaults on the note.

indirect taxes: Taxes on things, rights, and privileges, such as sales, franchise, and excise taxes, rather than taxes directly on people and organizations, such as income taxes.

individual proprietorship: See sole proprietorship.

Individual Retirement Account (IRA): A tax-advantaged pension plan arrangement available to individuals under Federal law. For many people this is the only kind of tax-advantaged pension plan available, although some are able to set up other kinds of pension plans, such as Keogh plans.

industrial average: See average.

industrial bank: A commercial bank primarily oriented toward the extension of consumer credit, in contrast to commercial banks pri-marily oriented toward business banking. Sometimes called Morris Plan banks, after Arthur Morris, a pioneer in the development of consumer credit financing, they are called industrial banks because they were originally conceived of as appealing to workers in indus-try.

industrialist: One who controls one or more industrial enterprises; usually implying the control of large enterprises and the manage-ment of large money and material resources.

industrialization: The development of widespread basic industry and mechanization within a country; a worldwide trend since the Industrial Revolution.

industrial migration: The movement of plants and whole industries to new geographical locations, spurred by such factors as the availability of less expensive labor, cheaper resources, and tax advantages.

industrial production index: A federally maintained index of the current level of national manufacturing, extractive, and utilities production, as measured against the currently used base period; a major indicator of the current state of the nation's economic health.

industrial revenue bond: A kind of municipal bond offered to investors, funding tax-advantaged arrangements as inducements for businesses to locate in municipalities. These arrangements are often very advantageous in terms of both taxes and plant construction costs. The bonds themselves are not federally tax-exempt to their purchasers.

Industrial Revolution: The beginning of the development of modern industry, in Western Europe as a whole and especially in England, during the 18th and early 19th centuries, and now often generally applied to any nation or group of nations in the process of industrialization.

industrial stock: The common stock of an industrial company, as distinguished from the common stocks of railroads and utilities.

industry: Firms involved in manufacturing, processing, and extraction; the term is used more loosely as a synonym for any kind of business.

inelastic demand: Demand for goods and services that does not fluctuate or that fluctuates relatively little in relation to price changes. For example, the demand for home heating oil is relatively inelastic in the short term; those who heat with oil can moderate their demand only slightly, even when faced with massive price increases.

in fee: See fee simple.

inflation: A rise in the general level of prices within an economy, accompanied by a decrease in the purchasing power of the unit of currency used in that economy. Inflation is often, but not always, accompanied by losses in real purchasing power, as when a cost of living index goes up by 10%, while average wages go up by only 5%, with a resultant 5% loss of purchasing power; in contrast, if average wages went up 15%, the net would be a 5% increase in purchasing power. But under conditions of rapid inflation, adulterations of quality and smaller quantities supplied at similar prices create hidden inflation as well, pulling the real purchasing power of the dollar down considerably more sharply than the standard figures indicate.

inflationary gap: The difference between available investment money from all private and public sources and the total amount of savings. In some economic theory, this difference is thought to be responsible for the pace of inflation.

inflationary spiral: A tendency within an economy experiencing inflation to accelerate the rate of inflation, as different interest groups struggle to raise their incomes to meet, and in some instances to exceed, the current rate of inflation. To increase their real incomes, businesses raise prices; workers demand higher wages; farmers demand higher prices; governments raise taxes; professionals raise fees; in a continuing spiral.

inflation hedge: An investment calculated to maintain the value of current holdings in spite of rapid inflation; for example, real estate when it is rising faster than the inflation rate, or government securities in a period when the interest paid on them is higher than the combined appreciation and dividends available in common stock investments.

infrastructure: The body of organizations, people, skills, and physical structures that binds together the economic operations of a nation and defines that nation's level of technology and socio-political sophistication. Infrastructure includes such factors as the level of technical skills available; the transportation industry; the telephone, telegraph, and broadcasting systems; the power systems; and the public health and education systems.

infringement: Violation by illegal use of the lawful rights of others who hold patents, copyrights, or trademarks.

inheritance: That which is received through a bequest from another; also that which is held and may be passed to another by bequest.

inheritance taxes: Taxes on the receipt of property by inheritance, and therefore paid by inheritors rather than the estate.

injunction: A writ prohibiting a defendant from doing or continuing to do something which is, or can become, harmful to a plaintiff. An injunction is often issued by a court to restrain a defendant from pursuing a certain course of action while a legal proceeding is being adjudicated. For example, an injunction may be issued to restrain a defendant in a patent or trademark infringement case while the suit is pending, as continued infringement could cause irremediable harm to the plaintiff during the time it takes to complete the suit, even if plaintiff ultimately wins. Injunctions have also been widely used by employers against unions in collective bargaining disputes.

inland bill: A bill of exchange drawn and payable entirely within one state, such as California, in contrast to a bill drawn or payable outside the state, known as a foreign bill of exchange.

input: Originally, all data entered into a computer; now popularly used to describe any kind of information or opinion from any source.

insider: One who, because of his or her relationship to a firm, has access to private information that may affect the market performance of that firm's stock, such an employee, member of the board of directors, attorney, or accountant.

insider buying: The amount of buying of their own companies' publicly traded stock done by those having an "inside" position in the companies, including principal stockholders, managers, directors, and outside professionals privy to company information not available to the general public.

insider selling: The opposite of insider buying.

insolvency: Inability to pay debts as they become due; usually a prelude to bankruptcy.

installment: A part payment on a financial obligation, often made periodically, as in part payment for a purchase or of a loan.

installment bond: A single bond that matures essentially piece by piece, the principal of which is paid in installments rather than all at once. It has the same net payment effect as a set of serial bonds, which mature one by one over a period of time, differing only in that it is a single bond.

institutional investor: An investing organization, such as a bank, mutual fund, pension fund, foundation, or other repository of substantial investment funds, that buys and sells large blocks of securities.

instrument: A document, embodying a formal and written legal entity, such as a contract, a will, or any of a whole range of financial obligations, such as checks, notes, and securities.

intangible assets: Assets that have no physical, determinable bodies, such as goodwill, patents, licenses, and trademarks, in contrast to such tangible assets as real estate, negotiable securities, and currency.

intangible value: The value of a business beyond its tangible assets, including such intangible assets as goodwill, patents, licenses, and trademarks.

integration: The extent to which related functions are joined in industrial enterprises, as in the instance of an aluminum company which is a producer, fabricator, and marketer of aluminum products, and therefore is responsible for every step of production and distribution.

Inter-American Development Bank (IDB): An international financing agency, formed under the auspices of the Organization of American States in 1959, in which most of the countries of North, South, and Central America participate. It raises money through bond issues and loans money for economic development purposes to both government and private organizations.

interest: 1. A legal right to all or part of something of value, as in an insurable interest, a beneficial interest under the terms of a will or trust, or an ownership interest, through ownership of all or part of a business. **2.** A sum of money paid for the use of money, usually expressed as a percentage of money borrowed, as when 10% of the principal of a loan is charged for the loan.

interest rate: The interest percentage charged by a lender for a loan, which varies with the kind of loan, the money market, general economic conditions, and the financial condition of the borrower, and therefore the amount of risk involved in making the loan. Stated and actual rates of interest being charged are often different, but true rates of interest charged retail borrowers must be clearly stated under the provisions of truth in lending laws.

interface: The facing and touching boundaries of two or more systems. Although originally used in business as a computer term, the term is now widely used to refer to the meeting place of any two or more contiguous systems, such as the government-business interface or the military-industrial interface.

interim: 1. Any period of time between fixed dates, such as the period between now and the first of next year. **2.** Describing a document, instrument, or function which by its nature is temporary, usually intended to be superseded by another, more permanent document, instrument, or function.

interim report: 1. A report covering less than a final report, issued as a temporary statement. **2.** In accounting, any report that covers less than a twelve month period.

interindustry competition: Marketplace competition between industries producing different kinds of products aimed at meeting similar consumer needs, as between aluminum and steel or cotton and synthetic fibers, in contrast to competition between companies in the same industry.

interlocking directorates: Company boards of directors that are related to each other by the same individuals holding seats on those boards. Though holding of seats on the boards of competing companies is formally prohibited by law, in practice many American corporations are so related through major stockholders and directors in common, often through bankers, lawyers, accountants, and retired executives, who may hold a dozen directors' seats, some of them in competing corporations.

interlocutory decree: A temporary or partial judgment of a pending legal action, which will be replaced by a final decree on conclusion of the action.

intermediate trend: A relatively short-term stock price trend, whether for a market or a single stock, within the context of longer-term price movements.

internal auditor: An auditor who is an employee of the organization being audited, responsible to company management for the performance of audit functions.

Internal Revenue Code: The body of statutes codifying the tax laws of the Federal Government.

Internal Revenue Service (IRS): That Federal agency responsible for enforcement of the tax laws of the United States, except as to several excise taxes, and for issuance of regulations interpreting those laws.

international balance of payments: See balance of payments.

International Bank For Reconstruction and Development: Also known as the World Bank, this is a major international financing agency, funded by a large number of participating nations, operating independently of, but affiliated with the United Nations. Formed at the Bretton Woods Conference of 1944, it has functioned since then to foster world-wide economic development, with special emphasis on the funding of economic take-off projects in developing nations.

international commodity agreement: An agreement between nations producing basic commodities to set a common market stance vis-a-vis those who consume their commodities, to achieve the best possible economic results from sale of their commodities on world markets, as when oil or coffee producers agree to limit production and set prices in common. Carried a step further, the nations participating in such an agreement sometimes develop more formal monopolistic combinations, as when oil-producing nations form themselves into a cartel.

international corporation: A company that does business in several countries, usually having major offices, subsidiaries, and affiliated corporations abroad. The term has to some extent been superseded by the term multinational corporation.

international creditor: See balance of indebtedness.

international debtor: See balance of indebtedness.

International Development Association (IDA): An international agency affiliated with the International Bank For Reconstruction and Development, also known as the World Bank; it functions as a conduit for funds from major industrial nations to developing nations, lending money to those nations' governments at little or no interest for a wide range of developmental projects.

International Finance Corporation (IFC): An international agency affiliated with the International Bank For Reconstruction and Development, also known as the World Bank; it lends money to private investors in underdeveloped nations to further the development of the private economic sectors of those countries.

international investment: Investment abroad of capital from any private or public source, whether for anticipated economic or political profit.

International Monetary Fund (IMF): An international financial agency, affiliated with the United Nations, which attempts to stabilize the world balance of trade and to smooth international money market fluctuations. Formed at the Bretton Woods Conference of 1944, the Fund has been especially active in attempts to aid developing nations.

international payments agreement: An agreement between two or more nations specifying the terms by which payments due between them are to be settled, often resulting in conservation of available foreign exchange through use of goods and their own national currencies for such settlements.

international payments disequilibrium: A tendency on the part of a country to develop a continuously unfavorable international balance of payments, usually resulting from a medium or long-term tendency toward an unfavorable international balance of trade.

International Telecommunications Satellite Consortium (INTELSAT): The international organization governing the development of the world communications system, involving joint use of communications satellites.

international trade: The trading of goods and services between the nations of the world.

interstate commerce: Commerce involving two or more states, which therefore may be constitutionaly regulated by the Federal Government. Court interpretations of what constitutes interstate commerce have widened very considerably in the last several decades, with the effect of bringing more and more commercial and related matters within the Federal Government's regulatory control.

inter vivos: Between living people; usually in law applied to the voluntary transfer of property from one living person to another through the establishment of a trust or the presenting of a gift.

intestate: Having died without having made a valid will; also, the individual who has died without making such a will.

in the black: Describing a business that is operating at a profit, in contrast to "in the red," which describes a business operating at a loss. The term stems from the use of black ink by accountants when summarizing profitable operations, while red ink was used to summarize unprofitable operations.

in the red: In a loss position; operating a business at a loss; from the accounting practice of noting losses in red ink; contrasts with "in the black," or operating at a profit.

intrastate commerce: Commerce carried on exclusively within a state, and therefore not subject to Federal regulation. Court interpretations in recent decades have greatly narrowed the scope of intrastate and greatly widened the scope of interstate commerce.

intrinsic: That which is inherent in something by the very nature of the thing itself; usually applied to matters of value, as in assessing the underlying value of a silver plate in terms of what the silver in the plate would bring at current market prices if the plate were melted down.

intrinsic value: See intrinsic.

inventory: To survey and record all things possessed; and the possessions so surveyed themselves. In this sense, a set of ideas, a body of trust property, a body of skills and people, or the material goods in the possession of a business may all be inventoried, and be inventory.

inventory change: The increase or decrease in the value of inventories carried from the beginning to the end of a given period. In economics, the quantity and kinds of inventory changes are thought to be important business cycle indicators.

inventory valuation: The process of assessing the value of an inventory as of a certain time; the accounting method chosen, such as fifo and lifo, often greatly affects the value stated.

inverted market: A market in which nearby futures contract prices are higher than deferred contract prices; also called "backwardation."

invested capital: The total value of the ownership shares held by the owners of a business.

investment: 1. In the widest sense, any attempt to profit from the use of money or other valuables. Generally, investment is the attempt to use money to make money, but such things as time and love are in popular usage described as having been invested as well, often for anticipated non-monetary rewards. **2.** A store of value.

investment advisor: One who is in the business of offering investment advice, usually for a fee, and is registered to do so with the Federal Government as well. Such advice may take the form of a published report, individual counselling, or both.

investment analysis: The evaluation of investment vehicles to determine key advantages and disadvantages in terms of profitability, risk, and investment goals, and the development of recommendations as to investment actions to be taken.

investment banking: The business of bringing securities to market, including both ownership equities and debt obligations, both private and public, either by issue to the public or by private placement to a few investors.

investment capital: See capital.

investment club: A group of investors who pool some resources and invest the resulting sum as a single fund, aiming to achieve better investment results than individual investing would bring.

investment company: A company formed solely for the purpose of selling shares in itself to investors, thereby creating an investment fund; either an open-end mutual fund selling as many shares as possible to the public or a closed-end fund which raises a fixed sum of money and uses only that fund for investment on the behalf of the fund's investors.

investment counsel: See investment advisor.

investment credit: In Federal taxation, tax credits allowed business for investment in machinery and equipment during a tax year.

investment property: See income property.

invisible export income: Income from both the sale of intangibles and investments abroad, in contrast to income from the sale of tangibles abroad, included in a nation's current account in computing the balance of payments. It includes such items as income from the sale of insurance, banking and other financial services; interest on deposits in foreign banks; and other investment income.

invisible import expenditures: Payments made by a country and its nationals for intangibles purchased from and investment return into other countries; included in a nation's current account in computing the balance of payments.

involuntary bankruptcy: See bankruptcy.

IOU: A written statement, signed by one, acknowledging a specific amount of debt to another, and constituting a legal, though informal and non-negotiable debt instrument.

IRA: See individual retirement account.

irrevocable trust: A trust which is permanent, and may not be revoked by its maker; the main form taken by trusts, constituting passage of title to trust property and removal of that property from the estate of the trust's maker.

IRS: See Internal Revenue Service.

issue: In the securities industry, a new body of stock or debt instruments placed on the market for public or private sale.

issued capital stock: The amount of a company's authorized capital stock which has been issued to its shareholders, the balance of a company's authorized and unissued stock being held by a company as its treasury stock.

issue price: The price placed on a new stock or bond issue by those who bring it to market, usually its underwriters.

J

joint account: A bank account held in common by two or more people or businesses.

joint endorsement: Endorsement of an instrument by two or more parties, made necessary by that instrument being payable to those parties.

joint float: An agreement among several nations to attempt to stabilize their currencies in relation to each other, causing their several currencies to rise and fall roughly together in international money markets.

joint note: A note signed by two or more makers, for which they jointly assume responsibility, each for the full amount of the note should all other makers fail to pay any share of that joint obligation.

joint ownership: Ownership of property by two or more persons, each holding equally and each taking sole ownership if being the sole survivor.

joint return: A Federal, state or local income tax return that joins the income of wife and husband, who then file together as one; in most but not all tax situations, the result thereby is smaller total taxes than if they had filed separate tax returns.

joint-stock banks: British commercial banks, incorporated and privately owned, taking their name from the form of equity ownership.

joint stock company: A business organization that issues transferable stock, but carries unlimited liability for stockholders, thereby having some of the features of a corporation and some of a partnership; not a widely used form.

joint venture: An undertaking for profit entered into by two or more people; usually but not always limited to the accomplishment of a single goal, such as the building of a factory abroad or the financing of a new mine; a general term, rather than a specific form of business organization, as such an undertaking may take any business form.

journal: In bookkeeping and accounting, any book originally recording transactions.

journal entry: In bookkeeping and accounting, any written entry recording a transaction in acceptable form and with enough information to be usable in constructing accounting data.

judgment: A court decision, complete and binding upon the parties to a matter before that court.

junior bonds: Bonds which have less claim upon the issuer's assets than do other bonds, and which therefore in a default situation can make claims only after the claims of those other bonds have been satisfied.

junior mortgage: A mortgage, such as a second or third mortgage, which has less claim upon the property mortgaged than do other more senior mortgages, and which therefore in a default situation can make claims only after the claims of those other mortgages have been satisfied.

K

Kaffirs: South African gold mining company shares, after a term of disparagement used by some whites to describe the black population of the Union of South Africa.

Keogh Plan: A kind of tax advantaged retirement plan, named after Congressman Keogh, the chief sponsor of its enabling legislation, which allows the self-employed and those in unincorporated businesses to build tax-deferred retirement funds.

Keynesian economics: A body of economic theory and proposed practice developed by John Maynard Keynes, aimed at control of unemployment and inflation and avoidance of depression, by means of government taxing and spending policies; an important element of national economic practice in the United States and many other industrial nations.

kickback: An illegal payment made to someone in authority by someone who has benefited from use of that authority, as when a government contractor covertly pays a government officer for the illegal granting of a government contract or a supplier covertly pays a purchasing agent for received purchasing favors.

knockdown: The consummation of a sale at auction.

knockoff: A copy of an antique or collectible, made considerably later than the original.

krona: The main currency unit of Sweden, hearing the same relationship to Sweden's national currency system as does the dollar to the United States currency system.

krone: The main currency unit of Denmark and Norway, bearing the same relationship to those national currency systems as does the dollar to the United States currency system.

L

lagging indicator: An economic indicator that, by its nature, moves some time after other indicators of economic activity have moved, as in the instance of new plant and equipment spending plans, which must, given the nature of the planning process in companies, move behind consumer buying patterns.

laissez faire: The belief that government should interfere as little as possible in economic matters; once a belief that government should not involve itself in economic matters at all, beyond tax collections, but now an attempt to limit government involvement.

lamb: An inexperienced and incautious investor, who imprudently takes the advice of others, loses much of his or her money as a result, and in some cases is victimized and therefore "fleeced" by the unscrupulous.

land banks: See Federal land banks.

land office business: A very active level of business, with a large number of transactions; usually, but not always profitable business.

lapping: A technique used to hide thefts or other account shortages, in which an employee enters the amount to be hidden in a future accounting period, does the same in that period with another amount and covers the amount previously hidden with current receipts. The original theft or shortage is then repeated in each accounting period, or until the employee can make up the shortage—or until the procedure is discovered.

last in, first out (lifo): A mode of inventory valuation that treats the cost of materials used in production as if those materials have just been purchased, no matter how long the materials have actually been in inventory. When prices are rising, the result is a considerable understatement of assets and profits, and a substantial reduction, therefore, in taxes paid.

last trading day: The last day on which a futures contract can be traded; after that day it effectively becomes a spot or cash contract, with delivery due at the time and prices specified in the contract.

last will and testament: The legal will of a decedent, superseding all previous testamentary dispositions.

late tape: A situation in which the recording of trades and prices on an exchange lags behind the pace of trading, due to physical inability to handle trading volume.

laundered money: Money that has been illegally obtained and then passed through other economic entities to hide its true origin; for example, money obtained from narcotics sales which is fed as cash into such high cash turnover businesses as restaurants to reappear later as seemingly legitimate profits.

lawful money: See legal tender.

leaders: Those securities which are trendsetters in a market, and which the rest of that market tends to follow up or down.

leading indicator: An economic indicator that by its nature moves ahead of the business cycle, and can therefore to some extent be used as a predictive tool regarding business cycle swings; for example, new building permits and common stock price indexes.

lead-lag indicator relationships: The fairly predictable relationships between leading and lagging indicators, with changes in lagging indicators following changes in leading indicators within a predictable time range, often as a direct result of the leading indicator changes; an example is the change in the value of orders for new plant and equipment that follows a change in spending plans.

lead time: The time between formal initiation of an action or plan and its completion, as in the time between completion of research and development and the start of commercial production of an item or between the placing of an order and its delivery.

lean buying: See hand-to-mouth.

lease: A formal and written contract between one who has the power to rent property and one who wishes to rent that property, setting up the relationship between them of lessor and lessee, on terms explicitly stated in the contract. Realty and equipment are the main kinds of business leases.

leaseback: See sale and leaseback.

leasehold: That property interest possessed by a lessee, as defined by the terms of a lease, including such matters as rights, obligations, length of lease, renewal options, and termination conditions.

lease-purchase contract: A lease that carries with it an option to buy the property leased, often with some allowance for rental paid under the terms of the lease if the option to buy is exercised.

ledger: A book of final entry used in accounting, into which is placed all information derived from original entry sources, such as journals and payment records; the size and complexity of a business' transactions will determine the number and kind of general and special ledgers needed.

legacy: In law, personal property that is passed by will; in general usage, anything, including both real and personal property, that is passed by will.

legal capital: The total value of the capital stock of a corporation, issued and unissued, stated as the total of that stock's par value; some part of the corporation's paid-in capital.

legal duty: A duty stemming from law or contract, and which undone may be found to breach a contract, violate law, or create liability for negligence.

legal entity: Any person or organization existing in law, and therefore capable of engaging in legal transactions, taking legal responsibility, acting, or being acted against in law.

legal interest: The highest rate of interest that may be charged by a lender; usually set by the usury statutes of the states, which have jurisdiction over interest rates.

legal investment list: An investment vehicle on a state-approved list of investments thought appropriate for fiduciaries and regulated companies, such as insurance companies and banks; usually composed of "safe" securities thought capable of withstanding almost all economic shocks.

legal liability: A liability enforceable at law, in contrast to a moral obligation, which although sometimes enforceable by mores and consequent social pressure, is not enforceable at law.

legal representative: One whom the law will recognize as representing another, as it does executors, administrators, and in some instances receivers in bankruptcy and some kinds of assignees.

legal reserve: The amount of cash or easily made liquid assets which must by applicable law be maintained by banks, life insurance companies and other firms as reserves against deposits and policies, and in compliance with other legal requirements.

legal residence: Any residence at which a person lives at least part of but not necessarily most of the time and which is chosen by that person as a legal residence; synonymous with domicile.

legal tender: Money that is recognized by government as a lawful medium of exchange and usable for payment of sums owed, and which therefore must be accepted by creditors when offered in payment, unless the sums owed are defined in other than money terms or in terms of other currencies. For example, payment of a debt specifically stated in Japanese yen or German marks must be made in the specified currency if demanded by the creditor; payment in United States dollars at the current exchange rate may legally be refused.

legatee: One who is to receive a legacy by the terms of a will.

lending institution: An organization wholly or largely in the business of lending money to others for profit, such as a bank or savings and loan association.

less-developed country: See underdeveloped country.

lessee: See lease.

lessor: See lease.

letter of credit: An instrument issued by banks and other financial institutions, guaranteeing payment of drafts up to a specified limit when made by the person or organization named in the instrument; commonly used in foreign trade transactions as a means of organizing payments between correspondent banks without large transfers of funds between them. In commercial transactions, letters of credit may be revocable at will by the issuing institution up to a stated date or irrevocable; may be guaranteed as to payment by the issuing bank and its correspondent bank or by the issuing bank alone; and may be for a fixed amount or constitute a line of credit. Individuals also widely use letters of credit when travelling; a traveller's check is such a letter of credit.

letters testamentary: A written instrument issued by a court of proper jurisdiction, authorizing an executor to proceed with execution of a will, and functioning as proof that the will has been through probate.

letter stock: Company stock that is unregistered with the Federal and state securities regulatory authorities and that is issued by letter between company and purchasers; it may subsequently be transferred only by private sale and not by public sale.

let the buyer beware: See caveat emptor.

let the seller beware: See caveat venditor.

leverage: The impact on a common stock's market price of substantial corporate financial obligations which must be paid before common stock can be considered for dividends. A company carrying relatively heavy debt obligations, such as large direct debts and bonds outstanding, with consequent very heavy interest payments, is said to be heavily leveraged. In times of high earnings, the company is making money on the borrowed money, and earnings relative to capital invested are high, pushing the market price of the stock up; in times of low earnings, the company may make little money or actually lose money on the borrowed money, and earnings relative to capital invested may be extremely low, pushing the market price of the stock down.

leverage buyout: The purchase of a going concern for cash, with the buyers financing most of the purchase price with borrowed money, often using the cash reserves and cash flow of the acquired concern to help finance much of the debt service and amortization resulting from the acquisition.

levy: 1. Any claim by government upon the property of its citizens, including all taxes and seizures. **2.** An assessment by an organization on its members or stockholders to meet organizational obligations.

liabilities: 1. Amounts owed by debtors to creditors. **2.** All items appearing on the credit side of a double entry accounting system, including all amounts owed.

liability: 1. In the law, one of the widest possible range of current, contingent, future, and possible responsibilities and hazards. **2.** In business, whatever is owed by debtor to creditor.   **3.** In accounting, any item appearing on the credit side of a double entry accounting system, including both current owings and future owings incurred but not yet due, and including the net worth items carried.

liable: Legally responsible, or likely to be so, for satisfying the claim of another, and obliged to respond to that claim by either contesting or settling it.

license: 1. A permit by government to do something which by law requires such a permit; granted as a matter of governmental discretion, rather than as a matter of individual or organizational right, for a limited time and subject to conditions imposed by government.   **2.** A permit granted by the owner of a patent or copyright to another to make use, usually commercial use, of patented or copyrighted materials or processes.

lien: A claim chargeable by one against the property of another, usually arising from a debt owed by the property holder to the lien holder. If that debt is unpaid, the claim may be pursued by legal action and the property sold to satisfy the debt, as when a mechanic holds an automobile for unpaid repair bills and is eventually satisfied out of the proceeds on sale of that automobile.

life estate: An estate granted to one who is not an inheritor under the terms of a will, and which is limited to the life of its holder or some other person, the estate then reverting to its grantor or some other party designated by the grantor.

life of the contract: Referring to the length of time left before a currently traded futures contract becomes a spot or cash contract.

lifo: See last in, first out.

limit: An instruction to a broker regarding securities to be bought or sold, setting the top price that will be paid or the bottom price at which securities will be sold.

limited (Ltd.): A British term describing the limited liability to stockholders accompanying the corporate form of business organization; attached to corporate names in Great Britain and throughout much of the English-speaking world, and used synonymously with the United States "Incorporated" or "Inc."

limited edition: An article which has been produced in specifically limited quantity, such as 100 copies of a lithograph or 10,000 copies of a silver plate, and of which its makers have guaranteed no further production, often by claiming destruction of the means by which more copies could be made.

limited liability: Any limitation on the liability of those jointly engaged in a business enterprise; the corporate form by its very nature offers limited liability to stockholders, whose liability as regards corporate obligations extends only to the value of their stockholdings.

limited partnership: A partnership form, in widespread use in the real estate industry and in real estate investing, in which one or more of the partners share liability only to the value of their holdings, take profits within stated limits, and participate only financially in the enterprise.

limited price order: See limit.

limit move: The price range within which a given exchange will allow a futures contract to move in single trading day, expressed as the highest or lowest price it will permit before it closes trading in that contract for the day.

limit order: See limit.

line of credit: See credit line.

liquid assets: Assets consisting of cash, notes minus an allowance for uncollectibles, and quickly marketable securities; for net liquid assets, current liabilities are also subtracted.

liquidate: 1. To terminate and dissolve an economic entity through sale of all assets, payment of all obligations, and distribution of the remaining liquid assets to those entitled by law to receive them.   **2.** To pay and discharge a debt.

liquidated damages: An amount previously agreed upon by parties to a contract or court action, representing damages that will be paid on breach of contract or judicial decision.

liquidating dividend: The distribution of remaining assets to equity holders on corporate dissolution, on a pro rata basis after satisfaction of all prior claims, such as those of creditors and bondholders.

liquidation: See liquidate.

liquidation sale: A sale of goods, sometimes including antiques and collectibles, at fixed prices, rather than at auction.

liquidation value: The estimated residual value of a business if it were to be terminated and dissolved, all assets turned into cash and all obligations paid.

liquidator: One appointed by law to liquidate a business; often used as a synonym for receiver.

liquidity: 1. The extent to which a security or market can resist selling or buying pressure without sharp price changes.   **2.** The ability to meet obligations out of liquid assets, rather than through debt creation or fixed asset sales.

liquidity preference: In Keynesian economic theory, the ongoing and ever-changing relationship between the demand for cash for current needs and security desires on the one hand and the desire to invest in income-producing investment vehicles on the other.

lira: The main currency unit of Italy, bearing the same relationship to Italy's national currency system as does the dollar to the United States currency system.

listed security: A security traded on and listed by a recognized stock exchange, such as the New York or American Stock Exchanges.

listing: 1. In securities trading, full recognition of a security by an established stock exchange. **2.** In real estate, the placing of a property for sale with a broker or group of brokers.

listing agreement: See listing.

listing requirements: Those rules and criteria of an organized securities exchange that must be met by a company seeking to have its securities listed for trading on that exchange, in such areas as the amount of stock outstanding and available for trading, size of company, and condition of company.

living trust: See inter vivos.

load: That proportion of an insurance company premium or mutual fund investment which is attributable to selling and other business acquisition expenses. In some mutual funds, these expenses are taken from investors' funds very early in the life of an investment program, and investors attempting to sell out their holdings soon after starting such a program find that their recoverable funds have dramatically diminished in a very short time.

loading: See load.

loan: Property owned by one which, by mutual consent, is used temporarily by another; also the transaction resulting in that use. In business, that property is usually money, which is by formal agreement passed from owner-lender to temporary user-borrower, to be repaid at specified times and at specified rates of interest.

loan capital: The loaned capital of a corporation, as distinguished from its equity capital. Loan capital consists of debt instruments, such as bonds and bank loans; equity capital consists of ownership shares.

loaned stock: Stock loaned by or through a broker to one selling short, so that the short seller can make timely delivery of the stock sold, even though the short seller does not own the stock at the time of sale. Interest is often payable by the short seller on stock so borrowed.

loan shark: A lender, operating illegally, charging usurious rates of interest, and normally indulging in unsavory collection practices.

locked in: A condition in which someone cannot move because the move will cause more adverse results than preserving the status quo; in securities trading, usually referring to an investor who has capital gains on a stock and is unwilling to sell because of probable adverse tax consequences.

long: Owning securities and commodities, usually purchased on margin and held in a margin account with a broker, which have been bought in expectation of a rise in their market prices.

long account: See long position.

long hedge: A futures purchase made by one selling commodities for cash now.

long interest: The amount of stock held by those with long positions, in a market, a group of similar securities, or a single security.

long position: The status of owning a security in expectation that the owner will be able to sell it subsequently at a profit.

longe-range forecasting: Systematic attempts to predict future trends and events beyond four or five years into the future, often using mathematical models and computer technology.

long term appreciation: Growth in the value of a security over a considerable period of time, rather than in the short term; thought to characterize the growth patterns of the securities of well-established, often blue-chip companies, carrying with them considerable safety as well as long-term growth possibilities.

long term debt: Debts which must be paid one year or more after signing of the loan agreement, in contrast to short term debts, which must be paid less than one year after the borrowing.

long term lease: A lease that runs for several years, usually three or more; a relative term and not sharply defined as to length.

long term liability: See long term debt.

long term trend: Describing the movement of securities and commodities prices over a considerable period of time, measured in months and sometimes years, rather than in days and weeks.

long the basis: Describing the position of one who holds cash commodities and has hedged that commitment by buying futures contracts short; if prices rise, profits will result from the short position.

loss: The difference between income and expenditure, when expenditure is larger; the net of the two is loss, in contrast to profit, which is the result when income is larger.

Ltd.: See limited.

lump sum payment: Repayment of a debt by a single payment, rather than by any installment payment mode.

M

M-1: The national money supply, defined in the most basic and narrow terms as the total of all currency plus all demand deposits.

M-2: The national money supply, using a somewhat broader definition than M-1, and including currency, demand deposits, and commercial bank time deposits.

M-3: The national money supply, using a somewhat broader definition than M-1 or M-2, and including currency, demand deposits, commercial bank time deposits, and savings held by savings institutions of all kinds.

macroeconomics: The study of economics in the large, using whole economies and large subsections of whole economies as objects of study, and focusing on how such large economic units behave; in contrast to microeconomics, or the study of small economic units.

Mafia: An alleged criminal syndicate, operating in the United States and many other countries. In a wider sense, used to refer to any group operating covertly and using violent methods to exercise control over other people and organizations.

mail auction: An auction conducted by letter or catalogue offer and met by communicated response, as by telex, telegram, telephone, or mail.

majority stockholder: One owning a controlling interest in a corporation; although earlier it referred to one owning more than 50% of a corporation's stock, it is now often used to describe those holding much smaller percentages, but in effective control.

major top: A situation in which a market is thought by many professionals in that market to have reached the highest price area possible before a decline sets in; always an estimate.

major trend: The main direction in which securities traded in a market are moving, over a relatively long period of time, measured in months, rather than days or weeks.

make a market: To act as primary trader for a specific stock, especially including moves aimed at regulating sharp fluctuations in the price of a stock, if possible. Dealers make markets in over the counter stocks; specialists make markets on the floors of stock exchanges.

maker: One who is the original signer of a promissory note, and therefore assumes prime responsibility for payment of that note.

maker's marks: See mark.

malfeasance: The commission of an illegal or otherwise wrongful act, the proving of which can lead to successful criminal or civil action against the malefactor.

managed currency: Any currency which is manipulated by government or its agencies in pursuit of national goals, rather than being left free to respond solely to marketplace conditions. All major modern currencies are so managed.

managed price: See administered price.

management: 1. In the widest sense, the operation and control of any function or organization, including the management of one's own time, a household, or the provisioning of an ocean liner. **2.** The operation and control of business organizations, aiming at attaining the over-all goals of those organizations at minimum cost and maximum profit. Management may participate in over-all goal setting and may in fact exercise many other ownership functions. 3. Those who are responsible for the operation and control of business orgnizations.

management accounting: Accounting systems designed to help management perform effectively by reporting financial information quickly, simply, and in forms usable by non-financial management people; usually the function of an internal financial officer, such as a controller, sometimes with the help of outside accountants.

management audit: A review of management's operations and control mechanisms conducted by independent outside reviewers, aimed at evaluating the quality of management's performance as compared with that of similar organizations, usually those head-quartered in the same country.

management by crisis: A technique of management purporting to favor the development of operating crises as a means of most effectively clarifying issues, developing effective management, and moving organizations ahead; normally far more an excuse for poor planning and ineffective management than a coherent management style.

management by exception: A technique of managing that focuses major attention on variations from plans and previous business patterns, in the main assuming that if plans are working out as budgeted, little attention need be paid to them, leaving more time for attention to the unforeseen.

management by objectives (MBO): A technique of managing that focuses on formal goal-setting and on reaching the goals set, featuring frequent planning, evaluation and reevaluation activities on the part of management people; usually accompanied by a good deal of organizational structuring and restructuring, as well as by the presence of a substantial number of internal and external consulting personnel.

management company: A company in the business of managing properties or investments.

management development: The process of attempting to train working managers to become better managers. Much of such development is self-development; much is relatively informal on-the-job skills training and self-training; some consists of formal in-company and outside professional training courses.

management game: Any problem-solving game using organizational models and case studies to develop alternative solutions to the kinds of problems managers face in real life; a widely used training and professional development technique.

management information system (MIS): A computer-based information system aimed at providing management with an ongoing flow of operating and financial data that will help provide the basis for consistently informed decision making.

management prerogatives: Those functions which management claims as solely its own, and not subject to the collective bargaining process; such as hiring, scheduling, and production control matters; all are very much matters of disagreement between labor and management in the United States and much of the rest of the world.

management rights: See management prerogatives.

management science: A body of formal techniques derived from the hard sciences and applied to the problems of management, most recently featuring mathematical models using computers as well as other complex mathematically based techniques. Also called quantitative management or scientific management.

manager: One who manages; in small businesses one who manages at any level; in larger businesses, one who manages above the first line supervisory or foremen's level.

managerial grid: A management self-assessment and development tool using a grid into which are positioned several variables, all within the constructs of "concern for people" and "concern for production" as major interacting factors in describing and evaluating management style and effectiveness.

mandamus: A court order commanding a court of lesser jurisdiction, governmental body, private corporation, other organization, or person to do or not do something, without delay; sometimes specifying the exact action to be taken and sometimes commanding that action in general terms, with the specifics left to the doer.

manipulation: In business the control or influence of market factors, such as the amount of a particular stock in public circulation or the price of a commodity or single product, for the economic benefit of those so operating. Some manipulations, such as the forcing up of a stock price, are illegal. Some, such as the control of world commodity prices by a group of commodity-producing nations, are merely factual, though deplored by those nations consuming the commodities in question. Some, such as control of money supplies by national governments, are widely regarded as beneficial instruments of national policy.

manner of: See school of.

margin: 1. The percentage of equity owned by an investor who has purchased stock on margin, that is by a combination of cash and brokers' loans; a 70% margin, for example, means that the equity holder has paid 70 ¢ on each dollar of stock and the broker has loaned 30 ¢, with the broker holding a lien on the stock to the extent of the 30 ¢ per dollar loan. If the market price of the stock goes up, so does the owner's equity; if down, so does the owner's equity, with the 30 ¢ loan remaining stable in dollar amount but varying in percentage. **2.** A synonym for gross profit.

margin account: A brokerage account, in which credit is extended by broker to customer for the purchase of securities, within rules set out by Federal and stock exchange regulations, which the broker may sell out as made necessary due to market conditions. The securities in the account may be, and usually are, used by the broker as collateral for bank and other institutional loans to cover the loans made to customers.

marginal analysis: An attempt to analyze the impact of changes in economic variables, such as cost and productivity, by isolating changes in individual variables for study purposes, while assuming that all other factors remain constant; often rendered extremely difficult in practice due to the multiple impacts of any change upon many of the variables in any situation.

marginal business: A business that operates at or close to break-even, generating very little profit or loss, carrying very little reserve for contingencies, and therefore always being close to failure.

marginal cost: The cost of adding a cost factor, assuming all other variables remain constant; often a theoretical rather than practical measure.

marginal costing: A costing technique that assigns only a marginal or incremental cost to a new cost factor, rather than assigning a full share of all costs being incurred; often used in evaluating new product results.

marginal productivity: The increase in amount produced caused by increase in a single factor of production; usually a theoretical rather than practical construct.

marginal revenue: The revenue resulting from a single additional sale. If revenue per sale remains constant, each additional unit sold yields as much as each previous unit, but if price decreases as units sold increase, revenue for each additional unit sold is less than a full unit price. For example, 5 units sold at $5 each yields $25. If 6 units are sold at $4.50 each the yield is $27, which is only $2 more than $25. The marginal revenue is $2.

marginal utility: The theory that the usefulness and therefore demand for a product may lessen with its increased availability.

margin call: A formal request from lender to borrowing investor or broker, calling for additional payments into a margin account, usually because a stock has lost market value, making the proportion of loan to equity too large to conform with legal requirements or lender policy.

margined securities: Securities that have been purchased on margin and held by broker in a margin account; such securities may not be taken in possession by their owner until they have been fully paid for.

margin of safety: The extent to which loans secured by collateral, such as those in a margin account, are protected by the value of the collateral above the amount loaned. For example, stock used as collateral is always subject to loss in market value, and the amount accepted as collateral must therefore considerably exceed the amount of the loan. In a wider sense, any allowance for error and shortfall.

margin requirements: The amount of cash required to buy securities or commodities, as a percentage of the purchase price; for example, a 70% margin requirement means that a purchaser must put up $70 cash for every $100 of securities purchased, the broker lending the purchaser the balance. Margin requirements are set by the Federal Government, the various organized stock exchanges, and in some instances by brokerage firms.

mark: An identifying insignia on an antique or collectible, such as a hallmark identifiably belonging to the firm that made the article, a maker's mark functioning as a signature on a piece, or an actual signature.

markdown: A lower evaluation of stores of value, such as securities held by institutions.

market: 1. Any placc at which goods and services are publicly traded, such as an open air market in which dozens of fruit and vegetable vendors sell their goods, a retail store, or the New York Stock Exchange. **2.** To sell, as when a company markets its goods. **3.** The demand for an item, as when the market for microcomputers is booming. **4.** A total of all trading activity in a designated area or kind of product, such as the Australian wool market or the world market for manganese.

marketability: 1. The likelihood that a product will be sold; its salability. **2.** The speed at which an asset may be made liquid without the substantial loss of value that would be caused by a distress sale.

marketable securities: Securities easily converted into cash, and carried as a current asset on the balance sheet.

marketable title: A title to real estate good enough to be conveyed and without which a valid real estate transaction cannot be legally consummated.

market basket: The price of a group of consumer goods, which moves as the cost of living changes. For example, a typical group of consumer goods, costing $1,000 this year, might be used as a base for computing changes in the cost of those kinds of consumer goods. The same group of goods two years later may cost $1,200, an increase of $200 or 20%.

market concentration: The extent to which the demand for a kind of product is concentrated in a specific geographic or kind of business area.

market equilibrium: The theory that prices reflect a balance between supply and demand, and that as supply and demand change and react against each other, prices tend to move in response to those changes.

market index: Any of the several indexes of securities market prices, such as the Dow-Jones or Standard and Poor's stock price indexes.

marketing: In the widest sense, the distribution function, including buying, selling, transporting, financing, and collecting. In modern business organizations, however, the term describes a group of selling and sales-related functions, including advertising, promotion, and direct selling.

marketing concept: A business planning approach that stresses the primacy of customer needs and wants, and regards the main function of the business as satisfying those needs and wants.

marketing mix: The set of marketing activities chosen by those responsible for marketing that they believe will most successfully sell their product or products, including the kinds of activities to be pursued, the amounts to be spent on those activities, and the integration of those activities into a coherent marketing plan.

marketing plan: The total plan adopted by marketing management for moving company products to market, including budgets, personnel, advertising, promotion, and direct selling plans.

marketing power: The relative ability of a firm to successfully sell its products in its markets; usually describing firms with relatively strong marketing organizations.

marketing research: See market research.

market leaders: See leaders.

market order: In securities trading, an order from customer to broker to buy or sell a security immediately upon receipt of the order at the best possible price then available in the market.

market penetration: The extent to which a firm has reached into a single market, and the share of that market to which it sells.

market position: The rank a firm occupies in its market relative to that occupied by other firms selling to the same market, assessed on the basis of such factors as sales volume, reputation and depth of penetration into specific areas. The term sometimes refers only to sales volume.

market potential: The sales possibilities for a product, in both present and future; a key assessment to be made by those developing new products.

market price: The price at which goods and services are currently selling in their marketplaces, such as the price of a security or commodity on an exchange.

market profile: A detailed description of the market or markets for a product, including such materials as demographic data and market survey results.

market rate of interest: The rates of interest currently being charged on loans by lending institutions.

market research: Information gathering and analysis bearing on any aspect of marketing, including such areas as consumer and industrial buying patterns and motivations, advertising, promotion, market definition, competition, and new product development.

market value: The price at which an asset or property will sell in its market now; often an estimate, as with real property, and sometimes a determinable amount, as with most securities.

markka: The main currency unit of Finland, bearing the same relationship to Finland's national currency system as does the dollar to the United States currency system.

markup: 1. The amount added to the cost of a product to cover additional costs and profits; for example, the amount added to the wholesale cost of a product sold at retail by the retailer, to cover operating expenses, other selling costs, and profits. **2.** A higher evaluation on stores of value, such as factory inventories and securities held by institutions.

married piece: A piece composed of two or more other pieces or parts; for example, a piece of furniture composed of a chest and legs made in China and other parts made subsequently in England.

Massachusetts trust: A firm owned by investors who hold transferable shares representing the value of their investments in the business and who have only limited liability, just as do shareholders in a corporation, but who have no control over management or management policies. The firm is organized as a trust, with shareholders passing the assets of the firm to management, who are called trustees, and retaining only beneficial interest in profits commensurate with their investments.

materiality: Relevance to the matter at hand, as when evidence presented in a legal action relates directly to the matter being adjudicated rather than being irrelevant to the main issues to be decided, or when a matter taken up or omitted on an accounting statement is relevant to proper understanding of company affairs by those who must be informed, such as directors, stockholders, the general public, and regulatory authorities.

mature economy: An economy that has experienced very substantial industrial growth in the past and has to some extent shifted its current emphasis away from basic industrial growth to consumer goods and services.

maturity: The point at which a financial obligation becomes due and payable, such as the date at which a debt becomes payable, or an insurance policy becomes payable due to occurrence of stated conditions.

maturity date: See due date.

MBO: See management by objectives.

mean: A measure of the central tendency of a set of statistical observations; especially important in analyzing normal distributions. The mean is calculated by totalling the values and dividing the result by the number of observations, so the mean of 3, 7, 4 and 12 is 26 divided by 4, or 6.5. In popular usage, the mean is often called the average, though that term can also refer to the mode or the median.

median: A measure of central tendency of a set of statistical observations; the median is the middle number of a series of numbers arranged in order, so that in the series: 1, 2, 16, 44, 56, the number 16 is the median. In a normal distribution, the median is theoretically the same as the mean, but when the data is highly variable, references to the median as "the average" can be misleading, since that term popularly refers to the mean.

medium of exchange: Anything that is accepted as money.

medium-range forecasting: Systematic attempts to predict the course of future trends and events, as far as two to three years into the future, often using mathematical models and computer technology.

melon: A relatively large sum of money to be divided among several people, whether proceeds or profits.

member bank: A bank that is a member of the Federal Reserve System.

member firm: A firm that is affiliated with the New York Stock Exchange.

mercantile agency: A company in the credit information business, such as Dun and Bradstreet and a substantial number of smaller firms.

mercantilism: A theory favoring extreme protectionism, in which trade barriers are encouraged, home industries are protected against competition from abroad and precious metal supplies are hoarded.

merchant bank: A bank engaged in a combination of investment banking, securities-related, and commercial banking functions, such as the international Rothschilds and Hambros banks; while active in Europe, they are not a United States banking form, for legal and historic reasons.

merger: The complete takeover of one business by another, whether accomplished by termination of the legal existence of the firm taken over or by its continued legal existence while under the complete control of the acquiring firm. A firm may maintain its name and be operated as a wholly owned subsidiary for public identification and marketing reasons, yet lose all legal existence in such a takeover.

microeconomics: The study of small economic units, attempting to generalize about economic behavior from that study; in contrast to macroeconomics, which is the study of economies in the large, using economies and large subsections of economies as subject matter.

milking: To systematically, intentionally and usually illegally strip a company of its assets; often prior to a change of ownership, bankruptcy, or dissolution; for example, by selling assets at bargain prices to a company owned by those in control of the company being looted.

minority interest: An ownership interest that is less than a controlling interest in a company. In some companies, a minority interest may be anything less than 50% of ownership; but in large companies, where a controlling interest may be as little as 10%, a minority interest may be anything under 10%. As a practical matter even substantial minority interests may be granted some share in policy-making.

mint: A coinage producing facility, as is the United States Bureau of the Mint.

mint condition: In excellent condition; like new. When referring to coins, literally the condition a coin was in when newly minted.

minus tick: See down tick.

MIP: See Monthly Investment Plan.

MIS: See management information system.

misfeasance: The improper and sometimes civilly or criminally actionable doing of an act which if properly done would be lawful; in practice, the term is often used to describe the doing of an unlawful act, and in that context is synonymous with malfeasance.

misrepresentation: A false statement of fact that is material to a transaction or agreement; such a statement may be explicit or capable of being constructed from actions; and it may be intentional or unintentional.

mixed economy: An economy including both public and private ownership of major industrial units, sometimes of units within the same industry, as when a government-owned postal industry and partially government-owned hospital system exist side by side with a telephone system and basic industries, such as steel and coal, that are privately owned.

mode: A measure of central tendency of the values in a set of statistical observations; in a data series, the number or value that appears most frequently; for example, in a series: 10, 11, 11, 11, 18, 19, 30, the mode is 11. A series of data in which two values appear with equal or near equal frequency is called bimodal.

model: A less-than-full-size representation, sometimes tangible, as in a ship's model; sometimes symbolic, as in a mathematical model; and sometimes symbolic but cast in technological form, as in a computer model.

monetary controls: Restrictions placed on the free exchange of currency between nations, by a single nation or a group of nations.

monetary policy: The set of policies by which a government attempts to manipulate the economy in pursuit of current national goals; in the United States, through the Federal Reserve System, and in many other countries, through their central banks.

monetary reserve: The stock of precious metal, usually gold, held by a government to secure its currency. The United States, in common with most other nations, secures its currency with only its full faith and credit, even though some gold stock is held.

monetary unit: A country's main unit of currency, such as the United States dollar, the British pound, or the Japanese yen.

money: A medium of exchange, generally accepted as having and holding a specified value against which the values of non-monetary items can be measured and expressed, as when a loaf of bread, which is non-monetary, can be bought for a dollar, which is a standard unit of money.

money broker: One in the business of finding money for those who wish to borrow some; normally one who puts private lenders together with borrowers, when normal lending channels are unavailable.

money market: A worldwide body of markets engaged in trading the short-term debt obligations of governments, financial institutions, and commercial firms, in such forms as commercial paper, bankers' acceptances, and treasury bills.

money market fund: A kind of mutual fund, trading mainly in the kinds of short-term debt obligations found in money markets, such as certificates of deposit, commercial paper, treasury bills, other United States Government securities, and bankers' acceptances.

money order: A money instrument purchased on a one-time basis and sent to its payee for conversion into cash; normally used as a means of sending money by mail by those without checking accounts or by those who want the payee to be able to use the proceeds of the order immediately, rather than having to wait for checks to clear.

money supply: The total amount of a nation's currency and demand deposits denominated in that national currency available for use at any time. The size of a nation's money supply relative to its productive capacity is often viewed as an important factor influencing inflation and deflation, boom and recession, so governments often tend to use money supply manipulation as a key element of national economic strategy, as does the United States government through the Federal Reserve.

money wages: Cash wages received, without adjustment for such factors as real wage changes due to cost of living fluctuations or dollar value changes due to international currency value movements.

monitor: To watch; for example, to continuously survey the pace of inflation, Soviet or United States nuclear weapons tests, the performance of a production line, or the operation of a computer system. Also refers to a device used in such observations.

monopolistic competition: Competition between several sellers who among them dominate a market, and whose products and prices differ little in function and performance.

monopoly: Effective control over a market by a single seller or a group of sellers, with no substantial competition and therefore no major buying choices available to purchasers other than refusal to buy at all—and no choice possible in the instance of monopoly—controlled necessities. United States examples are telephone services, power utilities, and postal service.

monopsony: Effective control over a market by a single buyer or group of buyers.

Monthly Investment Plan (MIP): A New York Stock Exchange sponsored installment stock purchase plan, in which investors buy small amounts of listed stocks on a regular basis, usually monthly or quarterly, with title to the stocks purchased passing as purchased, even when only a fraction of a share is purchased.

moral debt: See debt.

moratorium: A government-sanctioned postponement of debt repayment for a kind of debtor or debt, issued pursuant to government policy, as in the instance of Presidential declaration of a bank holiday in 1933, to forestall imminent collapse of the banking program.

Morris Plan: See industrial bank.

mortgage: A legally enforceable lien on property created by the pledge of that property as security for repayment of a debt or other obligation; also the legal document setting forth that lien, the terms of payment, and all other pertinent matters. In the common law, now largely superseded by state statutes, a mortgage was not a lien, but an actual transfer of property, voided by the mortgagee's performance of all obligations stated in the mortgage instrument.

mortgage bond: A kind of bond, secured by real or personal property, in contrast to unsecured bonds.

mortgage company: A company mainly engaged in the business of financing real estate and other property transactions through issuance of property secured loans.

mortgagee: One who holds a mortgage on the property of another, being named as mortgage holder in the mortgage instrument.

mortgage market: The aggregate of activity by those giving and getting mortgage loans in a given area; often referring to a state, as the states regulate mortgage loan rates and terms, but sometimes to the entire country. The term is sometimes used as synonymous with the rate of interest generally charged by lenders in a mortgage market.

mortgage premium: An extra charge, beyond the interest charges, attached to a mortgage transaction by the lender. It is often denominated in "points," that is, a specified percentage of the mortgage loan. For example, a bank or other lender might issue a mortgage loan of $20,000, at the going interest rate, plus 2 "points," or 2% of $20,000.

mortgagor: One who mortgages a property, usually in return for a loan.

most favored nation clause: A kind of preferential tariff, in which two or more nations, when making a trade agreement, agree to apply any favorable tariff treatment given any other nation in the future to each other as well.

moving average: An average or mean that is calculated in timed sequence using the same number of time periods but, at each calculation, dropping the oldest and adding the latest data; for example, a securities price average computed from twelve monthly averages, which is recomputed each month with data added from the most current month and dropped from the oldest month.

multilateral trade: Trade between more than two countries.

multinational company: A major international company, with operations, often including subsidiaries and associated companies, throughout the world, and managed as a single massive entity for all major corporate policy purposes.

multiplier principle: The theory that some kinds of expenditures impact on the economy far more strongly than the amounts expended, as when investment in new plant causes additional employment, retail purchasing, building, and other associated economic benefits.

municipal bond: A debt obligation of any unit of government in the United States, other than the Federal Government, including state and all other lesser governmental units. Such debt obligations are, with a few exceptions, exempt from Federal and sometimes from state and local taxes, and therefore are often attractive tax shelter devices for those of substantial income.

Murphy's Law: The colloquial expression that anything that can go wrong, will go wrong; it has become part of the everyday language of American management.

museum quality: Of such excellent quality as to be collected by museums as well as by private collectors.

mutual company: A company that distributes profits to its members in direct proportion to the dollar quantity of business they do with the company; there is no stock, but rather equitable holding that varies with that quantity of business, as when mutual savings banks distribute dividends proportionally to their depositors and mutual insurance companies distribute dividends proportionally to their policy holders.

mutual fund: An investment fund that pools the invested funds of others and invests those funds on their behalf, usually in a specific kind of investment, such as money market instruments, municipal bonds, or common stock.

mutual savings bank: A savings bank that issues no stock, but instead distributes its profits to its depositors. Although depositors become equity holders to the extend of their deposits, effective control is normally in the hands of trustees or management.

N

narrow market: A market, usually for a single security, which is characterized by a relatively small quantity of the security in circulation and relatively few trades, and which is therefore vulnerable to wide fluctuations in prices as trades are made.

NASD: See National Association of Securities Dealers.

NASDAQ: The stock quotation system operated by the National Association of Securities Dealers (NASD).

national accounting: The development and issuance of summary national economic information, including data on gross national product, foreign trade, savings and investments, government finances, and personal income and expenditure.

National Association of Securities Dealers (NASD): A securities dealers trade association, representing United States securities dealers, and holding some enforcement powers granted by the Securities and Exchange Commission, enabling it to regulate over-the-counter operations by dealers.

national bank: A bank chartered by the Federal Government to conduct a commercial banking business, in contrast to a state chartered bank.

national debt: The total of a national government's outstanding debt obligations.

national income: See gross national product.

nationalization: The process of government takeover of privately held property and organizations, with or without compensation, gradually or immediately. Examples are oil industry takeovers by nations in the Middle East and by Mexico, and industry takeovers following the Russian Revolution.

national product: See gross national product.

nearby contract: A futures contract that specifies delivery less than three months after current purchase, in contrast to a deferred contract, which specifies delivery three months or more after purchase.

nearby delivery: See nearby contract.

negative shelter: A tax shelter which has been in effect for so long that the tex shelter aspects of earlier years have reversed, and money formerly sheltered has now become an addition to current income; a result avoided by the use of other, later tax shelter arrangements to shield both current income and money returning to current income from previous tax sheltered investments.

negligence: In law, failure to do what a reasonable person would do under the same circumstances, with consequent actionable damage to another.

negotiable. 1. Legally transferable to another merely by delivery or by endorsement and delivery, the new holder then becoming owner for all legal purposes.   **2.** Open for bargaining, rather than being firm as stated; usually referring to prices and terms in a business situation.

negotiable instruments: Instruments, such as checks and promissory notes, which can be legally transferred merely by delivery or by endorsement and delivery, the new holder then becoming owner for all legal purposes.

negotiated price: A price fixed as a result of discussion and agreement between the parties to a purchase contract rather than fixed by the seller.

negotiation: 1. The act of transferring a negotiable instrument. **2.** The process of bargaining in any business situation, as in the development of a trade agreement satisfactory to the contracting parties.

net: The remainder, after all else has been added and subtracted; in business, always capable of being expressed discretely, almost always as a specific plus or minus number.

net assets: See net worth.

net asset value: In investment companies, the market value of all assets, minus all liabilities, divided by the number of shares, thus computing value per share.

net avails: The actual amount a borrower realizes from a discounted note, subtracting the amount of the discount from the amount borrowed.

net bonded debt: The net of bonds issued minus bonds in any way paid minus funds held in the issuing corporation or government as a reserve against repayment.

net business formation: The number of new businesses minus the number of firms going out of business for all reasons in any given period.

net change: The difference in the price of a security between the close of trading one day and the close of trading the next day.

net earnings: See net profits before taxes.

net foreign investment: The net of all investments in other countries owned by a country and its citizens, minus all investments owned by foreigners in the country.

net income: The income remaining in a business after deduction of all expenses and other deductions from all revenues.

net lease: A lease which rents only land or land and structures, with the lessee paying for all other costs arising from that which is leased, including such costs as taxes and all maintenance; for example, a lease of an entire shopping center from its owner by an operating company.

net liquid assets: See liquid assets.

net loss: The net of expenditures and revenues during a given period, when expenditures exceed revenues.

net national debt: The net of all debts owed by the Federal Government; does not include debts owed by the country's citizens or by state and local governments.

net national product (NNP): The net of gross national product minus depreciation, or the wear upon and using up of capital goods used in the process of creating gross national product.

net-net: A final net figure; synonymous with bottom line.

net position: The net of a trader's short and long positions, summarizing whether the trader is on balance holding a net short or a net long position.

net price: The actual price paid by buyer to seller for a purchased item, after all discounts, adjustments, and negotiations have been completed.

net proceeds: See net avails.

net profits: The net of revenues minus all appropriate costs. The term is often used as a synonym for net income, but in ordinary business usage may refer to either net profits before taxes or net profits after taxes.

net profits after taxes: The net of revenues minus operating expenses and taxes.

net profit before taxes: The net of revenues minus operating expenses but before deductions for taxes.

net sales: The net of gross sales minus all returns, allowances, and other appropriate deductions.

net working capital: See working capital.

net worth: The value of total ownership interest, the net of total assets minus total liabilities; expressed variously according to the form of business organization, as stockholders' equity, partner's equity or proprietor's equity. The net worth of an individual includes personal as well as business assets and liabilities, and is the net of all personal assets minus all personal liabilities.

new crop: The anticipated amount of crops of a kind about to be harvested; a significant projection for those investing in commodities and commodities futures.

new high: The highest price ever attained by a specific security, group of securities, or market; sometimes only the highest such price in a given period.

new issue: A securities issue that has just been put on the market, in contrast to a block sale of securities previously issued.

new plant and equipment spending: Total investment spending by the private sector on new plant and equipment; an important factor in smoothing out fluctuations in the business cycle, as actual spending in this area continues for some time after a period of high economic activity.

New York Curb Exchange: See American Stock Exchange.

New York Stock Exchange (NYSE): By far the largest securities exchange in the United States, and one of the world's largest stock exchanges; often referred to as "the Exchange" or "the Big Board."

night depository: A device by which bank depositors may make deposits after a bank's regular business hours.

NNP: See net national prodct.

no contest: See nolo contendere.

no limit order: A securities purchase or sale order at the market rather than at a specified price.

no load fund: A mutual fund that does not charge its investors heavy sales and management fees as soon as the investment is made, thus immediately sharply diminishing the value of the funds invested, in contrast to a frontloaded fund, which does make such charges.

nolo contendere: A plea of no contest made by the defendent in a criminal case, which operates for purposes of that specific case as a guilty plea, but which does not constitute an admission of guilt that can be used against the defendent in another case, criminal or civil.

nominal partner: Someone who gives every appearance of being a partner in a firm, such as being included on a firm's letterhead, but who in fact has no legal connection with that firm.

nominal price: 1 A price quoted on a lightly and infrequently traded security, reflecting a seller's estimate, rather than current market activity. **2.** A very low price.

nonassessable stock: Stock limiting the potential liability of its holders to the amount paid for that stock, and prohibiting the assessment of levies on that stock for additional monies by anyone.

noncallable bonds: Bonds that mature only at their stated maturity dates and that cannot for any reason be recalled or redeemed by their issuers before maturity.

noncumulative dividends: Dividends payable by a company to holders of its preferred stock which do not cumulate; if a specified date for dividend payment passes without dividend payment, the dividend is lost.

non-cumulative preferred stock: Preferred stock that does not accumulate dividends if dividends for any period are passed by a company; in that event the dividends are lost.

nonfeasance: Failure to perform a legal, usually contractual duty, but without intent to do so.

nonmember bank: A commercial bank that is not a member of the Federal Reserve System.

nonmember firm: A securities firm that is not a member of a specific securities or commodities exchange; non-membership refers only to that exchange. For example, a firm may be a member of one exchange, such as the American Stock Exchange, and not be a member of the New York Stock Exchange.

nonnegotiable instrument: An instrument that lacks one or more of the requisites for being negotiable, and that therefore, while being an instrument of value, is not capable of being freely negotiated.

nonoperating company: A company that engages in no operations of its own, being dormant or having converted its assets into leases, licenses, or investments.

nonoperating revenue: Revenue from all sources other than operations, such as dividends and land rental income for non-real estate companies.

nonperformance: Actionable failure to perform obligations under the terms of a valid contract.

nonprofit corporation: A corporation organized and chartered to be not-for-profit, from which no stockholder, manager, or trustee can legally take profit, and which often is wholly or partially exempt from Federal and some state and local taxes due to the nature of its socially and legislatively approved activities, in such areas as education and charitable causes.

nonrecourse loan: A loan by the terms of which a borrower makes only a promise to pay, supported only by any collateral that may be stated in the loan agreement. Should default occur, the creditor has no other recourse or claim against the borrower, and that is so stated in the loan agreement.

nonrecurring charge: A one-time expense, so treated on accounting statements.

nonrenewable resource: See wasting asset.

nonstock corporation: A corporation which by its natures does not issue stock as evidence of equity ownership, as when a mutual insurance company, mutual savings bank, or fraternal organization confers equitable shares in direct proportion to and measured by premium payments, deposits, or membership.

non-voting stock: Ownership shares in a corporation that have no voting rights as to the affairs of that corporation.

no par value stock: Corporate stock which has no stated par value, but is carried on the books of the corporation at a value set by its board of directors.

no protest: An interbank practice, in which a bank stamps "no protest" on a check or other collectible so that another bank collecting the check will not protest in case of nonpayment, but will return the instrument unpaid; usually for instruments carrying small face amounts.

norm: 1. A standard, such as a standard of performance or behavior. **2.** In statistics, the mean in a normal distribution.

normal distribution: In statistics, a frequency distribution, also called the Gaussian distribution, that has a characteristic bell shape—high in the middle, sloping sharply on either side, and then trailing off on both sides. According to the central limit theorem, for any kinds of data, the larger the sample, the more likely the distribution will assume this normal—that is, symmetrical—shape. In a normal distribution the main measures of central tendency—the mean, the mode and the median—all have the same value, and the measures of dispersion—the standard deviation and the variance—show the spread of data around that central value. Statisticians use tables based on the theoretical normal distribution to help them predict information about actual populations; applications range widely, from analysis of intelligence test scores to controlling quality of production processes.

normal probability distribution: See normal distribution.

nostalgia piece: A collectible that is thought to evoke the not-too-distant past, such as Depression glass.

notary public: A state-licensed person, legally authorized to perform a variety of document-related functions, including the taking and certification of affidavits, depositions, and oaths; of payment demands and protests of several kinds of financial instruments; and certification of documents. The notary's seal is admissible legal evidence.

note: A negotiable instrument in which the note's maker promises to pay a specified sum, at a specified time or on demand, to the note's payee. The maker may defend against making the promised payment for lack of a valid agreement as between the original maker and payee, but not against other holders in due course.

notes payable: The sum of all notes promised and owed by a business to its creditors, such as banks and suppliers.

notes receivable: The sum of all notes promised and owed by others to a business, such as customers.

notice of dishonor: A document which is issued by a notary public at the request of a note holder who has been refused payment of a note by its maker, and which functions as legal evidence that the note has been dishonored, or unpaid.

nuisance tax: A very low-yielding tax, which is usually more trouble and sometimes expense to administer and pay than it is worth to the taxing authority; many taxes so considered by those taxed are considered well worth levying by taxing authorities.

numbered account: A bank account designated by number, rather than by name, as a means of helping protect the anonymity of the account's owner, often as a means of soliciting bank business from those seeking to hide assets from their own government for tax avoidance and other purposes; available in several countries, notably Switzerland.

NYSE: See New York Stock Exchange.

O

obligation: 1. Any kind of legally enforceable duty to another. **2.** Any kind of money debt to another, for a specific sum and legally enforcable.

obsolete: That which is no longer used, having been superseded by other devices or techniques. In business, the obsolescence of physical assets means a sharp reduction in their value, even though they may be entirely usable for many years.

odd lot: Any quantity of securities other than 100 shares or a multiple thereof; trades of 10, 99, and 199 shares are all odd lot trades.

odd lot dealer: A stockbroker who buys securities in standard lots of 100 shares or some multiple of 100, and then sells odd lots, usually in amounts of less than 100 shares.

OECD: See Organization for Economic Cooperation and Development.

offer: To make a proposal to another, involving but not limited to buying or selling. For example, in the securities industry, one may offer or bid to buy a security at a proposed price, or offer to sell at a proposed price; and contracting parties, both in commercial contracts and in collective bargaining, may make and counter with offers.

offering: A securities issue, offered by its sellers to the public.

officer: One who is by charter and in law designated as a responsible official of an organization, capable of acting for that organization within specified legal limits; usual designations of officers in business include president, secretary, treasurer, controller, and vice president.

official exchange rate: A currency exchange rate set by a government, at which its currency is to be exchanged for other currencies.

offset: A sum balancing or reducing an opposite sum, as when damage claims and counterclaims by the parties to a lawsuit eventually, wholly, or partly negate each other, or when sums entered on both sides of a single account wholly or partly cancel each other.

off the board: A stock that is not listed on any stock exchange, but rather is traded directly in the over-the-counter market; an unlisted stock.

off the gold standard: See demonetization.

oligopoly: A group of producers effectively dominating a market, and engaged either in illegal collusive price-fixing or wholly legal price-fixing by unspoken but equally close consent.

oligopsony: A group of buyers effectively dominating a market, and using that domination to create favorable market conditions for themselves by driving down supplier prices and in some instances driving out small suppliers in favor of their own supply organizations.

on consignment: A mode of placing items for sale, in which a commission agent takes the items, sells them if possible and takes a specified commission for doing so, or returns them unsold after some period of time; one of the major ways of selling antiques and collectibles. Title remains with the owner of the items, until they are sold by the commission agent, although the commission agent's insurance normally covers, at least in part, the value of the items while in the commission agent's possession.

one-bank holding company: See bank holding company.

one-stop banking: A slogan put forward by commercial banks offering a wide range of services to depositors, in an attempt to attract customers by distinguishing commercial banking from savings banking, which has historically offered a more limited range of services.

on the block: See auction.

OPEC: See Organization of Petroleum Exporting Countries.

open: See opening.

open account: A credit arrangement, in which a seller delivers goods sold to a buyer without demand for cash with order, and the buyer settles amounts due in cash later; while not intended as a credit vehicle, but rather as a convenience for both buyer and seller, it often serves as a means of credit extension from seller to buyer.

open credit: A line of credit, in which a lending institution or seller extends credit to a customer or buyer up to a set limit, so that the credit is available and ready to be used as desired, without specific approval by the creditor each time it is used.

open door policy: In international trade, an attempt to maintain free access by all nations to a trading area, rather than allowing some nations to obtain preferential treatment, such as tariff concessions; originating as American policy toward China in the late nineteenth century.

open end mortgage: A mortgage that gives the mortgagee the right to borrow more from the mortgagor on the same mortgage, rather than being forced to undertake additional mortgages if a larger amount is desired.

open end mutual fund: A mutual fund that sets no limit on the number of shares available for public sale, usually selling as many shares as possible continually; the most prevalent form of mutual fund.

opening: The start of a trading day on an organized exchange; sometimes called the "open."

open interest: The total of all outstanding futures contracts currently held on an organized futures exchange.

opening price: The price of a security or commodity at the start of a trading day on a stock exchange, which may be and often is different from its price at the close of that exchange's previous trading day. Securities traded on several exchanges may open at different prices on different exchanges.

open market: A market open to all potential buyers and sellers, rather than effectively controlled by statutes or business organizations; often describes a main tendency rather than a pure state, as most markets are in some ways restricted.

open market operations: Federal Reserve bank trading of United States Government securities, usually short term securities, in markets open to all traders; part of central bank manipulation of credit supply in pursuit of current national economic objectives.

open mortgage: See open end mortgage.

open order: An order that has not yet been filled. In general business operations, that is often a back order, one placed previously but for supply reasons not yet sent to the customer. In the securities industry, it is a trading order that has not yet been executed by a broker, but that in most instances is executed within 24 hours of placement.

operating budget: A budget for current income and expenditures, rather than for capital items.

operating company: A company actively engaged in conducting one or more lines of business, in contrast to a nonoperating company, which is dormant, and has converted its assets into investments, leases, or licenses.

operating cost: A cost incurred while conducting business and attributable to the conduct of business.

operating expense: See operating cost.

operating profit: See operating income.

operating rate: The actual production of a company or industry compared to its potential to produce at full capacity, usually expressed as a percentage, as when a steel plant is described as operating at 75% of capacity. Capacity being hard to determine, the operating rate is almost always an estimate, rather than a hard and verifiable figure.

operating ratios: The relationships between items on an operating statement, usually expressing items related as percentages and multiples of each other; for example, sales costs as a percentage of net revenue or divisional operating revenue as a percentage of company wide operating revenue.

operating statement: A financial report on the operations of all or part of a business organization for a given period; for example, a rather detailed statement of income and expenditures or a cash flow statement.

OPIC: See Overseas Private Investment Corporation.

opportunity cost: The best return that might be realized from an investment, taking investment goals into account, expressed as a cost and contrasted with the return that is currently being realized; for example, the ability to invest surplus company cash in relatively safe securities yielding 8-10% as contrasted with current operating assets yielding 5%. The construct is often used in assessing major expenditures, such as new plants and acquisition possibilities.

option: 1. The right to buy or sell something at a certain price within a specific time, usually as stated in a written agreement enforceable at law, in which that right has been conveyed in return for some kind of consideration; for example, a tradable option to buy a security or commodity; an option to buy company stock offered as part of an employee's pay package; or an option to buy land.   **2.** A choice, such as alternative contract terms during negotiations, or of modes of payment in settlement of a life insurance claim.

optional bond: A bond that may be called in and redeemed by its issuer at some time or times before its final maturity date; a callable bond.

optional dividend: A dividend that stockholders may take in more than one form, as they choose; usually a choice between stock and cash.

option period: The time during which an option may be exercised according to the terms of the option.

options exchange: An exchange making markets in stock or commodities options, sometimes exclusively, sometimes as part of a regular stock exchange.

option spread: See spread.

option writer: An individual or institution supplying stock option contracts, which serve as a basis for options trading. The contracts are supplied to brokers dealing in puts and calls, who then resell them to option markets traders.

oral agreement: An agreement between contracting parties, that, in the absence of a written agreement, is legally binding upon the parties; sometimes, but rarely, enforceable at law, though never against a legally valid written agreement.

order: A legally enforceable buy or sell instruction; for example, a written or oral purchase order, buying goods from a supplier, or a customer's instructions to a broker to buy or sell securities for the customer's account.

ordinary depreciation: Losses in value occurring from normal aging and wear and tear, rather than from extraordinary factors, such as damage due to fire and natural causes.

Organization for Economic Cooperation and Development (OECD): An international organization for economic studies, sponsored by its member governments, including the United States; disseminates information through meetings and publications, aiming at the development of international cooperation to meet common problems.

Organization of American States (OAS): An international organization, formed by the governments of the countries of North, Central, and South America, which serves as both a forum and a vehicle for approaching such common problems as aid to the less developed nations of the hemisphere.

Organization of Petroleum Exporting Countries (OPEC): An international oil producers' cartel, formed by the governments of most major oil-exporting countries, which functions to set prices and fix other common policies in world oil markets.

original cost: The purchase price of an asset, as of its acquisition date, without any post-acquisition costs.

original entry: An accounting entry, recording a transaction and entering it into an accounting system for the first time.

other assets, deductions, income, or liabilities: Miscellaneous categories on accounting statements, summing up small amounts in all the major standard accounting categories.

Outer Seven: See European Free Trade Association.

outlay: An expenditure, in cash, cash equivalents, or property.

outside audit: See external audit.

outstanding: 1. A collectible or other current debt, due and collectible but as yet uncollected.   **2.** Company ownership shares or debt obligations held by anyone other than the company itself.

overage: Any amount more than is specified in a plan or on a document. The term may be used as either a plus or a minus; production may be over plan and budget, creating an overage; expenditures may be higher than plan or budget, creating an overage.

overbought: The condition of having bought more of something than was economically wise, and of now facing the necessity of selling at less than normal profit or at a loss, as when a retailer buys too much merchandise; sometimes applied to a whole market, as when a company stock is bid up by speculators and has nowhere to go but down.

overcapitalization: The existence of capital stock in a company valued at more than the company's assets are really worth, creating a situation in which company assets cannot possibly yield even a minimally reasonable rate of return on capital, thus forcing a reassessment and reorganization of capital structure.

overdraft: The amount by which a call on established credit exceeds the credit available; usually the amount by which a check exceeds the balance in the bank account on which it is drawn.

overdue: Any obligation that has passed beyond the date it was due to be fulfilled; usually refers to a debt obligation that has become due and payable but has not yet been paid, but can also refer to some other kind of timed contractual obligation, such as completion of a construction contract.

overexpansion: The development of far more productive capacity than is justified by current and near-term business prospects; consequently a drain on cash, profits, and sometimes credit and stockholder relations.

overextended account: A borrowing account in which the borrower cannot pay obligations due and payable.

overextension: Spending or borrowing far beyond prudent limits, as when so much has been spent on plant expansion beyond sales prospects as to endanger company credit relationships; or an investor has bought far more stock on margin than that investor's net worth indicates prudent; or so much has been borrowed, reborrowed, and expanded that current borrowings are far too great for prudent bankers to justify.

overhead: All costs that cannot be directly attributed to the output of goods and services.

overhead rate: A preset rate at which overhead costs are charged against production and other operating units; can be charged as a percentage of overhead incurred within a unit or a percentage charged for company-wide overhead costs or both.

overheated: Describing the condition of an economy experiencing an unusually high rate and volume of economic activity, accompanied by inflation.

overlying mortgage: A mortgage that is subordinate to other mortgages, and therefore a junior mortgage.

overnight loan: A short term loan extended literally overnight by a bank to securities dealers, to finance securities transactions consummated by dealers on which payment has not yet been received.

overproduction: More production than there is demand for goods and services; therefore always used as relative to consumption, dependent upon the level of consumption, and often called underconsumption.

Overseas Private Investment Corporation (OPIC): A Federal agency providing catastrophe insurance for American companies operating abroad, in such matters as nationalization, frozen bank accounts and damage resulting from terrorism.

oversold: Describing a stock or a market which is thought to have been sold more than is economically justified, and therefore to have declined in price to an unrealistic level.

oversubscription: Purchase by the public of more securities than the amount of a securities issue, resulting from simultaneous sale of the issue by a number of sellers; usually handled by pro rata cutting of buyers' purchases.

over-the-counter market: The market for securities not listed on any United States stock exchange, which are traded nationally and internationally directly between buyers and sellers, usually through dealers.

overvaluation: 1. The placing of a higher than reasonable valuation figure upon property; often the subject of property tax disputes. **2.** Governmental support of a national currency at exchange rates higher than those which would occur if that currency were allowed to float freely, to reach its value against all other world currencies as economic and world currency market conditions would determine.

owner: One who has legal title to property.

owner's equity: See net worth.

ownership: See owner.

P

package: A container, whether something physically holding goods or a document holding a group of ideas or agreements.

package mortgage: A mortgage that includes some items of personal property, such as kitchen and laundry equipment in a house mortgage, that mortgage then becoming a loan on house, land, and personal property, all treated as realty.

padding: Adding non-existent expenses, by falsely increasing real expenses or by stating wholly imaginary expenses; for example, adding imaginary cash out of pocket expenses to an expense account, or adding non-existent workers to a construction contract and then billing for costs beyond original estimates. Padding is usually actionable fraud.

paid-in capital: The total capital put into a corporation by its stockholders, including cash, property, service, and any other item of value than can be evaluated, and including both initial capital and any later contributions to capital.

paid-in surplus: The net of all capital put into a corporation by its stockholders minus the par value of the corporation's stock, including the difference between the par value of stock and the price at which it is sold to the public, plus all additional capital.

P & L: See income statement.

panic: A crisis in public confidence in the economy, triggering a depression, such as the Great Depression that started with the stock market panic of October, 1929; often used as a synonym for depression.

paper: A general description of such short-term loans as those evidenced by commercial paper and treasury bills.

paper money: Money issued by a government on paper, rather than in coins, which may or may not be convertible to precious metals. United States paper money is not so convertible, and is backed only by the full faith and credit of the federal government.

paper profit: A so far unrealized gain; usually used to describe increases in the value of securities since bought by their current owner. In one sense, the profits are real—securities used as collateral are valued at current market prices rather than prior purchase prices.

par: Full stated value, as indicated on the face of an instrument. Therefore, a stock's par value is its face value, and a check cleared at par is a check cleared at its full stated value, without discount or premium.

parent company: A company holding controlling interests in other companies, which are subsidiaries.

Pareto's law: The theory, developed by Vilfredo Pareto, that income distribution in a given economy tends to remain constant.

par exchange rate: See exchange rate.

parity: The principle, established as a matter of national policy, that prices for farm products shall be maintained by the Federal Government through price support payments to farmers. Parity is aimed at providing farmers with prices which will give them purchasing power, as consumers, roughly equal to their purchasing power in the years 1910-1914, which are used as a base period in computing parity payment rates.

Parkinson's Law: The rule that "Work expands so as to fill the time available for its completion," stated by C. Northcote Parkinson.

par list: A list of banks clearing checks at full stated value, without discount or premium, as published by the Federal Reserve, and consisting of most of the banks in the United States, including all Federal Reserve member banks.

parol contract: See oral agreement.

partially blind pool partnership: In real estate investment, a limited partnership in which some but not all of the assets to be acquired by the partnership are known to the investor at the time of purchase of the limited partnership interest.

participating bonds: Bonds that combine debt and some measure of equity participation, by paying both a fixed rate of interest and, under some conditions, dividends out of company earnings.

participating preferred stock: Preferred stock carrying both a fixed rate of interest and the right to a share of profits, under some conditions.

participation: 1. The share an investor or investing organization takes of a new securities issue. **2.** The share taken by a party to a joint venture, business organization, or any other pool of shared assets.

participation loan: A loan made by one bank in which another bank shares part of the risk and return, as when a large loan is made by several banks acting together, or when a large bank joins a smaller bank in taking a risk.

partition: The division of commonly owned or tenanted land, or of any commonly owned or held real or personal property, into separately owned units, as on dissolution of a partnership.

partner: One who has joined with others in some form of legal partnership.

partner's equity: See net worth.

partnership: The association of two or more people for the purpose of doing business together for profit. The main form is that of the general partnership, carrying with it unlimited liability, as well as the ability to bind and be bound by the commitments of individual partners, and needing no formal written agreements between the parties to be recognized in law as valid.

par value: The face value of a stock; usually quite different from market value, which normally is considerably higher.

passbook: A record-keeping book issued by a bank to its savings depositors, in which deposits, withdrawals, interest, and current balances are recorded and updated as transactions occur; also sometimes used in combined savings-checking accounts, but rarely in purely checking accounts.

passbook loan: A bank loan using as collateral the deposit balance in a savings account as shown in a passbook.

passed dividend: A regular dividend payment that, when due, is not voted by a corporation; usually due to business problems, and rarely otherwise done, as it is often seen as a clear indication that the corporation is in trouble.

past due: See overdue.

patent: A document issued and recorded by government, attesting that all rights to the invention patented belong to the specified patent holder, including manufacture, distribution, and licensing; patents are also protected by international agreements, signed by most nations.

patent pending: A statement by government that a patent has been applied for; usually printed or otherwise affixed to a product or process for which patent has been applied for and not yet granted to serve as a warning to others against patent infringement, because patent protection will be considered in effect retroactively since registration, when and if granted.

pawnbroker: One who lends money, holding personal property as collateral for the loan, and charging relatively high rates; used by those borrowers who are otherwise virtually unable to borrow from conventional lenders.

pay as you go: The payment of financial obligations on a current basis, rather than incurring debts; increasingly rare in modern business, personal and governmental financial practice.

payback period: The time it takes for a capital investment to return the amount invested, in terms of savings, increased productivity, or any other investment result that can be reduced to number quantities.

payee: That person or organization to whom a debt instrument, such as a note, check, or money order, is made payable.

payment: A sum paid another in settlement of an obligation, or pursuant to an agreement, whether complete or partial; also the act of paying.

payment terms: The way in which payment is to be accomplished, as specified in the agreement between payer and payee; for example, repayment of a loan in installments or cash on delivery in payment for a purchase.

payoff: Money paid for illegal purposes, such as bribes and kickbacks; also called payola.

payola: See payoff.

payor: One who is responsible for payment, and is so named on a debt instrument, such as a note, check, or money order.

payout period: See payback period.

PC: See professional corporation.

peak: The highest point, whether of a mountain, a business cycle, or market.

peculation: See embezzlement.

pecuniary: That which relates to money, the word most often being used as a synonym for money, as in pecuniary benefit, meaning money benefit, or pecuniary exchange, meaning exchanging money or goods for money.

pegging: Price fixing and price maintenance, using a variety of devices to hold prices at or very near a predetermined point; sometimes illegal, as in the instance of collusive price fixing by United States companies selling domestically; sometimes a matter of national policy, as in the fixing of currency exchange rates or farm prices; sometimes the result of international agreement, as in the fixing of oil export prices by an international cartel.

penny stocks: Very low priced, usually highly speculative common stocks, most often sold in over-the-counter markets, rather than on stock exchanges.

pension: A long series of payments made to a retired person or former employee, usually for the balance of a lifetime, by former private or public employers, or by government. Pensions may be payable only upon retirement from a job, upon a combination of retirement from a job reaching a specified age, or only upon reaching a specified age alone, as in the instance of Social Security benefits.

P/E ratio: See price-earnings ratio.

per capita: Latin for "per head." An average, computed by dividing a total sum by the amount of people in a given group to find the amount per person; for example, per capita income is average income per person.

percentage depletion: A Federal income tax allowance for the depletion or using up of resources in the extractive industries, such as oil, gas, coal, metals, and minerals, allowing income tax deductions based on a specified percentage of gross income, with no direct relation to the cost of the property being so depleted. Percentages allowed vary with the kind of resource.

percentage lease: A business lease providing for computation of rentals to be paid wholly or partly as a percentage of gross business income; very often used in franchise agreements.

percentile: A 100-unit system of ranking items in a frequency distribution, often used in testing, with the percentile indicating the number of people at or below the point specified; for example, a score in the 91st percentile means that only 9 percent of those tested scored better. Related ranking systems are the decile, which used a 10-unit ranking system, and the quartile, which uses 4 units.

perfect competition: See pure competition.

performance: The results shown by an investment vehicle or company, in terms of such indicators as market price, earnings, yield, and other key indicators of present health and future prospects.

performance fee: Fees paid to those managing investments based upon the performance of those investments; usually as a bonus in addition to normal compensation arrangements. Sometimes such fees are paid to management organizations, rather than to individual managers.

performance fund: A mutual fund focusing on investments in speculative securities, taking high risks for anticipated high profits.

period cost: A cost that is attributable to a time period, rather than to a product; usually a fixed cost, such as real estate or interest.

period income: Income attributable to a time period, and spread out for accounting purposes over the time properly attributable to it; for example, future interest on bonds already purchased.

perjury: The giving of false information knowingly, under a legally recognized oath in or out of court, before a judge, or any other official empowered to give an oath, or in legally sworn writing; a crime.

perpetual bond: A bond that is an open-ended promise to pay interest indefinitely, and that has no maturity date; or a bond that has such a long life that it is effectively perpetual.

personal check: A check drawn by an individual upon a checking account either in that individual's own name or one that is shared with one or more other individuals.

personal consumption expenditures: Total national spending by the public for consumer goods and services.

personal finance company: See finance company.

personal holding company: A tax avoidance device, now little used because of tax law provisions attacking it, consisting of a corporation formed by a high income individual to circumvent high individual tax rates by holding income in undistributed corporate earnings after paying the lower corporate taxes.

personal income: Gross individual income from all sources, including all income derived from work or property ownership, after expenses and before taxes.

personal loan: A loan made to an individual by a lending institution, such as a bank, credit union or finance company, carrying unlimited obligation to repay, with or without collateral; includes both specific sums loaned and lines of credit.

personal property: All property owned, other than ownership interests in realty and relatively immovable structures attached to realty; includes both tangibles, such as vehicles, books and toothbrushes, and intangibles, such as securities, copyrights, and insurance policies, as well as less-than-ownership interests in land, such as leaseholds.

personal property taxes: See property taxes.

personal service: Legally valid service of such legal process as a subpeona by personal delivery to the person for whom it is intended.

peseta: The main currency unit in Spain, bearing the same relationship to Spain's national currency system as does the dollar to the United States currency system.

peso: The main currency unit of a substantial number of primarily Spanish-speaking countries, including Mexico, Argentina, Bolivia, Cuba, Colombia, and the Phillippines, and bearing the same relationship to those national currency systems as does the dollar to the United States currency system.

Peter Principle: The rule that "In a hierarchy, every employee tends to rise to his level of incompetence," stated by Dr. Laurence J. Peter and Raymond Hull.

petition in bankruptcy: A document filed by a debtor or creditors in court of bankruptcy, asking the court to place the creditor in a legal state of bankruptcy.

petrocurrency: Money paid to oil-producing countries by oil consumers, accumulated in very large quantities and deposited in financial institutions throughout the world; used for a wide variety of purposes by the oil producers, including foreign investment and the purchase of goods and services.

petty cash: A small amount of cash kept on the premises of a business or a small bank account maintained as a matter of convenience in making minor expenditures for miscellaneous small items, such as the office coffee, messenger service, and minor stationery items.

physical life: The potential producing life of a machine or some other inanimate element of production, in contrast to its economic life, which may be cut short by such matters as technological developments causing obsolescence while it is still in good operating condition.

picker: One who finds for and supplies items to dealers and auctioneers, searching for specified items as well as speculatively wherever seems appropriate.

pie chart: A chart representing its object of study as a circle, and its components as wedge-shaped pieces of that circle in varying sizes to show their proportion to the whole.

piracy: Once the illegal taking by force of vessels at sea by unaffiliated robbers, without the legitimization of war or national policy. In our time, the stealing of people, ideas, and processes, whether legally or illegally, as when a patent or copyright is illegally appropriated or an employee is quite legally stolen away by a competitor offering higher pay.

pit: The trading floor of a commodities exchange.

pit trader: One who deals in commodities on behalf of his own account in the pit or on the floor of a commodities exchange.

placement: The sale of securities, whether to the public through public issue or by some private sales means.

planned economy: An economy in which all major economic planning is done by the state, and in which supply and demand operate, if at all, only in some consumer products areas which do not significantly affect the main course of the state's economy; an example is the Soviet Union.

planned obsolescence: Any manufacturing policy and set of devices that are aimed at making products rapidly obsolescent that would otherwise be quite capable of further use, sometimes for years; examples are high fashion clothing, designed and redesigned for quick replacement, and some United States automobiles.

plant: In the widest sense, all fixed assets, including land, buildings, and equipment; but more often used to describe buildings or both land and buildings.

plant and equipment spending: See new plant and equipment spending.

plant capacity: The maximum productive capacity of a given plant, assuming that it is worked seven days a week, 24 hours a day, and 52 weeks a year, but including an estimate of down time for necessary repairs and maintenance.

play: An investment vehicle or opportunity; for example, a silver "play," means an investment in silver, or "the state of the play in gold," means an analysis of the current gold investment situation. The term is synonymous with "action," but without negative gambling overtones in the investment industry.

pledge: The passing of collateral from borrower to lender as security for a loan, with the borrower keeping title but giving actual possession over to the lender, as when an object of value is pawned or securities are held by a bank as collateral on a loan.

plow back: To use profits as money available for investment, rather than money to be distributed to owners; to put profits back into the business.

plunger: One who invests heavily in speculative securities, enterprises, or transactions.

plus tick: A securities trade made at a higher price than the last previous such transaction.

point: 1. In United States securities trading, a dollar. When a stock starts a trading day at 100 and goes up to 102 by the end of that trading day, it is up 2 points for the day. In the stock markets of other countries, a point is the normal currency unit used for describing trades.   **2.** A percentage point, as when a lending institution demands an extra "point," or 1%, of a mortgage, in a lump sum at the start of the payback period before granting that mortgage.

point and figure chart: A graphic representation of price changes in an investment vehicle.

pool: A group of companies formally working together to control any aspect of their business; for example a group of insurance companies may share risks and premiums on certain large and high risk insurance cases, or a group of transportation companies may quite legally set prices together under the provisions of an applicable federal statute. All but a few such pools are outlawed as restraint of trade.

pooling of interests: A merger of interests, often for a limited time or specific purpose, in which those merging truly merge, rather than one party buying out another, with the resulting company reflecting the relative values of each party before merger.

portfolio: The total securities holdings of an inividual or organization, including all stocks, bonds, options, limitcd partnership shares, and any other securities held; in a wider sense, all debts owed by others and all ownership equities.

portfolio management: The professional management of investment portfolios, within discretionary limits agreed upon between the owner of the portfolio and the manager, if the manager is functioning as an independent investment advisor hired by the portfolio owner; also the management of the investment portfolio of an organization by its employees.

position: 1. A commodities or commodities futures holding of any kind.   **2.** The aggregate of all commodities and commodities future positions held by an investor.

positioning: Strategic placement to maximize opportunities and minimize risk; for example, a company considering introduction of a major new product or creating a market image for the product, must consider its positioning.

postdate: To date a document later than the actual date it is executed; most often done on a check so that it cannot be cashed until the date specified, as banks cannot cash postdated checks until they become due.

postindustrial state: John Kenneth Galbraith's descriptive term for an economy thought to be past a major stress on industrialism and the development and maturation of basic industries, focusing more on the quality of life.

pound: The main currency unit of many countries, including Great Britain, Ireland, Israel, Lebanon, Egypt, and Turkey, and bearing the same relationship to those national currency systems as does the dollar to the United States currency system.

power of attorney: Written authorization by one to another to act as an agent capable of making binding decisions regarding assets owned by the authorizer; may be limited to certain assets or for a limited time, or may be unlimited and revocable only by specific act of the authorizer.

power of sale: A mortgagor's or trustee's right, as specified in a mortgage or deed of trust, to sell mortgaged property at public auction to satisfy the debt when mortgage payments have not been kept up and the mortgage is thereby in default; the mortgagor or trustee satisfies as much as possible of the debt from the auction proceeds, with any remainder going to the mortgagee.

predate: To date a document earlier than the actual date it is executed; an act which may invalidate a contract, and which may in some instances lead to violation of law, as in the instance of checks predated to place deductions in a closed tax year for tax evasion purposes.

prediction: See forecast.

pre-emption: 1. The power of government to buy anything for sale ahead of its citizens, at a reasonable valuation.   **2.** The power of a government at war to seize property belonging to neutrals and to conduct a forced sale of that property to its own citizens; just short of confiscation without compensation.   **3.** The power of any individual or institution to buy ahead of others as a matter of right.

pre-emptive rights: The right of present stockholders to buy newly issued stock, as provided by corporate charter; usually granted in some fixed relationship to their current stockholdings.

preference bonds: Bonds on which interest is payable only out of corporate earnings, after all other expenses, including more senior debt obligations, have been paid.

preferential tariff: A tariff that provides preferential treatment for one or more nations as against all others, as when a country charges a former colony considerably lower import duties than it charges other countries.

preferred stock: Stock conferring equity ownership senior to that conferred by common stock, in that it receives dividends in stated amounts before any dividends can be distributed to common stock; sometimes also in that it carries more control over corporate affairs than does common stock. It may be cumulative, receiving dividends owing from previous unmade distributions, or non-cumulative, losing past unmade distributions; it may be participating, sharing to some extent in profits beyond specified dividends, or non-participating, not so sharing; it may be convertible, or capable of being exchanged for common stock at the owner's option.

premium: 1. The amount by which the price of a security or commodity is larger than its face value. **2.** The amount by which a new securities issue exceeds its selling price shortly after issue. **3.** The actual price of an option contract. **4.** Something of value, given by buyer or seller beyond the stated terms of a transaction, such as a toy enclosed in a box of cereal or an extra interest charge on a real estate transaction.

prepaid expense: An expense incurred currently, but properly attributable to future periods for profit and loss statement purposes, unless profit and loss are figured on a cash basis; for example, rent paid in advance for future occupancy; advance payment of insurance premiums or advance payment against anticipated royalties or commissions.

prepayment: Advance payment of obligations that will be due in the future, such as property taxes, mortgages, and debts. When such payment of future obligations operates to reduce future interest payments, there may be prepayment penalties; therefore prepayment is often a privilege specifically covered by contract.

prepayment penalty: A money penalty imposed by contract on a debtor prepaying an installment loan, to compensate for the lender's foregone interest.

prepayment privilege: The right of a debtor paying off an installment loan, such as a mortgage or personal loan, to pay all or part of the balance due earlier than the payment schedule specified in the loan, so effecting a total interest reduction, without a money penalty charged by the lender for prepayment, as partial compensation for that foregone interest.

presentation: The physical presenting of an instrument due to be paid to the party responsible for paying it.

present value method: See discounted cash flow.

pretax dollars: Income before taxes; often describing money used for investing purposes which is in some way tax sheltered and accumulating for the present untaxed or little taxed.

pretax income: Net income before taxes.

price: 1. The amount of money, goods or services offered or asked in return for goods, services or money, that are for sale. Asking prices are prices quoted on that which is for sale; offering prices are bids by potential buyers. **2.** Also, the amount for which something is sold, which is often somewhere between what is asked and what is offered.

price control: The setting of maximum prices for goods and services by government, sometimes as a means of curbing wartime excess profits, often as a means of fighting inflation.

price-earnings ratio (P/E ratio): The relationship between the current market price of a stock and its most recent yearly earnings per share; for example, a stock selling for $20 per share, with previous year's earnings of $2 per share, has a ratio of 20:2, reduced and stated as 10:1.

price fixing: The setting of specific prices to be charged by groups of sellers for goods and services. It is legal when done by government during wartime, in peacetime to curb inflation, or in a regulated industry; if done by private industry, it is an illegal combination in restraint of trade.

price index: A measure of how prices for certain goods and services, or for all goods and services, have risen or fallen in a geographical area during a period of time, when measured against a previous period used as a base or comparison period. The Consumer Price and Wholesale Price Indexes are major national and regional economic indicators.

price leadership: The pricing position held by one firm or relatively few firms in an industry, which act as trend setters for the rest of the industry when making price changes; for example, a few large banks will initiate prime interest rate changes, and most other banks will follow.

price level: The average price paid for any group of goods or services, or for all goods and services, in an area or throughout an economy, measured in money actually paid.

price limit: The price or price range at which a customer instructs a broker to buy or sell securities or commodities.

price performance: The performance of a security, commodity, or market as to market price during any given period, however short or long.

price range: The range within which a security, commodity, or any other item bought or sold on a market is traded within any given period, however short or long, the range consisting of the difference between high and low prices for the period.

price rigidity: The tendency of some goods and services to hold prices within a relatively narrow range, without responding to supply and demand swings; a characteristic of markets dominated by a few large producers or suppliers.

price stabilization: The holding of prices within a narrow range; usually effected by government action, ranging from pressure on business to voluntarily hold current price levels to complete price controls.

price support: Government support of the price levels of specified goods or services, using any of a wide range of devices, including direct payments to producers and a variety of indirect means; used to support the prices of a substantial number of agricultural products.

pricing: The process of establishing prices which will be quoted for goods and services.

pricing policy: The price structure and selling arrangements quoted by a business for the goods and services it sells, usually including such matters as prices, terms, credit arrangements, and discounts.

prima facie: Something which will be presumed to be true unless there is evidence to contradict that presumption, as when evidence presented in a case at law builds a case that will stand, unless successfully rebutted.

primary distribution: See primary issue.

primary issue: A stock issue sold by a company directly or through its underwriters, in contrast to a body of previously issued stock being sold through any distribution channel, known as a secondary issue.

primary market: 1. The market for a new securities issue.   **2.** A main market to which any kinds of goods are sold; for example, the automobile industry is a primary market for steel.   **3.** A first market in which goods are sold; for example, grain to cities containing major grain-milling facilities.

primary offering: See primary issue.

primary reserves: That portion of legally required bank reserves consisting of cash, money held in banks, and money held by the Federal Reserve.

prime: 1. Of very high quality; for example, some bonds, and some commercial paper.   **2.** Sometimes used as an abbreviation of the term prime rate.

prime cost: Direct cost, including materials and labor, but not including any items of indirect cost, such as overhead.

prime mortgage rate: The lowest general interest rate charged on mortgage loans by lenders in a given period, extended to those thought to be excellent credit risks.

prime rate: The lowest interest rates charged by commercial banks to their most favored borrowers, usually extended only to large, well-established, and low risk corporations. As the prime rate changes, all other interest rates in the private sector of the economy tend to follow suit.

primitive: An art work or antique that is thought by professionals in its field to have been produced by relatively untrained creators. Some such works may be substantial works of art, highly prized, and command high prices.

principal: 1. The amount of a loan or note, on which interest is charged.   **2.** An amount invested, on which earnings, such as profits and interest, may accrue.   **3.** One of the parties to a transaction.   **4.** The holder of a substantial ownership share in an enterprise.

principal distributor: A securities firm carrying primary responsibility for selling securities underwritten by others; sometimes a firm which is both underwriter and main distributor. The term is most often encountered in reference to firms selling mutual funds and real estate limited partnerships.

priority: The order of preference enjoyed by creditors and other claimants against bankrupts and estates.

private bank: A bank organized as a partnership or sole proprietorship, rather than as a corporation, and chartered under state banking laws; a very old and widely used form in European banking and in United States investment banking.

private corporation: See closed corporation.

private enterprise: Businesses owned by individual owners, not by government, whether organized as sole proprietorships, partnerships, corporations, or in any other form; such enterprises may be highly regulated or even partly owned by government and still be in the main privately owned.

private enterprise system: See capitalism.

private placement: The selling of stock or debt obligations to a limited number of investors and investing organizations by an issuing company or by a securities firm, but not by public offering.

private property: Property owned by individuals and private organizations, rather than by government.

private sector: That portion of the national economy which is privately rather than publicly owned, including those portions of the economy that are substantially financed by government sudsidy, but owned privately, such as portions of the health care industry.

probate: The validation of a will by act of a court of appropriate jurisdiction, and associated actions by a probate court.

proceeds: The amount actually received by a party to a transaction, such as a borrower or a seller.

process: 1. A production system, in which a series of planned and codified steps results in an end product; usually so codified as to be patentable. **2.** To convert materials into other, usually more refined materials, as in the conversion of metal ores into metals, petroleum into oil products, or harvested agricultural products into fibers and food. **3.** A legal proceeding, including all the steps in that proceeding, from beginning to end. **4.** A legal document summoning a defendant to court.

produce exchange: See commodity exchange.

producer goods: See capital goods.

product cost: See direct cost.

product development: The process of developing new products and processes, of changing the nature and sometimes the market images of old products, and of finding new uses for old products and processes.

production: The process of making goods, as in mining and otherwise extracting or growing raw materials, manufacturing, and otherwise creating finished goods.

production capacity: See capacity.

production method of depreciation: Depreciation based on an estimate of the number of units that can be produced during the useful life of a machine, with each unit to be produced assigned a percentage of total depreciation and that depreciation taken as units are produced.

productivity: The amount of output relative to input involved in producing that output; normally measured for land, labor, or capital, or any component thereof.

productivity of capital: The yield produced by invested capital, as when money invested in securities nets 10% per year or money invested in capital goods yields 9%, but without adjustment for tax factors, which may very significantly alter the real money yield of an investment.

productivity of labor: The quantity and quality of goods produced by labor, usually measured as output per working hour, but varying with such factors as technical levels and techniques of production.

productivity of land: The crop yield of land, usually measured on a per acre basis; varies not only with the quality of the land but also with the quality of labor, machines, techniques and nutrients put into the land.

product liability: The liability of a product's maker or any others involved in the chain of distribution for damages directly or indirectly caused by that product; covers a wide range of possible causes of action, from food containing harmful foreign matter to construction materials containing cancer-causing substances.

product life cycle: The stages of a product's life in its markets, from introduction through maturity through eventual withdrawal by its maker.

product line: A group of related products. A single company may have several product lines; sometimes all of the products of a firm are described as its product line, even though not all products are related.

product mix: The products sold by a company; sometimes the result of planning a series of complementary products, but equally often a group of loosely related products developed separately over the lifetime of the company.

professional corporation (PC): A corporation organized to conduct joint professional practice by several practitioners, such as doctors or lawyers; for many years barred by law, but now authorized in many states, and increasingly used by professionals in many fields.

profile: An outline, briefly describing main characteristics, such as a company profile, outlining the nature, personnel, products, financial structure, and prospects of a company.

profit: 1. The net of revenues and costs, which may be expressed as a plus or minus figure. **2.** Any yield on capital or on entrepeneurial effort, such as the value of a small business built by a combination of a little capital and a great deal of time and effort.

profitability: 1. The net earnings of a business organization. **2.** The extent to which operations produce earnings, usually expressed as a percentage of sales.

profit and loss statement (P&L): See income statement.

profit center: Any portion of a business that is treated by that firm's management and accounting system as a source of costs and revenues, and therefore is capable of being evaluated in profit and loss terms; may apply to a very wide range of activities and unit sizes, and several profit centers may be included within a larger profit center.

profiteering: The taking of unconscionable profits through exploitation of a social or national emergency, such as war or epidemic; in normal times very much in the eye of the beholder.

profit margin: The net of revenues and costs, described in percentile terms.

profit sharing: A kind of additional compensation paid by a company to its employees, in the form of a distribution of some share of current profits to employees, usually as stock, stock options or cash, and often in deferred form, to be held until employee retirement or termination of employment.

profit squeeze: A situation in which profits are dropping, because costs are rising and, for whatever reasons, prices cannot be raised to offset those higher costs; often occurs while volume continues at previous or even higher levels.

profit taking: In securities trading, the selling of securities on which paper gains have been made, to turn those paper gains into real profits; often used to describe selling in a market that has been rising, helping to trigger a levelling off or downturn in prices.

pro forma: Latin for "as a matter of form." In the law, a decision rendered to pave the way for appeal.

pro forma statement: In accounting, a financial statement that, at least in part, makes assumptions as to future events, and that therefore serves only as a model, rather than as a financial statement reflecting reality.

progressive tax: A tax that increases in percentage as taxables increase. For example, Federal income taxes tax income at progressively higher rates as taxable income rises; in contrast, fixed rates of tax, such as many sales taxes, tax all purchases of the same kind at the same rate.

promissory note: A written promise to pay another or the bearer of the note a specific sum, at some time in the future or on demand.

promoter: One who takes an entrepreneurial role in the development of an enterprise, such as the development of a new company or a single event, such as a boxing match; used most in describing those who organize sports events.

propensity to consume: The proportion of income people tend to spend, at various income levels and as incomes rise.

propensity to hoard: See liquidity preference.

propensity to import: A country's tendency to import more as national income rises, but limited by government policy in planned economies.

propensity to save: The proportion of income people tend to save at various income levels.

property: That which can in any way be legally owned, by any individual, organization, or by the state, including real and personal property, tangible and intangible property.

property tax: Any tax imposed by government on real or personal property; most often on real property.

proprietary: 1. Exclusively owned. **2.** Relating to a specific owner, or to owners and ownership generally.

proprietary accounts: In accounting, those accounts containing ownership amounts.

proprietary interest: An ownership interest, as in the interest held by an equity holder in a company or a patent holder who licenses use of the patent by others.

proprietary lease: A lease which grants certain proprietary rights to the lessee, but continues ownership in the lessor, as in the instance of a cooperative apartment lease.

proprietor: 1. An owner of a business or one who has legal title to something, such as a patented process or design. **2.** In general usage, any business owner.

proprietor's equity: See net worth.

proprietorship: See sole proprietorship.

pro rata: Proportional division of amounts, as in the division of overhead costs among several products or of utility charges among users sharing a single meter.

prospectus: A fully detailed description of every significant aspect of a business offering stock for public sale and of that stock, including financial matters, personnel, products if any, and all other pertinent business data.

prosperity: Good times, characterized by peace, growth in gross national product, growing real wages, increasing profits, a low inflation rate, and general optimism as to the economic future.

protective tariff: A tariff aimed at protecting domestic businesses from competition in domestic markets by products from abroad.

protest: A statement in writing and certified by a notary public, declaring that a negotiable instrument has been presented for payment or acceptance and has been rejected.

provenance: The history of a work of art, antique, or collectible; often of major importance in assessing authenticity and establishing market value.

proximate cause: That which is the prime, immediate cause of the happening of an event, and without which the event would not have happened.

proxy: A written statement, legally authorizing another to vote stock capable of being voted by the authorizer; a normal arrangement in many publicly held corporations, with management routinely soliciting the proxies of shareholders, but also used by those trying to win control of a corporation away from its current management.

proxy statement: An explanatory written statement required by law to be attached to a proxy solicitation by whomever is soliciting the proxy.

prudent man rule: A general guide to legally acceptable investment action on the part of those investing funds in some sort of fiduciary capacity, indicating that those funds should be invested in such securities as a "prudent man" would invest in, rather than in speculative securities; in practice, the rule results in considerable conservatism on the part of those so investing.

public corporation: 1. A corporation which has issued stock through general sale to the public, and which is therefore at least partially owned by those shareholders. **2.** A corporation set up by government and owned wholly or partially by goverment.

public debt: The total of all debts owed by every governmental body in a country; in the United States, the total of Federal, state, and local debts.

public finance: The formal study of the financial activities of government, in such areas as borrowing and spending policies and procedures, public debt management, and tax policy.

public housing: Housing that is financed, built under the direction of, and operated by government; usually but not always aimed at meeting the housing needs of people of small to moderate income.

public offering: An offering of an original issue of stock through public sale.

public ownership: The ownership of any organization by government, as in a federally owned public utility, such as the Tennessee Valley Authority or a city-owned transportation line.

public property: Anything owned by any government, including both real property and that which would otherwise be personal property.

public sale: The disposition of property at a sale open to the public, at auction, or at fixed prices.

public sector: That portion of the national economy which is occupied with the economic activities of government, including all ways in which a government spends or receives money and the entire public payroll.

public service commission: The most common name for state agencies charged with the regulation of and rate-setting for public utilities in the best interests of state citizens, while allowing the utilities reasonable profits.

public spending: The amounts spent by government for all or any purposes.

public utilities: Those basic functions so directly supplying public needs, and at the same time so prone to becoming monopolies, that government recognizes their essentially monopolistic nature and by law regulates their prices and other activities, such as telephone, power, water, and some transportation companies.

public utility bonds: The debt obligations of such public utilities as gas and electric companies; often secured by mortgages on company plant and equipment, and generally regarded as high quality bonds.

public utility commission: See public service commission.

public utility stocks: Ownership equities in such public utilities as gas and electric companies; due to the protected and regulated position of these companies, usually regarded as high quality, relatively stable stocks.

public works: A wide range of projects funded by government to serve public interests, such as canals, bridges, dams, roads, and power projects.

pump priming: An attempt by government to stimulate business activity and economic growth in times of recession or depression by direct spending, usually on the kinds of public works that create substantial numbers of immediate jobs for the unemployed.

purchase money mortgage: A mortgage accompanying a property sales transaction, given by buyer to seller as all or part of the purchase price.

purchase syndicate: See underwriting syndicate.

purchasing power: How much a unit of currency, an individual, a group, or an entire economy can buy, relative to some previous period.

pure competition: A market in which all sellers compete equally, supply is high, and no one has any influence on supply, demand, or price; a largely theoretical construct.

put: A stock option contract, enabling its holder to sell a stock at a specific price at any time during the contract period; often used as a hedge by bears, those who believe that the market or that particular stock will drop in value.

put and call: A double option, to either buy or sell the same stock at different specified prices within the same period.

put and call broker: An options broker.

pyramiding: 1. The selling of dealerships, distributorships, or franchises essentially for resale, resulting in short-term high profits for promoters and early investors, and ultimately in the defrauding of later investors.   **2.** The building of equity positions on paper profits, by using the profits in margined accounts to buy more stock.   **3.** A corporate acquisition technique that builds a chain of controlled companies, by using the assets and borrowing power of some acquired companies to buy others.

Q

qualified indorsement: 1. An indorsement that in some way limits the free negotiability of the indorsed instrument, such as "for deposity only." **2.** An indorsement "without recourse," which attempts to remove or limit the liability of the current indorser if the instrument is ultimately unpaid or for some reason not accepted for payment.

qualified stock option: An employee benefit, enabling employees to buy shares of their corporations at stated prices within a specified future period, making it possible for the employees to buy stocks at lower than market prices within the option period or to forego buying if market prices should drop below option prices; subject to legal restrictions imposed by laws and regulations, and qualifying for special tax treatment through compliance with those laws and regulations.

quantity theory of money: The theory that the amount of money in circulation will directly affect prices and spending, less money in circulation causing higher prices and more money in circulation causing lower prices.

quartile: See percentile.

quasi-public corporation: A privately owned corporation recognized in law and practice as having public responsibilities, such as a public utility; therefore a corporation that is very highly regulated and expected to behave at last partly in the public interest.

quick asset ratio: See acid test.

quick assets: Assets that are quickly and easily convertible into cash, such as cash and readily marketable securities.

quick knock: At an auction, rapid consummation of the sale by the auctioneer after a bid considered final, signified by a rap of the auctioneer's gavel with little time allowed for those still uncertain to make another bid.

quick ratio: See acid test.

quick turn: A rapid sale following a securities purchase; normally a speculative purchase followed by a sale to turn a quick profit.

quitclaim: 1. A release given by one to another, giving up any claim against the other as to a specific matter. **2.** A release giving up claim to title; for example, title to land.

quitclaim deed: A deed given by one to another, passing claim, interest, or title to that other, but not claiming to have clear title to pass. If title is legally capable of being conveyed, the quitclaim deed serves to pass title.

quota: A limit, such as the maximum amount of a certain kind of import that may be brought into a country in a given period.

quotation: The current market price, both bid and asked, of securities and commodities.

quoted price: The current market price of a security or commodity, determined by the price of the last purchase in that market; somewhat different prices may be quoted in different markets at the same time.

R

raid: An attempt by securities speculators and traders to cause the price of one or more securities to drop; an illegal market manipulation.

rally: A turnaround in stock market prices, in which previously dropping prices bound upward; applied rather indiscriminately by traders to both large and small upward price movements.

rand: The main currency unit of the Union of South Africa, bearing the same relationship to South Africa's national currency system as does the dollar to the United States currency system.

R and D: See research and development.

rate: A seller's quoted price.

rate base: The amount thought to be invested in a public utility, which provides a base upon which a fair rate of return may be calculated, when determining a regulated public utility's proper rates.

rated capacity: See capacity.

rate of exchange: See exchange rate.

rate of interest: See interest rate.

rate of return: See yield.

rate regulation: The process of setting public utility rates engaged in by state and local public utility commissions.

ratings: See bond ratings.

ratio chart: A type of statistical chart that presents relative, rather than absolute, changes, often using special types of graphing paper such as semi-logarithmic paper.

ratio-to-moving-average technique: In statistics, a way of developing measures of seasonal and other fluctuations by comparing moving averages with historic trends.

reacquired stock: Stock that has been sold by the corporation to shareholders and then in some way acquired by the company to become treasury stock; usually because of a decision to buy back outstanding stock but sometimes due to gift or bequest.

reaction: A decline in securities prices, thought to be caused by some event or combination of events; for example, a decline following a sharp rise in prices, a decline following a major political event, or a decline following a rise in interest rates.

readjustment: The restructuring of a corporation's debt and capital structure by voluntary act of the corporation; in contrast to reorganization, which is involuntary and results from legal process.

real account: In accounting, an account that is carried forward from one fiscal period to another, and is a balance sheet item, in contrast to a nominal account, in which transactions are completed within a single fiscal period.

real cost: 1. The cost of an item measured by its relationship to other items, as in a barter system; for example, one sack of grain is worth two bags of salt.   **2.** The cost of an item measured in money terms, but adjusted to allow for that money's inflation or deflation; for example, one sack of grain worth $10 in 1967 may be worth $22 today, but its real cost may still be only $10 in terms of base year 1967 money.   **3.** A synonym for opportunity cost.

real cost of borrowing: The net of true interest minus the rate of inflation, without allowing for hidden inflation, which does not show up in government figures indicating the current rate of inflation.

real estate: Land and anything held in law to be permanently attached to that land, including structures and some kinds of fixtures and equipment; real property, as distinguished from personal property.

real estate bond: A bond secured by a real estate mortgage; a debt obligation of its issuer backed by the issuer's promise to pay and further backed by the underlying value of the mortgaged property.

real estate fund: A publicly owned real estate limited partnership.

real estate investment trust (REIT): A fund dedicated to real estate investments, and accorded special federal tax treatment; in practice operating much as does a mutual fund.

real estate tax: A kind of property tax, levied on real estate; part of a considerable body of state and local taxes.

real income: Income adjusted for the impact of inflation and deflation on purchasing power, usually calculated by comparing price changes with income changes, using a specified year as a base year for both; for example, apparent income may have doubled between 1970 and now, expressed in dollars, but prices as measured by the Consumer Price Index may have risen 100% in the same period, yielding a net result of no change in real income—though such change may also be affected by changes in other factors, such as the proportion of income spent on tax payments.

realize: To convert something of possible or anticipated value into cash or near-cash equivalents; for example, to sell stock that has gone up in value since purchased, or to sell goods in stock to a consumer.

realized appreciation: The difference between the purchase price paid by the seller of something of value and a later higher selling price; for example, on stock or land sold.

realized depreciation: See recaptured depreciation.

real national income: See real income.

real property: An ownership or other legal interest in real estate, including land, structures and some kinds of fixtures and equipment.

real wages: See real income.

recapitalization: A substantial change in the amount or nature of the securities issued by a corporation, especially as regards capital restructuring to cover debts or deficits with new capital.

recapture of depreciation: For Federal tax purposes, that part of the net selling price minus book value which is due to depreciation deductions taken by the seller while the asset was in its hands, and on sale is to be treated as ordinary income by the seller.

receipt: 1. A written acknowledgment that something has been received, capable of being used as legal evidence of such receipt; for example, a warehouse receipt for goods delivered to that warehouse, or a store receipt for goods purchased from that store.   **2.** The act of receiving cash or any other assets, to be recorded on books of account.

receivables: 1. That which is now or will be collectible, in the forms of accounts and notes receivable.   **2.** In accounting, a statement of the total of all accounts and notes receivable.

receiver: A court-appointed custodian of the assets of a debtor, charged with saving whatever of the debtor's assets can be used to satisfy creditors; limited to the custodial role, as the trustee in bankruptcy is appointed by the court to maintain and restore as much of a going business as is possible.

receivership: In law, the position of an insolvent business, one being managed by a court-appointed receiver, rather than by its previous management.

recession: A strong and relatively long-term downturn in the national economy, characterized by increased unemployent and a lower level of business activity, but less deep and protracted than a depression, such as the Great Depression of the 1930's.

reciprocal business: Orders placed with favored customers, in return for reciprocal orders. In the securities industry, securities orders placed in return for reciprocating orders, and in some instances as hidden payment for services rendered.

reciprocity: A principle stated in some international trade arrangements, in which nations agree to supply each other with goods and services on mutually agreed-upon favorable terms.

reconciliation: The process of balancing related accounts in a double entry bookkeeping system, and the documents evidencing that such balancing has been completed.

record: Any written or otherwise stored information, usually in sequential form for multiple items; examples include accounting information stored in books of record and legal proceedings, often referred to in the law as the record.

record date: The date officially set by a corporation for a dividends or rights distribution; stockholders must be recorded as such on the corporation's books on or before that date to participate in that distribution.

recorder of deeds: A government official responsible for the recording of documents relating to real estate transactions in official books of records.

recourse: The extent to which one who has an obligation can be legally held to that obligation. For example, the maker of a personal note has unlimited liability to pay that note, but if the note is "nonrecourse,'' the lender has agreed to accept only the borrower's promise to pay, backed by whatever collateral is specified, if any, and has no ability to compel payment from other borrower resources.

recovery: 1. Something, usually of value, awarded by a court to a plaintiff as a result of a successful action at law.   **2.** The collection of all or part of a debt that had been treated as uncollectible.   **3.** An upward move to a previous higher level, as when securities prices fluctuate.   **4.** The move of a whole economy toward relative prosperity after a recession or depression.

redeemable bond: A bond that may be recovered by its issuer before its maturity date, on payment of its face value and usually an additional premium amount to its holders.

redemption: 1. The recovery of a debt instrument by its maker through repayment of the debt it evidences; for example, the recovery of a note after payment, or the retirement of a bond issue at maturity or at full payment before maturity.   **2.** The right to buy back an obligation, by payment of money or performance of an obligation, as provided by law and the specific provisions of applicable contracts.

redemption fund: See sinking fund.

redemption price: The price at which something may be bought back; for example, the price at which a bond may be retired by its issuer before maturity.

red herring: A preliminary prospectus, offering a new issue of securities for public examination; but without some of the details offered in the final prospectus, which actually offers the securities for public sale.

red ink: Referring to a minus entry in accounting records, which was traditionally written in red ink; but in a wider sense indicating losses rather than desired profits.

rediscounting: The act of making second and subsequent discounts of commercial paper passing between banks or between banks and Federal Reserve banks; for example, the discounting of a note by a bank when paying it and passage of that note to a Federal Reserve bank to raise funds in a second or rediscounting transaction.

rediscount rate: The interest rate charged to member banks by the Federal Reserve on rediscounted paper only; synonymous with discount rate.

referee in bankruptcy: An officer appointed by a bankruptcy court, responsible for fact finding, hearing, and preliminary adjudication steps under the supervision of the court, and who, if bankruptcy is declared by the court, functions as temporary administrator of a bankrupt's assets.

refinancing: The replacement of existing debts with new debts, usually extending the term of debt repayment, whether as a matter of convenience or economic necessity on the part of the borrower; for example, the replacement of an existing mortgage with a larger mortgage, supplying needed cash, more and smaller payments, or both; or the replacement of corporate or government bonds about to mature with new bonds carrying a maturity date years in the future.

reflation: A governmental policy aimed at moving economic activity, prices, and wages to higher than current levels, usually by means of inflationary money, tax, and credit policies and usually in the presence of recession or depression.

refunding: See refinancing.

regional stock exchange: A stock exchange operating in a limited geographic area, listing the securities of companies headquartered in its region as well as those of companies listed on other, major exchanges.

register: A body of information about a specific kind of thing or transaction, maintained in writing in sequence or in a data base capable of being called forth in sequence. Examples are sequenced accounting entries, usually kept in book or journal form; a list of ships registered as vessels of a particular country; a list of lawyers, accountants, doctors, or dentists practicing in a geographical area; or a corporation's stockholders list.

registered bond: A bond carrying the name of its owner on its face, and so recorded on the books of its issuer. It may not be negotiated unless endorsed by its owner and transferred on the books of its issuer.

registered check: A check purchased from a bank rather than drawn on funds deposited with that bank, in practice functioning as a money order, though called a kind of check.

registered coupon bond: A type of registered bond that is registered to its owner, but carries interest-paying coupons negotiable by delivery, as do non-registered bonds.

registered representative: One who is licensed by the Securities and Exchange Commission to sell securities and is employed by a brokerage firm doing business on the floor of a stock exchange, through its own floor broker or by arrangement with another securities firm. Registered representatives buy and sell securities for customers through floor brokers.

registered stock: Stock that is recorded on the books of its issuer in the name of its owner, and which cannot be transferred without that owner's signature and transfer on those books.

register of deeds: See recorder of deeds.

registrar: An agent, employed by a corporation issuing securities, usually a banking organization, to perform all authentication and checking functions in relation to an issue, to prevent issuance of unauthorized, counterfeit, or otherwise illegal securities.

registration: The process of officially registering securities with the appropriate Federal and state regulatory authorities, involving a series of documents and clearances, so that the securities may be offered for public sale.

registration statement: A document filed by a prospective securities issuer with the appropriate regulatory authorities, which must grant official clearance before those securities are cleared for public sale; such a statement includes substantial financial, other business, and personal information relating to the securities issue, its issuer, and the leading people associated with the issue.

regression analysis: In statistics, a way of examining and predicting the behavior of unknown factors by casting them against the behavior of known factors, the unknown factor being called the dependent variable, and the known factor being called the independent variable. For example, assembly line error rate might be predictable if cast against the speed of the line, with the percentage of error increasing as the speed of the line increases. The casting of one known against one unknown is simple regression analysis; of one or more unknowns against one or more knowns multiple regression analysis.

regressive tax: A tax that is proportionately heavier on those of small income than on those of large income. For example, a sales tax, on which all pay equal amounts of tax per dollar spent, is regressive, contrasting with a progressive tax, in which tax rates rise with income.

regular dividend: A dividend that is customarily and regularly paid by a corporation, usually on an annual, semi-annual, or quarterly basis. It may be paid out of current profits or reserves; it may be unchanged in amount for many years, or raised or lowered at any time of payment by the corporation's Board of Directors. If not paid when scheduled, it is passed and lost.

Regulation Q: The Federal Reserve regulation specifying the top limit on interest payable by member banks on regular savings accounts.

Regulation T: The Federal Reserve regulation specifying the top margin credit allowable by brokers and dealers to their customers.

Regulation U: The Federal Reserve regulation specifying the top amount of credit bankers may advance their customers for the purpose of buying listed securities; a regulation that is companion to Regulation T, aimed at preventing the use of bank credit in circumvention of margin requirements.

reinvestment: The investment of funds stemming from other investments rather than taking those funds out of investment; for example, the investment of funds resulting from maturing bonds or stock sales in other bonds or stocks; or the investment of funds resulting from dividends paid on stock and interest paid on bonds in more of the same stocks and bonds.

REIT: See Real Estate Investment Trust.

remainder: A future interest in an estate after all prior interests have been satisfied. The person who holds such an interest, under the terms of an estate, is called a remainderman.

remainderman: One who is to receive the remainder of an estate after all prior interests set up by the terms of the estate have been satisfied; for example, a child who takes the remainder of an estate that, on the death of one parent pays income to the other parent for life, with the entire estate and its income going to the child on the second parent's death.

remittance: A payment, usually on a debt or other financial obligation; sometimes used more widely to describe any sum of money sent by one party to another.

remonetization: The restoring of a metal to the status of money, after having removed it from that status; for example, bringing back gold as money and issuing a currency fully recoverable in gold after having gone over to a paper money backed not by gold, as it once was, but rather solely by the full faith and credit of the government issuing that paper money.

remuneration: Pay, in whatever form; for tax purposes, including a wide range of non-cash items, such as many, though not all, kinds of fringe benefits.

renewal: The extension of a debt, by its replacement with another debt; for example, the replacement of a loan due to be paid to a bank with another loan to be paid later. A loan may be renewed again and again, in practice constituting a line of credit.

rent: Payment for the right to use anything tangible, including land, buildings and equipment, usually for a specified period of time, but sometimes for the use itself, as when a machine is rented for a single use rather than for a period of time.

rentier: From the French, someone whose income is largely dependent on the proceeds of investments yielding fixed dollar amounts, rather than varying with economic conditions; a highly vulnerable economic position in periods of inflation.

reorganization: The involuntary restructuring of a corporation's debt and capital structure, as ordered by a court of law, under circumstances of insolvency and pursuant to the bankruptcy statutes; in contrast to readjustment, which is voluntary.

reorganization bonds: Bonds issued by a company as part of the process of reorganization, replacing previous debt obligations.

replacement cost: What it would cost to replace an asset, usually part of plant and equipment, at current prices.

replacement method of depreciation: The addition of straight line depreciation and a factor for replacement cost, when replacement cost is estimated higher than original cost; for example, when replacement costs are estimated as $5,000 higher than the original cost of, and the depreciable life of the item is 10 years, $500 per year for ten years would be added to the straight line depreciation of the item. Generally not an acceptable mode of depreciation to accountants and taxing authorities.

repledge: To use a borrower's collateral as collateral for a loan to the original lender. For example a bond that has been pledged as security for a loan may be used by the original lender as collateral for a different loan. Repledging requires some form of consent by the original borrower, who owns the collateral although it has been so pledged.

reporting period: The period of time covered by a report; usually applied to a report issued regularly, such as a quarterly or annual report.

representative money: Paper money issued by a national government that is backed to its full value by stores of precious metal, in contrast to paper money that is backed wholly or partly only by the full faith and credit of the government.

reproduction cost: An estimate of the cost of reproducing a specific kind of fixed asset at current prices.

repudiation: The act of refusing to fulfill an obligation; usually a refusal to pay a debt. As a practical matter, legally enforceable private debts cannot be repudiated, as legal process will result, but governments can and do repudiate debts.

repurchase agreement: A legally enforceable contract between buyer and seller that specifies the seller's right to buy back what is being sold on specified prices and terms; a device often used in sale and leaseback agreements.

research and development (R and D): Investigation aimed at developing new products and processes, whether directly through applications research or indirectly through basic research.

reserve balances: Reserves held by member banks of the Federal Reserve System in the form of Federal Reserve bank deposits.

reserve currency: A national currency recognized as so stable that many nations keep their foreign exchange reserves in that currency, as well as in gold or any other internationally recognized medium of exchange; for example, United States currency in the period following World War II.

reserve fund: A fund set aside for a specific purpose, consisting of cash or cash equivalents, and recognized as such for accounting purposes.

reserve price: See upset price.

reserve ratio: The relationship between the deposits of a commercial bank and its vault cash or deposits in a Federal Reserve bank; that ratio is set by each Federal Reserve bank.

reserve requirement: The amount of commercial bank deposits that each Federal Reserve bank requires be held by those banks in each Federal Reserve District; a primary means of Federal money market manipulation.

reserves: 1. Actual funds held to meet obligations or potential obligations; for example, bank reserves, national gold reserves, company reserves held for special purposes, and legally required insurance company reserves held to meet potential claim obligations. **2.** In accounting, a series of accounts set aside for specific reasons, such as reserves against amortization, bad debts, contingencies, depletion, and repairs.

residence: A place where one lives or maintains some kind of abode. One may have many residences, in fact and for legal purposes, but only one domicile, which for legal purposes is recognized as the principal living place.

residuary estate: That portion of an estate that remains, if any, after disposition of all that has been specifically covered by the terms of a will and satisfaction of all debts and expenses in connection with the estate.

resistance level: Any securities or commodities price level, whether for a single security or a whole market, at which advances or declines have previously tended to stall.

restoration: Any and all repairs, refinishing, and rebuilding aimed at restoring an art work, antique, or collectible as nearly as possible to its original condition.

restorer: One who is professionally engaged in the practice of restoration.

restraint of trade: The concept that businesses may attempt to control competition, and by so doing limit freedom of competition; a basic concept in the development of the entire body of United States anti-trust law, which attempts to make combinations and other actions in restraint of trade illegal.

restricted stock: Stock which by the terms of its issue cannot be freely traded; for example, stock offered under an employee compensation plan, which must be held conditionally for some time, or unregistered stock, which is restricted as long as it is held.

restrictive convenant: A contract provision limiting free use of property by its owner, usually encountered in real estate contracts; for example, requirements that new home styles in a housing development be approved by a homeowner's committee, or the now-illegal restriction of the sale of homes to whites.

restrictive endorsement: An endorsement on a negotiable instrument that limits or destroys its further free negotiability; for example, "for deposit only to the account of . . . " is a common restrictive endorsement on the back of a check.

retained earnings: Company earnings after taxes that are held by the company rather than being distributed as dividends to shareholders; such earnings often fuel long-term capital needs.

retaliatory tariff: A tariff levied by one country on the products of another, or on products heavily exported by another, because of tariffs previously levied by that other; sometimes part of an escalating series of protective tariffs between several countries, sharply limiting trade for a period.

retire: To remove from circulation and end the life of financial instruments, such as bonds paid at maturity.

retrenchment: Cutting back on expenditures, usually in the face of adverse business experience or prospects.

return: 1. Earnings on investment, expressed as a percentage of investment; sometimes used imprecisely to describe also dividends paid relative to the current market value of a stock, even though the stock itself has fluctuated since its acquisition. **2.** A document supplying a taxing authority with information on matters relating to taxables and with tax computations, accompanied by tax payments as necessary.

return on investment (ROI): Earnings on investments, expressed as a percentage of the amount of the investment; for example, an investment yielding a 4% yearly dividend and 2% in the form of increased market value in the year of investment would have returned 6% if that investment had been turned back into cash at the end of a year.

revaluation: To change the stated value of a national currency in relation to the values of other national currencies by formal action of a national government.

revenue: The total of income received from all sources, but the term is used variously in business and government; for example, in government it includes tax and miscellaneous income while in public utilities it generally means only sales.

revenue bonds: State and local bonds backed by revenues to be received from state and local income-producing facilities, such as port authorities and power plants, rather than backed by the full faith and credit of the governments issuing them.

revenue stamp: A stamp placed by a taxing authority upon a taxed item, indicating that taxes have been paid.

revenue tariff: An import duty aimed mainly at raising money for government, rather than at protecting home products in domestic markets; in practice, many import duties perform both functions.

reverse split: The calling in of an existing stock issue by its issuer and its replacement by an issue containing less shares than the issue recalled, resulting in a smaller number of shares outstanding; a consolidation of shares rather than a split.

reversionary interest: An interest that reverts to an owner after an interest granted to another has ended, for whatever reason; for example, real property occupied by another under the terms of a lease.

revocable credit: A specific amount or line of credit extended by a lender, usually a bank, that may be revoked at any time and without notice.

revocable trust: A trust which may be revoked by its grantor; usually one that involves a trust fund paying trust income to its beneficiary while its grantor is alive and that is revocable either at will or under stated conditions.

revolving fund: A fund into which receipts go and from which disbursements are made, causing the size of the fund to continually change as funds flow in and out of it; for example, a government working fund, into which tax dollars flow and from which expenditures are made; in the widest sense, any current working fund.

rial: The main currency unit of Iran, bearing the same relationship to Iran's national currency system as does the dollar to the United States currency system.

rigging: The manipulation of a price by collusion between two or more parties; for example, the manipulation of securities prices by stock speculators or the rigging of a bid by collusion between bidders.

rights: **1.** In general, justified claims, supported by law or tradition. **2.** The option, extended by a board of directors to current shareholders of a corporation, to buy a new issue of corporate stock at a discount; such an option is something of value, which can be bought and sold in the securities marketplace.

ring: A group of collectibles dealers who purchase together and then resell as a group.

ringgit: The main currency unit of Malaysia, bearing the same relationship to Malaysia's national currency system as does the dollar to the United States currency system.

risk: 1. The extent to which loss is possible. In a somewhat wider sense, the amount of danger or potential loss in a situation in personal and business terms.   **2.** That which is covered by insurance, if it is insurable.

risk arbitrage: That branch of investment banking involved in taking risks associated with anticipated growths in securities values arising from corporate takeover situations; for example, when a corporation has just received a purchase bid from another company, the purchase of its common stock by arbitrageurs anticipating a substantial rise in that current market value.

risk capital: Capital invested in high or relatively high risk securities and enterprises, in expectation of commensurately high returns.

risk management: The management of insurable risks, including both insurance and the prevention of loss.

riyal: The main currency unit of Saudi Arabia, bearing the same relationship to Saudi Arabia's national currency system as does the dollar to the United States currency system.

ROI: See return on investment.

rollover: A refunding of debt by the replacement of existing debt with new debt; used frequently by governments as a means of continuing debts, paying only interest on them, while at the same time normally incurring new debts as well.

rouble: The main currency unit of the Soviet Union, bearing the same relationship to the Soviet Union's national currency system as does the dollar to the United States currency system.

round lot: A standard securities or commodities trading unit; for example, the standard New York Stock Exchange common stock trading unit is 100 shares, and most trades are conducted in multiples of 100 shares.

royalties: Amounts paid by one to another as compensation for the use of the other's property; for example, a percentage of net or gross receipts paid by a publisher to an author for use of the author's work, or a percentage of revenue paid to a landowner for the right to extract natural resources.

runaway inflation: A very high rate of inflation that cannot be brought under control, even with use of whatever manipulative tools are available to government.

runner: See floor man.

run on the bank: See bank run.

rupee: The main currency unit of several countries, including India, Pakistan, and Mauritius, bearing the same relationship to those currency systems as does the dollar to the United States currency system.

rupiah: The main currency unit of Indonesia, bearing the same relationship to Indonesia's currency system as does the dollar to the United States currency system.

S

safe deposit box: A vault in which valuables are kept, in some remote location, usually a bank.

safety: The anticipated relative ability of an investment to hold its buying price; for example, of a blue-chip common stock to hold its price, compared to the stock of a small, volatile company.

sag: A minor dip in securities prices.

sale: A contract passing title to goods or undertaking an obligation to supply goods or services in return for stated consideration, usually in the form of a price.

sale and leaseback: The sale of a property by its owner to a financing organization, accompanied by the leasing of that property on a long-term basis by its former owner; a financing technique used to remove both ownership and debt obligation from the books of the former owner, while allowing full use of the property for business purposes.

sales: Income from goods and services sold, appearing as such on financial records and statements.

sales forecast: An estimate of sales that will be made within a specified period; a guess that is a vital part of all budgeting and other planning.

salvage: 1. The value of something tangible that is sold as scrap. **2.** In accounting, the estimated value of property if it were to be resold, whether for use as originally designed or as scrap.

salvage value: See salvage.

satellite banking: The development of a web of dependent relationships between relatively small banks outside a large metropolitan area and a larger, centrally located bank.

savings: Income held for future use, rather than being spent as received, forming a basis for accumulation and investment.

savings account: A bank account devoted to the accumulation of savings and paying interest on the money held in it, in contrast to a checking account, which is devoted to handling transactions and pays no interest; but the difference between the two is blurring, as more and more bank accounts combine both features.

savings and loan association: A savings banking institution specializing in home mortgage loans, and organized on a mutual basis, with account holders actually shareholders holding equity proportional to the size of their accounts.

savings bank: A bank that holds depositor's money in interest-paying savings accounts and uses that money in the main to make mortgage loans, as well as making relatively small investments in high grade securities; but the distinction between savings and commercial banks is blurring, as savings banks undertake more and more service functions, such as checking accounts and life insurance sales.

savings bond: A United States Government bond paying a fixed rate of interest and holding a fixed value; it cannot be traded on bond markets, and can be redeemed only by the government.

SBA: See Small Business Administration.

SBIC: See Small Business Investment Company.

scaling: The placing of a series of orders to buy or sell securities at specific amounts and at specific price levels, in contrast to the placing of a single order to buy or sell at a specific price or at current market prices.

scalper: One who attempts to profit on small price changes in securities prices, buying and selling on a short-term, quick in-and-out basis.

scarcity: The condition existing when the supply of specific goods or services is considerably short of current demand; for example an insufficient supply of oil, whether that short supply is a real condition or artificially created.

schedule: 1. In general a detailed list of any kind.   **2.** A body of supporting data, especially as used by accountants in supporting financial statements.

schilling: The main currency unit of Austria, bearing the same relationship to Austria's national currency system as does the dollar to the United States currency system.

school of: Describing an art work not done by a well known, named artist, but thought by some experts in the field to have been done by those associated in some way with that artist, as students, as employees, or as part of a circle of associates; often a modern attribution following an earlier attribution, now thought erroneous or questionable, to the named artist.

scout: See picker.

scrip: 1. Substitute money issued by a government with promises to redeem it in real money at some future time; for example, the "occupation money" used by the victors in Europe after World War II.   **2.** Substitute dividends issued by a corporation, constituting a promise to pay a specific amount per share at some future date.

SDRs: See Special Drawing Rights.

seat: A membership on an organized stock exchange, such as the New York Stock Exchange.

SEC: See Securities and Exchange Commission.

secondary distribution: The offering for sale of a block of stock, one that is so large as to probably depress the market in that stock if offered on the open market, by means of a special sale to other brokers and dealers, after filing and receiving permission to do so from the Securities and Exchange Commission.

secondary market: See after market.

secondary offering: See secondary distribution.

secondary reserves: Bank reserves that can easily be turned into cash on very short notice; for example, short-term high grade commercial paper and short-term government securities.

second mortgage: A mortgage on real property which already has a first mortgage. Such a mortgage is subordinate to the first mortgage, and in the event of foreclosure has no right to satisfaction until the first mortgage has been completely satisfied.

second mortgage bonds: Bonds secured by second mortgages and subordinate to bonds secured by first mortgages.

secured bond: A bond that is secured by some kind of collateral, such as a mortgage, thereby becoming more than a mere promise to pay on the part of its issuer.

secured creditor: A creditor whose claim against the debtor is secured wholly or partially by some property of that debtor.

secured loan: A loan that is secured by collateral or mortgages capable of being liquidated in the event of default in order to satisfy the debt created by the loan.

securities: Documents of ownership or debt, such as common and preferred stocks, bonds, and notes, some of which are negotiable and tradeable in securities markets.

Securities and Exchange Commission (SEC): A Federal agency responsible for registering and regulating securities traded interstate and people and firms engaged in trading or counselling others as to any aspect of those securities; the SEC carries wide investigative, regulatory, and quasi-judicial powers to help it carry out its statutory charge.

self-liquidating: Describing an investment or asset which is thought to be capable of repaying its purchase price in cash during some defined period; always an estimate, one that often fails to take properly into account the rate of inflation.

selling against the box: A short sale against an equal amount of stock held, to guard or hedge against decline in the value of the stock held.

selling climax: A wave of extremely heavy selling of securities at or near the bottom of a market decline; often followed by a buying surge and an upward price movement.

selling off: Describing a market in which substantial selling is driving market prices down.

selling pressure: A market situation in which sellers considerably outnumber buyers, and the selling trend seems to be growing.

sell order: An order from customer to representative, such as bank, broker, or portfolio manager, to sell securities or commodities.

sell out: To liquidate an investment position, by selling all securities, commodities, or other assets held in connection with that position; for example, to sell all owned shares of a specific common stock.

senior bonds: Bonds carrying a primary claim upon a corporation, being secured by such assets as land and buildings, with no other bonds carrying prior claims; for example, first mortgage bonds, as contrasted with second mortgage bonds, which are junior obligations.

sensitive market: A market in which investors are unsure of current trends, respond erratically to market and market-related developments, and cause the market to fluctuate relatively rapidly and usually within a fairly narrow range.

serial bonds: Bonds that are issued at one time, but mature serially; for example, a $5,000 issue that matures in five equal $1,000 installments over a period of five years.

service industries: Those industries that produce services, such as the professions, and the finance, entertainment, and transportation industries, in contrast to those that produce goods, such as the steel, automobile, and mining industries.

service life: The anticipated useful life of an asset to its owner, forming a basis for computation of straight line depreciation. Physical life does not always equal anticipated service life, because an asset may become fully depreciated and still be in use, or an asset may be not yet fully depreciated when it is scrapped due to obsolescence.

session: A scheduled trading period on an organized exchange, usually a day.

settlement: A finishing up of a transaction or group of transactions; for example, the transactions accompanying the closing of a brokerage account, or the finishing of a single trading transaction by physical passing of securities and cash between brokers representing the parties to the transaction.

settlement date: The date on which a commodities or securities transaction is physically consummated.

settlement price: The daily closing price set by a commodities exchange on those contracts traded on that exchange.

shakeout: 1. A business or financial trend forcing some companies into troubled business positions, and others out of business. **2.** A securities or commodities market trend causing a downward price trend, characterized by substantial selling pressure.

share: An evidence of equity ownership in a corporation, that ownership being divided into equal parts.

shareholders' equity: See: stockholders' equity.

shaving: 1. Discounting a note at a higher than normal rate, when that note is of relatively low quality or market conditions make such action possible for the lender. **2.** Making an extra charge for allowing late delivery of securities in securities transactions.

shill: One who works with an auctioneer to drive up auction prices, by posing as a bidder and making fraudulent bids; in general, anyone fraudulently posing as a customer or winner, as when a gambler seems to be winning, thus encouraging others to gamble, but is actually in collusion with those running the gambling game.

short: One who has sold securities or commodity futures short, hoping to buy back later at a lower price.

short account: 1. A brokerage account functioning wholly or largely as a vehicle for handling the short sales of its principal. **2.** See short interest.

short covering: The act of buying stock or commodities to cover the borrowings made by a short seller.

short hedge: See hedging.

short holdings: Stocks and futures sold short that have not yet been covered.

short interest: The total number of short securities or commodities futures contracts sales open and uncovered at any given moment in a specific market or single exchange.

short position: The position of a short seller, who is on balance holding a short interest in a trading account. Also see short interest.

short-range forecasting: Systematic attempts to predict the course of future trends and events for only a year or less into the future, often using mathematical models and computer technology.

short sale: A securities or commodities sale in which the seller sells securities not yet owned, in expectation that the securities will go down in price between the time they are sold and the time the seller purchases equal amounts of the same securities for delivery to the buyer of the securities sold short. The seller will often, through a broker, borrow securities, on which interest must be paid, to deliver to the buyer if no purchase has been made to cover the securities sold short when they are due to be delivered; then delivery must eventually be made back to those from whom the securities were borrowed. Should the securities sold short go down before eventual delivery, as hoped by the short seller, the short seller profits; should they go up, the short seller must eventually cover at higher prices than the original sales price, and loses, then being in what has sometimes been called a "short squeeze."

short seller: One who is selling short, in one or more markets, in anticipation of price declines in those markets.

short squeeze: See short sale.

short term: A relative description, depending upon the subject, but in all instances referring to a time period of less than one year.

short-term capital gain: For tax purposes, capital gain that is treated as if it were ordinary income, because it has resulted from sale of an asset held too short a time to qualify for long term, more favorable tax treatment.

short term debt: 1. All debts and debt instruments maturing in less than one year.   **2.** For accounting purposes, all debts maturing in less than one year, including long term debts coming to maturity in that period.

short the basis: The opposite of "long the basis."

show dealer: One who sells primarily at auction or at fixed prices during shows, rather than through a retail or wholesale establishment.

sick market: A market in the course of a prolonged price decline, with no end in sight.

silent partner: A partner who is inactive in the conduct of a business and may be anonymous except to the other partners, but who is a general partner and therefore carries unlimited liability for the obligations of the business, as do all other general partners, whatever the extent of their activity.

silver certificate: A paper currency unit fully backed by national silver holdings; an important form of currency during the latter part of the nineteenth and early part of the twentieth centuries; now superseded by Federal Reserve notes, backed only by the full faith and credit of the United States Government, rather than by any precious metal.

silver standard: See silver certificate.

simple interest: An interest charge computed by multiplying the rate of interest by the principal, without any kind of compounding, or piling of interest upon interest.

simple regression analysis: See regression analysis.

single option: A single put or a single call.

sinking fund: A fund created by an organization to pay long term debts or retire preferred stock, consisting of earnings set aside in a separate fund and held in cash or quite conservative investments easily convertible into cash.

sinking fund bonds: Bonds that by their nature require that a sinking fund be set up to retire them, that fund to be deposited with an independent holder, such as a bank, and to be large enough, with anticipated interest, to pay principal in full at maturity.

sleeper: An investment that unexpectedly, and usually rather quickly, moves up in market price; usually a security that has had little recent investor attention.

sleeping partner: See silent partner.

slipping: Describing a market or investment experiencing a small price decline after a period of rising or generally level prices.

slope of change: The rate of change in a price or prices, as it might be represented graphically; the sharper the change, the steeper the line on the graph.

slowdown: A deceleration in the pace of national economic activity.

sluggish: Describing a market characterized by relatively small trading volume and a relatively narrow trading range.

slump: 1. When describing a whole economy, a synonym for recession or depression. **2.** When describing a unit smaller than an economy, such as an industry or regional economy, a slowdown in business activity, characterized by lower gross revenues and layoffs.

small business: Any very small to modestly sized business, such as a single pushcart or a family grocery store; but as defined by the Small Business Administration, may also refer to a manufacturing firm grossing some millions of dollars a year and employing scores of people.

Small Business Administration (SBA): A Federal agency responsible for administering a wide range of loan and information programs aimed at fostering the growth of small businesses, pursuant to statute and public policy.

Small Business Investment Company (SBIC): An investment company supplying capital, loans and management advice to small businesses; such companies are partially financed by Federal money, but privately owned.

smart money: Those presumed by others to possess expert knowledge and inside information on business and investment possibilities.

snake in the tunnel: A multinational agreement to float several currencies within an agreed-upon range, using one of those currencies as a center, around which the other currencies might fluctuate within that range.

snowballing: Describing any set of changes that is accelerating. In securities and commodities markets, particularly referring to a set of stop orders that trigger subsequent stop orders, forcing an acceleration factor into short-term upward or downward price trends.

socialism: State ownership of major elements of the means of production and distribution, in such basic industries as mining, metalworking, and transportation, along with substantial central planning of economic activity. Some countries have mixed forms, including elements of both private and public ownership.

soft currency: A national currency that is losing value relative to other, more stable currencies in a given period; for example, the American dollar in the late 1970's, which diminished in value very sharply relative to the values of the German and Japanese currencies.

soft landing: A slowdown in national economic activity that does not turn into a recession; so far in the main only a theoretical construct.

soft loan: An international loan made on relatively easy interest and repayment terms, and often repayable in the currency of the borrowing nation; sometimes a lightly disguised grant rather than a real loan.

soft market: A market that is declining; often used to describe the short-term price tendencies of securities or commodities markets.

soft spot: A declining investment vehicle or group of investment vehicles in a market that is otherwise rising.

software: See computer software.

sol: The main currency unit of Peru, bearing the same relationship to Peru's national currency system as does the dollar to the United States currency system.

sole proprietorship: A major form of ownership, in which a single person is the only owner of a business, and carries both unlimited rights and liabilities in regard to that business.

solvency: The ability to pay debts, implying the ability to pay those debts when they are due out of relatively liquid assets without damaging the underlying structure of a business; for example, selling fixtures may enable a small store to pay current debts, but may make that store unable to continue in business, which in practical terms makes it insolvent.

sources and applications of funds statement: See flow of funds statement.

special assessment: See assessment.

special assessment bonds: Special purpose local and municipal bonds, issued to raise money for such projects as sewers, waterworks, and libraries, and backed by special taxes levied upon those within the areas affected by those projects.

Special Drawing Rights (SDRs): An international reserve fund maintained by the International Monetary Fund for participating nations, serving as a vehicle by which nations can pay their balance of payments deficits, with maximum loans set by the IMF; the values of the SDRs are determined by averaging current values of a group of the world's major country currencies.

specialist: A stock exchange member who works as a primary trader for very few stocks on the floor of that exchange, attempting to hold markets in those specialized stocks relatively stable, minimizing sharp price fluctuations.

specialist's book: The order book of a specialist in a single stock; there are as many books for that stock as there are specialists in it.

special offering: See secondary distribution.

special partner: A securities brokerage firm partner who has a limited partnership in the firm, accompanied by liability limited to the value of that partner's investment in the firm; a legal status much like that of a limited partner in a real estate venture.

special situation: A security thought to possess unusual profit possibilities because of special circumstances accompanying it and the company issuing it; in many instances merely so described by eager brokers who want to sell these securities.

specie: Metal money, as distinguished from paper money; sometimes also used to describe any precious metals that may be used as money.

specific tariff: An import duty stating a specific amount to be charged for each unit imported, as contrasted with a percentage of value; for example, a duty charging $2 for each bottle of perfume of a particular size imported, rather than a percentage of the value of the bottles of perfume, is a specific tariff.

specified asset partnership: In real estate investment, a limited partnership in which all of the assets to be acquired by the partnership are known to the investor at the time of purchase of the limited partnership interest.

speculation: High risk purchases of any kind of property in hope of high profits at least commensurate with the risks; for example, purchase of volatile common stock in hope of quick, profitable sale or the purchase of land either for quick resale or coupled with willingness to hold it for a substantial length of time, but in either case risking large losses in hope of high profits.

spinoff: The transfer of some portion of corporate stock and some corporate activities to a newly formed corporation, for such purposes as preparation for sale or liquidation of the operations involved, or for expansion of those operations.

split: See stock split.

splitoff: See spinoff.

splitup: See split.

spot: Immediate, as in describing a spot market, which handles transactions involving immediate payments and deliveries, in contrast to future transactions.

spot market: A commodities market handling transactions involving immediate payments and deliveries of real goods.

spot prices: The prices of goods traded on spot markets; for example, the prices of quantities of crude oil bought and sold daily in those markets.

spread: 1. The difference between two related prices; for example, between the bid and asked prices of stocks traded over the counter, between the price paid by a retailer and the price charged by that retailer for the same goods, or between the interest paid by a bank to secure loanable money and the interest charged to borrowers for that money. **2.** In commodities trading, the difference between current prices, known as cash or spot prices, and the prices of future contracts. **3.** Also in commodities trading, to have two futures positions in the same, or in some instances different, commodities simultaneously.

squeeze: Describing a wide variety of situations in which some are caught by economic circumstances; for example, the kind of squeeze that occurs when profits are curtailed by rising inventories and faltering sales during a recession, the investment squeeze that occurs when short sellers who have sold in expectation of declining securities or commodities futures prices are confronted instead with rising prices and have to buy to cover at ruinous prices, or the borrowing squeeze that occurs when lenders are less willing than before to lend at other than very high rates of interest.

stabilization: The condition of a market investment vehicle or economy that has for some considerable time achieved steady growth without substantial fluctuation.

stabilize: To move to moderate the pace of price changes, as when a government moves to ease the velocity of changes in the value of its currency in international markets, or a stock exchange floor trader acting as a specialist buys or sells to smooth out fluctuations in the price of a single security.

stagflation: A combination of economic stagnation and inflation; a term coined by Gunnar Myrdal in an attempt to describe the condition of most Western economies in the last fifteen to twenty years.

stagnation: An economic condition in which annual growth rates are relatively small, capital formation and investment slacken, and real income diminishes.

stamp taxes: Taxes levied in the form of stamps that must be purchased and attached to items sold by sellers before legal transfer can be effected; examples include stamps on deeds, securities certificates, and cigarettes.

Standard and Poor's Index: A composite index maintained by the Standard and Poor's Corporation of the price movements of a group of 500 industrial, rail, and utility stocks.

standard cost: The normal cost estimated for producing goods and services, serving as a comparative measure of efficiency and productivity.

standard of living: The level of material well being of the people in an economy and of economic strata within that economy, as indicated by the goods and services consumed. An attempt to measure the quantity of life rather than its quality, it is by no means a precise or even a determinable measure, but varies both in level and goal structure between countries and regions.

standby authority: The right to take specified actions, or actions within a specified range, conferred on officials by legislating bodies; for example, the right to impose certain kinds of tariffs, or to impose or lift some kinds of price controls, granted to an American President by act of Congress.

state bank: A state-chartered commercial bank able to perform all commercial bank functions, in contrast to federally chartered commercial banks; sometimes state banks are members of the Federal Reserve System and usually they are members of the Federal Deposit Insurance Corporation.

stated value: See face value.

state holdings: Property and industries owned by a national government; mainly used to describe government holdings in wholly planned economies, but sometimes used to describe government-sector holdings in mixed economies as well.

state of the play: See play.

state planning: See centralized planning.

state trading: International trading conducted by a government organization rather than by a private trader, though it may be conducted with both other governments and private traders; for example, all the foreign trade conducted by the People's Republic of China is conducted through state agencies, as are most major United States arms sales abroad.

steady: Describing a market or investment vehicle that is holding prices at roughly equal levels during a given period, with trading occurring within a relatively narrow price range.

sterling area: Those nations, located throughout the world, in which the British pound is used as the main reserve currency, many of them formerly members of the British Commonwealth.

stock: 1. An ownership share in a corporation, whether that corporation is publicly held, privately held, or both. Ownership is divided into shares of equal value, and the quantity of shares held indicates the proportion of ownership held. **2.** The inventory carried by a company, with particular reference to goods held by wholesalers and retailers for resale.

stockbroker: A dealer in securities, who buys and sells stocks for customers and sometimes for house accounts.

stock certificate: A proof of ownership of a specified number of shares in a corporation, in the form of a document issued to its shareholders by that corporation.

Stock Clearing Corporation: A clearing house for securities transactions maintained by the New York Stock Exchange, organized as a subsidiary of the Exchange.

stock dilution: See dilution.

stock dividend: A corporate dividend paid to stockholders in the form of additional stock, rather than in cash.

stock exchange: An organized securities trading market, such as the New York Stock Exchange, in which members trade on behalf of their own and customer accounts.

stockholder: One who owns some share of a corporation, through ownership of one or more shares of company stock.

stockholder list: A list of the current stockholders in a corporation, maintained by the corporation or its outside stock transfer agent, or both.

stockholder of record: A stockholder whose ownership interest is registered on the books of record of the corporation; significant in terms of dividend payments and other corporate actions which are often stated as applying to stockholders of record as of a specific date.

stockholders' equity: The value of total stockholder shares in a corporation, expressed as the net of assets minus liabilities.

stock market: 1. Any stock exchange that is an organized market for trade in securities. **2.** The New York Stock Exchange, widely described as "the market" for stocks and bonds.

stock option: A right granted by a corporation, usually to employees or underwriters, to purchase corporate stock, under specific price and timing conditions; for example the right granted corporate officers to buy 1,000 shares of common stock at $10 a share, a right that must be exercised no later than 90 days from its date of issue. When the option is issued to an employee at a price below the current market price of the stock, it is compensation, and Federal tax law applies.

stock purchase plan: A fringe benefit, in which a company encourages and sometimes contributes to the purchase of corporate stock by employees, usually on a regular payment basis, much like a savings program.

stock purchase right: See warrant.

stock split: A corporate action increasing the number of its own shares in being, by dividing the outstanding shares; for example, the split of 200,000 outstanding shares on a 2:1 basis, creating 400,000 shares out of the previous 200,000. A split does not directly affect the total market value of all outstanding shares, so that a share selling at $20 before a 2:1 split becomes 2 shares worth $10 each.

stop limit order: A securities order carrying instructions to buy or sell at no less or more than specified price, but carrying additional authorization to buy or sell at a little less or more than the price stipulated, often a point or half a point more, the final acceptable price being the stop limit. As a practical matter, the stop limit price then becomes the ultimate stop price.

stop loss order: A securities order carrying instructions to sell specified securities at the point where their market value declines to a stated price.

stop order: A customer instruction to a broker to buy or sell securities at a specified price, rather than at the market price at the time of the order; for example, to buy a stock at $10 if it goes down to $10 from its current $12 or to sell stock currently at $12 if it goes down to $10.

stop payment: An instruction to a bank from a depositor to withhold payment on a check drawn on that depositor's account, as when a check has been issued in error, or has been lost in the mail and must be replaced by a new check.

stopped out: Describing the status of a security that has been sold pursuant to a stop order.

stop price: The price specified in a stop order; when the security reaches that price, the stop order becomes a market order, and the security is bought or sold.

straddle: A simultaneously held put and call, specifying a price at which its owner will either buy or sell a security.

straight line depreciation: A method of depreciating property that assigns equal proportions of value to each of the years it depreciates. For example, an asset worth $10,000 depreciating over a ten year period will depreciate at the rate of $1,000 for each of the ten years.

straight loan: A loan granted on the basis of the anticipated ability of the borrower to repay, without any kind of collateral.

straight paper: Any note, acceptance, or bill of exchange, that is secured by nothing but its issuer's promise to pay.

strap: A combination of two calls and one put.

street name: The name of a broker, holding securities belonging to a customer at the customer's request, or as collateral for securities bought on margin. The securities are held and traded in the broker's name, rather than that of the customer.

striking price: The contractually fixed price at which an option may be bought or sold.

strip: A combination of two puts and one call.

strong: Describing a market that is advancing, rather than declining or holding relatively steady.

studio of: See school of.

style: The characteristic appearance of artifacts made in a specific place and period; often used to describe the period.

sublease: A lease from a lessee, who in turn has leased from the owner, as when someone takes over the remaining portion of a lease; original leases normally specify that such a sublease requires the consent of the owner of the property.

subordinated debenture: A debenture which by its terms of issue becomes junior to such other debts as bank loans in the event of bankruptcy, reorganization, or dissolution.

subordinate interest: An interest in property which, by its nature and from the start, is of lower rank than some other interest; for example, a second mortgage which may be satisfied by sale of the property securing it only after an existing first mortgage is fully satisfied.

subpoena: An order to appear before a court to testify in litigation before that court.

subpoena duces tecum: An order to produce a document in court relating to litigation before that court.

subrogation: The substitution of one creditor or other claimant for another; for example, the substitution of one creditor for another when a note is made payable to another.

subscriber: One who agrees to buy a new securities issue.

subscription: An agreement to buy a new securities issue.

subscription capital: Money received from subscriptions to capital stock.

subscription rights: The right to purchase capital stock; a form of stock rights.

subscription price: The asking price placed on a new securities issue by its issuers at public sale.

subscription warrant: The right of current securities holders to purchase specified amounts of new securities being offered by the corporation within stated time limits and at a stated price.

subsidiary: A corporation that is wholly owned or directly controlled by another corporation

subsidy: Direct or indirect financial support by government of business organizations or individuals, as directed by public policy and statutory authority, including a very wide variety of supports and insurances for farming and farm prices, domestic producers, transportation companies, and public utility companies.

substitution of collateral: The replacing of collateral by other collateral that is equally acceptable to the lender, often occurring when owners of securities pledged as collateral want to trade those securities and must free title so that sale can be accomplished.

summons: A notification that a court action has been started against a defendant, and that judgment against the defendant will be issued by the court if he or she fails to appear to defend the action.

sum of the years digits method: An accelerated depreciation method in which the estimated life of an asset is used to figure progressively smaller depreciation amounts; for example, an asset estimated to have a depreciable life of four year will have these digits— 4, 3, 2, 1, totalling 10. First year depreciation will be 4/10, or 40%, second year 30%, third year 20% and fourth year 10%.

sunspot theory: The theory that substantial sunspot activity adversely influences investing attitudes and causes stock values to decline.

support level: A price level at which securities price declines may stop and a buying trend may begin; always an estimate, based on previous market behavior, and very often a hope rather than a real analysis.

support price: The government-supported price of a commodity.

suppressed inflation: Inflation that is held back for a period by governmental action, such as price and wage controls.

surety: One who agrees to guarantee the actions of another, usually the payment of a debt or the performance of a contractual obligation; such a guarantor may be an insurer acting for a fee or one acting without fee, such as the voluntary co-signer of a note.

surety bond: An instrument formally guaranteeing performance of an obligation, issued by an insurer to an insured for a fee.

surplus: 1. The net of assets over liabilities, constituting shareholders equity in a corporation. **2.** Any net of pluses over minuses, such as a larger supply of wheat than there is demand for wheat.

surtax: An extra tax, levied periodically on top of regular taxes; for example, excess profits taxes, which have been occasionally levied on top of regular corporate income taxes.

suspense account: For accounting purposes, an account that holds income and expenditures until they can be identified and properly entered on the books.

suspension: A penalty, involving the halting of rights for a period; for example, of the right of a firm to handle securities transactions for a specified period by action of the Securities and Exchange Commission or a state regulatory commisison, or of the right to handle transactions on a single exchange for a specified period by action of the officials of that exchange.

suspension of trading: The action of an exchange in halting trading for a time in a single listed stock or in all stocks, in order to attempt to stabilize a market and smooth out price fluctuations to some extent; normally used to moderate wide swings in a single stock due to unusual circumstances, such as takeover attempts and bankruptcies.

swap agreement: When there are official exchange rates, an agreement between two countries to exchange their currencies at those official rates, in order to ensure supplies of each others' currency to meet currency outflow and valuation problems as they arise; normally these are agreements to swap as needed up to specified maximums, rather than actual exchanges.

swap fund: A mutual fund that under certain conditions may receive securities which have appreciated in value from their owners and issue fund shares in return, effecting a tax-advantaged sale of the appreciated securities.

swing: A financial or economic fluctuation, such as stock, commodity and currency price movements and economic activity movements.

switch: In commodities trading, to sell a contract specifying one delivery month for a contract in the same commodity specifying another delivery month.

switching: Moving to other securities and commodities, by selling holdings and buying new holdings with the money realized.

switch order: An order to purchase one stock and sell another, substantially at the same time, though practical considerations sometimes preclude nearly simultaneous transactions.

syndicate: In the securities industry, a group of investment bankers joined to handle the marketing or placement of a securities issue; a means of sharing risk and marketing strength when bringing a large issue to market.

synergy: The achievement of far more through the combination of two or more factors than could have been accomplished by those factors alone; for example, the achievement of very substantial business successes resulting from the combination of two companies, successes that could not have been achieved by either company acting alone.

T

take a bath: To lose a good deal of money on an investment.

take a position: To make a commodities or commodities futures investment.

takeoff period: The time in which an economy rapidly moves into industrialization, a period characterized by large investments in a rapidly developing manufacturing system, and development of a large body of skilled people capable of handling the needs of a modern industrial state.

takeover: The acquisition of one business by another; whatever the form used in making the transaction, and whether or not the transaction was effected amicably.

takeover arbitrage: The purchase or sale of securities in hope of realizing gain from the stock fluctuations resulting from takeover attempts, having little to do with arbitrage and much to do with speculation in takeover situations.

takeover candidate: A company that is being studied by one or more potential acquirers, in terms of the desirability and feasibility of a takeover attempt.

take up: To pay balances due on margined securities and by so doing take full control and unencumbered legal ownership of those securities.

tangible assets: Those assets that have physical being, such as machinery, in contrast to assets that are not physical and therefore are intangible, such as good will.

tangible value: The value to a business of such tangible assets as plant and equipment, while that business is in operation, in contrast to their value once that business has ceased to be a going concern.

target company: A takeover candidate company that has been selected by a potential acquirer as a desirable and feasible takeover target, whether or not that company has evidenced any desire to be taken over.

tariff: A tax by government on imports or exports, for revenue, purposes of national policy, or both.

tax: See taxes.

taxable estate: That portion of an estate remaining and subject to taxes after all deductions of any kind from the gross estate.

taxable income: That portion of income remaining and subject to taxes after all deductions of any kind from gross income.

tax anticipation obligations: Any of several interest-bearing financial instruments sold by governments to raise money in advance and in expectation of tax revenues, and which aim to smooth out government income over the year, rather than having that income concentrated in periods of high tax receipts.

tax avoidance: The legal minimization of taxes due government by application of a large number of tax planning devices; in contrast to tax evasion, which is illegal.

tax base: For tax purposes, the value of all the property within a jurisdiction subject to taxes; for example, the value of all taxable real property in a township, which would not include such nontaxable property as church-owned land.

tax burden: The extent to which a kind of tax or group of taxes impact upon a group, usually stated relative to other groups; for example, one of the aims of the progressive income tax is to lessen the impact of the income tax on the poor and disadvantaged, compared to the impact on those thought better able to pay.

tax credit: A sum that may be directly deducted in full from taxes due, in contrast to a deduction, which is subtracted from taxables; for example, an investment tax credit allows businesses to deduct certain sums spent for capital investment directly from corporate income taxes that would otherwise be due.

tax deduction: A sum that may be deducted from taxables, lowering those taxables; for example, certain sums spent for charitable purposes, taxes, and medical and dental payments are deductible from taxable income on Federal income tax returns.

tax equalization: The adjustment of property taxes payable among taxpayers in a taxing jurisdiction, in an attempt to fairly apportion taxes, usually by adjustments of valuations, rates, or both.

taxes: Charges imposed by government on those under its jurisdiction, including charges on income, imports, exports, sales, estate and trusts, gifts, licenses and fees, and property.

tax evasion: The illegal minimization of taxes due government; in contrast to tax avoidance, which is legal.

tax exempt bonds: Bonds that pay income that is not taxable, including Federal, state, and local bonds that are not in any way taxable and Federal bonds not subject to state and local taxes.

tax exemptions: Sums deductible from Federal, state, and local taxable income for each taxpayer and each legal dependent of that taxpayer.

tax fraud: Failure to pay taxes legally due, with intent to defraud the taxing authority, through such actions as failure to report income and misstatement of deductions; no statute of limitations applies to tax fraud.

tax free income fund: A mutual fund wholly or almost entirely invested in tax free securities.

tax haven: A country that levies little or no income tax on foreign individuals and businesses and so, under some conditions, offers foreigners the possibility of legal tax avoidance in their own countries; but in many situations the line between tax avoidance and tax evasion is a fine one, and is subject to considerable litigation.

tax lien: A lien placed on a taxpayer's property by government for nonpayment of taxes due; the lien is satisfied by payment of taxes due or by forced sale of the property for back taxes.

tax loophole: A provision of a tax law that makes it possible to avoid taxes that might otherwise be due, sometimes due to government inadvertence, sometimes pursuant to legislative intent, and often as a result of special interest legislation with application far beyond the interests of the lobby that forced through the legislation.

taxpayer: 1. An individual or business liable for the payment of taxes, now or in the future.   **2.** A property developed just enough to pay the taxes due on it, such as a single story row of stores on a piece of prime commercial property that is awaiting development into an office building.

tax rebate: Government return of taxes already paid to a class of taxpayers, usually as part of an attempt to stimulate the economy.

tax refund: Government return of taxes already paid, due to overpayment or error.

tax roll: A record of all taxable property within a taxing jurisdiction, with ownership and tax information.

tax sale: A sale of private property by government to satisfy unpaid taxes.

tax selling: The selling of securities to achieve advantageous tax results, whether to take loses on which tax deductions may be gained or to take gains on which taxes will be paid; always a feature of the last quarter of the year, when planning is most often done, but a factor at other times of the year as well.

tax sharing: The sharing of Federal or state tax revenues with the governments of smaller jurisdictions; a means of moving some tax money back into localities, sometimes to provide a higher proportion of that money to the needier localities.

tax shelter: A form through which income can be developed tax-free or in a tax-advantaged way, such as a pension or profit-sharing plan, an investment in tax-advantaged oil drilling activities, or certain real estate investments.

technical analysis: A school of stock market analysis stressing the primacy of such market data as price trends and trading volume in market trend analysis, and using a wide variety of charts and other graphic representations as tools of analysis.

technical assistance: Aid to other, usually underdeveloped, nations in using materials, techniques and processes and in developing those kinds of skilled people necessary to form the infrastructure of a developed nation.

technical factors: Those factors influencing market price behavior stemming from market-related rather than from fundamental or external factors; such matters as the extent of short interest in the market, trading volume, and the nature of short-term price fluctuations are thought to be such market-related factors.

technical indicators: A wide range of market-related indicators, including such matters as short interest, trading volume, and the nature of short-term price fluctuations.

technically strong market: A market featuring rising prices and relatively large volume when the general price level is rising.

technically weak market: A market featuring declining prices and relatively large volume when the general price level is declining.

technical patterns: See technical indicators.

technical position: Describing the relationship of technical factors to the current status of a market.

technician: In securities and commodities markets, one who bases analysis and action primarily upon technical, rather than fundamental factors.

technology: The practical application of the scientific method to the solution of production and distribution questions, and to the development of all those machines and machine-oriented processes that characterize industrial society.

technostructure: The body of managers and technical personnel that collectively forms the infrastructure of large modern corporations, and provides their day-to-day management.

teller: One who is employed by a bank in the actual handling of currency for customers in a variety of transactions, including deposits and withdrawals.

temporary injunction: A preliminary injunction restraining a defendant from doing or continuing to do an act until such time as the injunction is dissolved by the court or replaced by a permanent injunction.

tenancy: A legal right or interest in the holding and occupany of real estate, which may be with or without a written lease. Tenancy terms may vary widely, including a specified lease period, month-to-month and year-to-year terms; and tenancy may take many forms, including individual, joint and corporate tenancies.

tenant: One who has a legal right or interest in the holding and occupany of real estate, with or without a written lease.

tender: 1. An offer to pay a debt or perform a contractual obligation. **2.** An offer to purchase, often encountered in company takeover situations, in which one company makes an offer to buy the stock of another at a stated price.

tender price: The price at which an offer to buy is made; for example, the price at which a company offers to buy outstanding shares of a company it wishes to acquire.

tenor: The time period between the date a financial obligation, evidenced by a financial instrument, comes into being and the date it is due to be paid, at maturity.

term: Any time period; in finance and investment, the length of time a debt or debt instrument, such as a bond, is in being.

testament: A synonym for "last will," meaning the legally valid last will of a deceased person; therefore "last will and testament" is redundant.

testamentary: Pertaining to a testament.

testamentary capacity: That soundness of mind and memory necessary for one to be able to make a legally valid will.

testamentary disposition: Property given by the terms of a will, and not passed until the testator dies.

testamentary trust: A trust created by the provisions of a legally valid will, becoming effective after the testator's death.

testator: The maker of a legally valid last will.

The Big Board: See New York Stock Exchange.

The Exchange: See New York Stock Exchange (NYSE).

The Market: A general description of all securities markets; but when describing stock market fluctuation, usually used to describe the price movements of securities listed on the New York Stock Exchange.

The Street: Wall Street, as a symbol for the entire New York City financial district, center of the American financial community.

thinly held: Describing a stock that is held by relatively few people and institutions, and which is therefore subject to considerable fluctuation on a modest transaction volume.

thin margin: Describing a security or commodity held with very little equity investment and very large borrowings.

thin market: A market for anything generally sold, such as securities and commodities, that is characterized by relatively few buy and sell orders, and for modest quantities, and is therefore subject to considerable fluctuation on a modest transaction volume.

third market: A market in which large blocks of securities exchange hands, sold by dealer to dealer and customer at small negotiated commission rates.

ticker: A remote printer used to transmit messages simultaneously to many locations. Examples are a stock ticker, which transmits stock prices to brokerage offices, and newswires, which transmit news stories to newspapers and broadcasters, often widely separated.

ticker tape symbol: A symbol identifying a security, carried on a stock exchange's communications system; the ticker tape formerly used has now generally been replaced by more sophisticated communications devices.

tied loan: An international loan carrying the condition that the borrower must use all or a specified part of a loan proceeds to buy goods and services originating in the lending country.

tight money: A government policy that attempts to slow inflation by restricting the amount of money and credit in circulation through exercise of a number of money-manipulative devices, especially manipulation of the Federal Reserve rate, which directly affects the prime rate.

till money: See vault cash.

time bill of exchange: A bill of exchange payable at a specified future date.

time deposit: An interest-bearing bank deposit, which may be withdrawn only upon notice to the bank as specified by the terms of the deposit, and which pays a rate of interest dependent upon keeping the deposit in the bank for a minimum time; if the deposit is withdrawn early, there are substantial interest penalties.

time draft: A bank draft payable at a specified future date.

time loan: A loan repayable in full at a specified future date, in contrast to an installment loan, which is payable in a series of equal payments.

tip: Advice to take buying or betting action based on purported inside information as to the affairs of a company or the probable outcome of a horse race.

title: Legally valid ownership of real or personal property, and the documentary evidence of that ownership, such as a deed, certificate of title, or bill of sale.

title insurance: Insurance against passage of legally invalid title, issued by a title insurance company after a title search by that company has established that legally valid title exists in the seller, who then is able to pass that title to the insured.

token money: Metal money that is worth less than its face value, as is true of all United States coins currently issued; in contrast to some gold and silver coins currently being issued by other countries and to gold and silver United States coins formerly issued.

tombstone: A black bordered advertisement announcing a new securities offering, placed in periodicals by its underwriters or, if done directly by its issuing corporation, by that corporation. The advertisement does not sell the new issue; that can only be done by formal prospectus.

topheavy market: A market thought by some to be characterized by securities prices that are higher than it will be able to maintain, and which is therefore on the verge of a declining price trend.

topping out: Describing a market that is thought to be approaching its top currently possible price levels after a period of rising prices, and which will therefore tend to hold steady or begin to decline.

tort: A private or civil wrong to another, actionable at law for damages, such as unintentional harm to a person or property caused by negligence; such an action does not preclude a criminal action arising out of the same set of circumstances.

tortfeasor: One who is judged by a court to have committed a tort, that is an actionable private or civil wrong done to another.

total demand: See composite demand.

tracer: A procedure aimed at tracking down an instrument, mailing, or shipment that has not reached its intended destination within a normal length of time, such as a check passing between banks.

trade: The exchange of one item of value for another, including the exchange of goods and services for money; of money for money, as in a currency transaction; of goods and services for goods and services, as in barter; and of financial instruments for other financial instruments.

trade acceptance: A bill of exchange signed by the purchaser of goods in favor of the seller of those goods, usually functioning as a check drawn on the purchaser's bank; a negotiable instrument.

trade barrier: Any impediment to the full and free development of international trade among all nations equally, including protective tariffs, import quotas, currency restrictions, and political restrictions.

trade credit: Credit extended by business sellers to buyers on a regular basis, in anticipation of payment within a normal period, usually thirty days.

trade deficit: A larger volume of imports than exports for a country in a given time period; one of the key elements in the balance of trade.

trademark: A mark, logo, or other design so distinctive as to be capable of being registered with the United States Patent Office and accepted as the mark associated with a company or product. Once it is so registered, others may not legally use that mark without the permission of its owners, and may be enjoined from use or be liable for damages resulting from illegal use.

trade name: The name under which a company markets a product or the name of the company itself; although not a trademark, such a name may be legally protected against misleading use of identical or substantially similar names by others to capitalize on the established business reputation of the company and its products.

trade paper: See business paper.

trade relations: The web of commercial and financial relationships between countries trading with each other, as expressed by treaties and other written agreements; by governmental presence in the form of embassies, consulates, and missions; and by a miscellany of public and private contacts and arrangements.

traders: Those who buy and sell goods, services, and instruments of value for themselves or on behalf of others; they often are also wholesalers and distributors, as in the securities and automobile industries.

trader's market: A market conducive to the making of quick in-and-out trades for limited speculative profits, and characterized by very short term price moves within a narrow price range.

trade secret: A product, formula, recipe, or any other item which has been developed or legally acquired by business; which is held uniquely by that business; and which can be successfully asserted at law as unique and valuable, providing the basis for injunction or damage suit against any who might steal or otherwise illegally acquire it.

trade surplus: A favorable balance of trade.

trading floor: That portion of a market on which trades are actually consummated, such as the floor of the New York Stock Exchange.

trading limit: The maximum extent to which commodities futures prices will be allowed to fluctuate during a single trading day; set by the rules of each exchange. Once a trading limit has been reached, either the high or low limit, trading will be terminated for the day by the exchange, though every exchange has the ability to suspend its rules in this area in special circumstances.

trading post: A station on the floor of a stock exchange at which trades for designated securities are consummated.

trading volume: The total amount of stock or of a single stock traded on an exchange in a given time period; usually describing that volume in a single trading day.

transfer: The legal conveyance of title to property from one party to another, whether by act of the parties or by operation of law.

transfer agent: An organization or individual engaged by a corporation to physically handle and record all transactions involving the stock of the corporation; such agents are often banks or other outside organizations, but sometimes are employees of the corporation.

transfer tax: A Federal or state tax on the value of stocks transferred, payable each time the stocks are transferred.

transit number: The identifying number placed on checks by each bank as it moves checks into the clearing process; a uniform system throughout the United States, with each bank having its own number.

traveler's letter of credit: A credit instrument issued by a bank on behalf of a depositor, guaranteeing the extension of credit up to specified limits; usually issued to named correspondent banks.

Treasury bills: Short-term United States Government obligations issued by the Treasury Department, bearing no interest but sold at a discount, that discount therefore effecting a rate of return for investors; for example, a bill issued in denominations of $10,000, sold at a 10% discount, sells for $9,000. The rate of return is 10/90, or 11.1%. Such bills are fully negotiable.

Treasury bonds: 1. Any bonds issued by the United States Government through the Treasury Department. **2.** Bonds previously issued by a corporation, bought back before maturity, and held in the corporation's treasury.

Treasury certificates: Short-term United States Government obligations issued by the Treasury Department, bearing interest and maturing in one year or less.

Treasury Department: The department of the United States Government responsible for major policy formulation, administration, and regulation of a wide range of tax and financial policies and functions, including tax collection, administration, and enforcement; supervision and printing of the physical money supply; protection of the President and the President's family; participation in international financial organizations; and a wide range of other duties.

Treasury note: Medium-term United States Government obligations issued by the Treasury Department, bearing interest and maturing in one to five years.

treasury stock: Stock previously issued by a corporation, and then bought back; such stock may be held indefinitely, earning dividends, or may at any time be resold.

trend: A relatively well-sustained set of securities or commodities price movements, of whatever duration.

trial balance: A listing and summary of all account totals in a double entry bookkeeping system, to determine whether total debits equal total credits, preliminary to balancing the books.

trickle down theory: The idea that stimulants applied to a lagging economy by Federal, state, and local governments are best given to business to induce economic growth that will benefit citizens indirectly, rather than being given directly to consumers to spur purchasing power.

triple bottom: Describing the movement of a market down to nearly its most recent substantial bottom three times within a short period, without going through the level of that recent bottom to new lower price levels.

triple top: The opposite of triple bottom.

trough: A bottom reached in some area of economic activity; always an estimate and an approximation, even after the fact.

trust: 1. A right or interest in property held by one or more for one or more others; the holders, or trustees, have the right and responsibility to handle that property in the best interests of the others, or beneficiaries. Also refers to the instrument creating that right or interest. **2.** An illegal monopoly, the intended target of antitrust activities.

trustbusting: Federal antitrust activity of any kind, attacking trusts, combinations, and activities alleged to be unfairly competitive and in restraint of trade.

trust company: A financial institution, usually a bank as well as a trust company, which handles many kinds of trusts and trust investments; sometimes as trustee and sometimes as agent for trustees; commercial banks perform all major trust company functions, and the line between them and trust companies has now blurred so much as to practically disappear.

trustee: See trust.

trust fund: A fund set up under the terms of a trust, in which the trustee holds the principal and distributes some or all of the trust's income to the beneficiaries. Such a fund is often for the benefit of a surviving spouse for the remainder of a lifetime, with principal then to surviving children or others, and often to surviving children until they have reached specified ages, with principal then to them.

trust receipt: A financial instrument created for the purpose of financing purchase of goods by a bank's depositor for resale; a bank advances money to its depositor to buy goods, to which the bank takes title through the form of the trust receipt, with the bank then passing title back to the depositor or directly to the purchaser when the goods are sold.

turn: A new price trend in a market, moving from declining to rising prices, or vice versa.

turnaround situation: Describing a company thought to be capable of being moved from a losing or declining position to one of profits and growth, and therefore a company very much worth investing in at its current low stock price levels; always a speculative move, as many such companies do not in fact turn around, but continue on their well established downward courses—as do the market prices of their securities.

turnover: 1. The volume of securities or commodities traded on a given exchange in a given period. **2.** The number of times an asset or group of assets is replaced during a stated period, often a year; expressed, for example, as a ratio of sales to net worth, so that with sales of $1,000,000 and net worth of $200,000, the rate of net worth turnover is 5 to 1.

turnover tax: A tax on total sales made by the kind of business being taxed, usually expressed as a percentage of those sales.

two dollar broker: A securities broker who handles orders for other brokers for a fee based on the value of the transaction.

tycoon: A powerful and wealthy financier or businessperson.

U

uncollected funds: See float.

uncollectibles: Debts that cannot be collected due to the inability or unwillingness of the debtor to pay; reserve for such debts is normally carried by businesses selling products and services.

undercapitalized: Describing a business that has insufficient capital to properly meet its needs, and sometimes insufficient capital for survival. Often, the description is inapt, as what is really being described is a business that may have considerable capital and enough to meet its needs if that capital were easily made liquid, but has instead a cash crisis.

underconsumption: The idea that downswings in the business cycle are caused by economic inability to consume what has been produced, resulting in a downward production spiral, which is self-correcting only at the bottom of a business cycle. From the opposite vantage point, often called overproduction.

underdeveloped nation: A country that is economically less developed than the industrial countries of the world, as measured by industrial output, per capita income, infrastructure development, and capital available for investment; often characterized by an explosive increase in population and decreasing ability to feed that population.

underinvestment: A situation in which a smaller portion of available savings is used for investment than is healthy for an economy.

undervaluation: The lower than reasonable evaluation of securities being traded, or other property for sale, and consequent creation of investment opportunities.

undervalued asset play: A special situation in which the assets owned by a corporation are thought by some analysts to be carried on the books of that corporation at considerably less than their real worth, creating a presumption that the publicly traded stock of that corporation is likewise undervalued, and therefore an excellent investment opportunity.

underwriting: The guaranteeing of the sale of a securities issue by a firm or group functioning as purchasers of the entire issue of that security and subsequent resellers of the issue to the public or to private parties.

underwriting syndicate: A group of investment banking firms joined together to purchase and resell a securities issue.

undistributed profits: Earnings that have been retained in the corporation rather than distributed to equity holders.

unearned income: Revenue that has been physically received but is as yet unearned, such as payment for subscriptions not yet fulfilled, and therefore must be treated as deferred income for accounting purposes.

unearned increment: An increase in the value of property that results from conditions out of the control of the owner of that property, rather than through additions to value brought about by action of the owner; but not including a general rise in property values due to the impact of inflation; for example, a rise in the value of real estate located near a superhighway entrance.

unearned revenue: See unearned income.

uneconomic: That which yields poor economic results, in terms of profits, growth, efficiency, and other economic factors.

unencumbered: That which is entirely free of legal claims and obligations; for example, realty that is sold with clear title, and free of all debts and liens.

unenforceable contracts: Contracts which cannot be enforced by legal action, such as contracts creating obligations to do acts that are in themselves illegal, as well as contracts which are invalid for any of a wide range of reasons.

unfair competition: Competitive activities that create competitive advantages which are at law deemed unfair, and usually are illegal as well, such as deceptive competitive comparisons and the use of misleading trade names.

unfavorable balance of trade: A balance of trade between nations in which a nation has more total imports than exports.

Uniform Commercial Code: A national codification of major laws concerning commerce and finance, which has been adopted by almost all states, covering a very wide range of matters, such as sales, contracts, commercial and bank paper, bank deposits, and receipts.

unissued stock: Stock that has been authorized but not yet issued by a corporation; such stock is not treated as an asset, in contrast to treasury stock, which is also held by the corporation, but which has been issued and repurchased by the corporation.

unit cost: The cost to a producer, distributor, or retailer of a single designated unit in a group of substantially identical units; for example, the cost to the producer of automobile parts produced on an assembly line; or the per-ounce cost to the producer of instant coffee.

United States depositaries: Those Federal Reserve and commercial banks used by United States Government departments and agencies as sources of banking and financial services, and in which federal funds reside.

United States Government bonds: All bonds issued as debt obligations of the Federal Government.

United States Government securities: All securities issued by the Federal Government, including bonds, bills, certificates, and special debt issues.

unlimited liability: Liability that extends to all of a debtor's business and personal assets; the corporate and limited partnership forms of doing business substantially limit liability, but the sole proprietorship and general partnership forms generally carry unlimited liability.

unlisted security: A security traded on the over-the-counter market, and not listed on any organized United States stock exchange; a corporation may be listed on an exchange functioning elsewhere in the world, but be an unlisted security in the United States.

unload: To sell securities in the belief that their prices will soon decline sharply; often done in an attempt to cut losses by those who believe the course of a downward price trend is accelerating.

unpaid dividend: A dividend which has been declared by a company and therefore is an obligation of that company, but which has not yet been paid to equity holders.

unrealized profit: See paper profit.

unregistered stock: See letter stock.

unrestricted sale: An auction sale at which everything up for auction will be sold, without any reserve or minimum prices in force.

unsecured: Describing a debt instrument, such as a bond or note, that is not backed by any kind of collateral, but is backed only by the debtor's promise to repay.

unsubscribed shares: That portion of a new securities issue which has not been sold by the underwriters, and is held by the underwriters for future sale, unless so much stock is unsold that a contractual provision cancelling the issue comes into play.

upgrading: 1. The placing of a new, higher rating on a security, usually a bond, by a rating service. **2.** The weeding out and replacement of those securities thought weak in a portfolio with securities thought to be of higher quality; often a move to more conservative securities from securities thought to be speculative.

upset price: The minimum price at which a sale will be made, such as the starting price set at auction, to be met by bidders or the item will be withdrawn from that auction.

upside potential: The extent to which a security is thought by an analyst or investor to be capable of quick and sustained appreciation.

upswing: A turn upward in stock or commodity market prices, after a period of declining or relatively level prices.

up tick: See plus tick.

urban renewal: Attempts to develop or redevelop sections of cities, often center city sections that have severely deteriorated; usually financed either directly by Federal, state and local governments or by private industry with substantial help from those governments in the forms of direct payments or tax concessions.

useful life: See service life.

use tax: A tax on the use of an item, rather than on its sale; for example, automobile registration fees in some states.

usury: The charging of illegally high rates of interest by a lender; such rates are governed by state laws, and allowable rates vary from state to state, creating some imbalances in periods of rapid inflation, when money may be available to borrowers in one state and very difficult to secure in another, because of higher allowable rates in one than another.

V

valuation: 1. The process of establishing the value of an asset, usually for sales or tax purposes; for example, the highly formalized practices associated with setting real estate values for tax assessment purposes, or the process of evaluating items in an estate, including such items as antiques and collectibles. **2.** The value established for an asset, for sales or tax purposes.

value: 1. The worth of something, in terms of a reasonable assessment of what price it might bring if sold under current market conditions. **2.** The actual price paid for something just sold.

value added: The amount of value added to raw and semi-finished materials during the process of manufacture.

value added tax (VAT): A tax on the net of sales minus materials costs, levied successively at each stage of sale, from the first sale of processed raw materials to the final sale; for example, where value added taxes are in effect taxes are levied on the sale of paper to make a book, on the value added by the publisher when that book is sold to a jobber, on the value added by the jobber when the book is sold to a retailer, and on the value added by the retailer when the book is sold to a consumer.

variable costs: Operating costs that vary with changes in the levels of production and sales; for example, power, labor and materials, which depend significantly on the volume of business being done.

variable overhead: See overhead.

variance: 1. The difference between estimates and actuality; for example, the difference between sales forecasts and sales realities. **2.** In statistics, the square of the standard deviation; a basic measure of dispersion of values around the mean in a normal distribution, used in tests designed to determine if the difference between items or groups, whether people or widgets, is statistically significant, at various levels of probability.

VAT: See value added tax.

vault: A security room, for keeping valuables; usually a literally armored room in a bank.

vault cash: Currency held by a bank in its vault and cash drawers to meet current operating needs, such as check cashing.

velocity of money: The rate at which money changes hands during a given period, usually a year; significant in terms of assessing the level of economic activity.

venture: A new business undertaking, whether a single move by an established business or a whole new business, and always implying some entreprencurial risk.

venture capital: Capital employed in the establishment of a new business, always implying some entrepreneurial risk and hope of a relatively substantial rate of investment reward.

vertical integration: The process of acquiring or developing organizations handling more steps in the production process than the company was previously able to handle; for example, the acquisition of ranching and cattle-feeding facilities by a company formerly solely in the business of wholesale meat marketing, or the development of retail outlets by the same firm.

vested interest: An interest arising from an existing right or set of rights; for example, the right to receive payments from a company pension on retirement after working for a company for a minimum number of years, even though leaving the employ of that company long before retirement and holding other jobs.

visible items: Tangible goods traded internationally, and literally visible as exported and imported goods, in contrast to invisible items, which are intangibles, such as banking and financial services.

volume: See turnover.

volume of money: See money supply.

volume of trade: See trading volume.

voluntary bankruptcy: A bankruptcy applied for by an insolvent debtor, in contrast to an involuntary bankruptcy, which is applied for by the creditors.

voluntary export quota: A voluntary agreement by exporters of a country to limit exports of certain goods, usually arrived at through pressure and negotiation between themselves, their government, and foreign firms and governments.

voting right: The right of a stockholder to vote in corporate matters requiring a vote, usually on the basis of one vote for each share of stock owned.

voting stock: Stock which by its nature gives its owner the right to vote in corporate matters requiring a vote; common stock is voting stock, but preferred stock is not, except for exceptional circumstances specified in the corporate charter.

voting trust: A trust to exercise on a continual basis voting rights stemming from corporate stock ownership of stockholders who have passed those rights into the trust; in contrast to stockholders' passage of proxies, which enable proxyholders to vote stock owned by others only once.

W

wage-price spiral: The idea that wages are the main cause of inflation, and that wage increases feed price increases, which in turn feed further wage increases, and so on; one of several theories as to the causes and cure of inflation.

waiver: The voluntary and unilateral abandonment of a right or claim which would have been legally enforceable.

Wall Street: See The Street.

warehouse receipt: A receipt issued by a warehouse to an owner of goods stored there, stating that the goods are stored in the warehouse and are the property of the owner; if it further states that the goods will be duly returned to the owner or to anyone else indicated on the receipt, it is a negotiable instrument.

warehouse receipt loan: A loan accepting warehouse receipts as proof of collateral, in which the lender holds the receipts and the goods so used remain in the warehouse; a standard commercial loan form, but also the basis of several major financial frauds, when warehouse receipts so used have proven false.

warrant: A stock purchase right that gives its holder the right to purchase a specific amount of stock at a specific price within a specified period or in perpetuity. Such a right functions much as a stock right, but it is normally attached to debt obligations and preferred stock, and can be exercised over longer terms. If attached by coupon to another instrument, it is non-negotiable; if issued alone, it is negotiable.

warranty: An assurance by a seller or other contracting party, whether expressed or implied, that property transferred is acceptable, using generally accepted standards of measurement; while not the central matter of the transaction, such an assurance is very often so material as to invalidate a transaction if a warranty is breached, or to give rise to successful damage actions.

warranty deed: A written statement accompanying a deed, stating that title to real property is clear, and that the property is unencumbered.

wash sale: A sale and purchase of stock at the same time and by the same party, creating a false impression of great activity in a stock, with the aim of manipulating the price of the stock upward; an illegal practice.

wasting asset: An asset that by its nature diminishes with use, such as oil or natural gas, and that is recognized as such by tax law, which makes allowances for the progressive depletion of such assets.

watered stock: Stock issued with aggregate value very considerably higher than the total asset value of the issuer.

weak market: A market experiencing a somewhat declining general price level, usually on a short-term basis.

wealth: The aggregate of personal, business, or national assets.

wealth tax: See ability to pay principle.

weighted average: An average in which some of the items used to compute the average are figured in more heavily than some of the other items; for example, in a study of buying motives, comparative price might count twice as much as esthetic satisfaction.

wellhead tax: A tax on the value of oil or gas, as it leaves its producing well.

when issued: The status of securities that have been announced to the public, not yet formally issued, and are being actively traded on a prospective basis.

whipsawed: Losing twice in one price swing; for example, buying just before prices drop and selling short just before they rise.

white knight: In corporate takeover situations, a company asked by the management of the takeover candidate to bid against an unwanted acquirer, in an effort to either frustrate the aims of that acquirer and keep control or to replace the unwanted acquirer with a presumably more friendly acquirer.

wholesale banking: That aspect of commercial banking that handles accounts and transactions for large institutional and business customers and for wealthy individuals. Today most commercial banks handle both large and small customers, and the distinction between wholesale and retail banking has all but disappeared, except as a description of a commercial bank's thrust in building its business.

Wholesale Price Index: A monthly national price index indicating wholesale price trends, using a weighted group of goods sold at wholesale; issued by the Bureau of Labor Statistics.

will: A legally valid document disposing of its maker's property after death; once accepted by a court of appropriate jurisdiction, the wishes of its maker are carried out as far as possible.

windfall: An unexpected gain, such as that resulting from a sudden price rise in a stock or commodity held.

wiped out: Having lost one's investment; sometimes meaning having lost one's entire financial stake, as happened to so many investors in the 1929 Crash.

wire house: A very large stockbroker, operating many offices throughout the United States and usually throughout the world, directly or indirectly through arrangements with other brokers; originally referred to a large securities house that maintained its own communications network.

withdrawal: The reclaiming of funds held in a bank deposit.

won: The main currency unit of South Korea, bearing the same relationship to South Korea's national currency system as does the dollar to the United States currency system.

working capital: The net of current assets over current liabilities; a major factor in assessing a company's financial health.

working capital ratio: The relationship between current assets and current liabilities, expressed as a ratio; for example, a company with current assets of $1,000,000 and current liabilities of $500,000 has a working capital ratio of 2:1.

working control: Ownership by an individual, group, or company of enough stock in a company to reach and maintain effective direction of the company's policies and activities; in many widely held companies, this is often far less than a majority or near-majority stockholding, and can be as little as 10-20% of ownership.

working papers: The research notes and other underlying data supporting a more formal and extended statement, such as those developed in connection with publication of a scholarly work or development of a substantial accounting statement.

work in process: For accounting purposes, work that is currently being manufactured; generally, any work in the process of being produced.

World Bank: See International Bank for Reconstruction and Development.

world trade: The trading of goods and services between the nations of the world, and the total of all such trade.

writ: A court-issued document directing or empowering a sheriff or other officer of the court, an official body, or any citizen, to act in some specified way or within specified bounds.

write down: To cut the value at which an asset is carried on the books of a business, to confirm it with current estimated value, for such reasons as obsolescence, unusual depreciation, or price decreases.

write off: To cut the value at which an asset is carried on the books of a business to zero, reflecting that estimate of the current true worth of the asset; for example, an uncollectible debt.

write up: To raise the value at which an asset is carried on the books of a business, to conform it with current estimated value, for such reasons as unanticipated price increases on stock in inventory.

X

x-dividend: See ex-dividend.

Y

yardstick: A set of prices charged by one business that is used to set a standard for prices charged by other businesses in the same field; such use is generally informal, and in some instances would be quite illegal if formal, being considered price-fixing in restraint of trade.

year-end dividend: A dividend paid at year end to stockholders of record as of the end of the calendar or fiscal year, whichever is used. Usually it is a special dividend declared by the board of directors, regular yearly dividends normally being paid more frequently; for example, quarterly.

yen: The main currency unit of Japan, bearing the same relationship to Japan's national currency system as does the dollar to the United States currency system.

yield: That which is actually returned by an investment, but not including the investment itself; examples are the rate of return on securities investments and the crops harvested from land under cultivation.

yield spread: The difference between the yields currently available from differing investments.

Z

zloty: The main currency unit of Poland, bearing the same relationship to Poland's national currency as does the dollar to the United States currency system.